Vitality and Renewal

A Manager's Guide for the 21st Century

Vitality and Renewal

A Manager's Guide for the 21st Century

Colin Hutchinson

With Forewords by
Philip Sadler and Chris Baines

Praeger Studies on the 21st Century

Westport, Connecticut

Published in the United States and Canda by Praeger Publishers
88 Post Road West, Westport, CT 06881
An imprint of Greenwood Publishing Group, Inc.

Printed in the United States of America

The paper used in this book complies with the
Permanent Paper Standard issued by the National
Information Standards Organization (Z39.48–1984).

10 9 8 7 6 5 4 3 2 1

English language edition, except the United States and Canda,
published by Adamantine Press Limited, 3 Henrietta Street, Covent
Garden, London WC2E 8LU England.

First published in 1995

Library of Congress Cataloging-in-Publication Data

Hutchinson, Colin.
    Vitality and renewal : a manager's guide for the 21st century /
Colin Hutchinson ; with forewords by Philip Sadler and Chris Baines.
        p.   cm.—(Praeger studies on the 21st century, ISSN
1070–1850)
    Includes bibliographical references and index.
    ISBN 0–275–95233–9 (alk. paper).—ISBN 0–275–95234–7 (pbk.)
    1. Sustainable development.   2. Organizational change—Management.
3. Industrial management—Environmental aspects.   I. Title.
II. Series.
    HD75.6.H88   1995
    658.4′063—dc20   94–46201

Library of Congress Catalog Card Number: 94–46201

ISBN: 0–275–95233–9 Cloth
        0–275–95234–7 Paperback

This book is dedicated with love to Christopher, born 19 May 1993 and to his generation.

Contents

Summary of Charts

Foreword

Philip Sadler CBE

I congratulate Colin Hutchinson on his achievement in linking and integrating three major issues facing contemporary society: the nature and implications of the environmental crisis, the development of appropriate strategic responses, and the processes of managing individual and organisational change.

He aims to convince businessmen and managers of the urgent need to take the threats to the environment seriously, to persuade them to choose the path leading to wealth creation by means of sustainable development, and to give them the tools and techniques to bring about the needed changes in values, attitudes and behaviour.

He is to be commended for having the courage to cross the boundaries of disciplines and schools of thought, thus providing a uniquely broad-based approach to these matters. We tend to live our lives too much in compartments – business people, academics, ecologists, conservationists and others inhabit their own worlds with seldom more than a glimpse into the worlds of others. The result is appalling ignorance, misunderstanding and conflict where the need is for shared knowledge, common ground and cooperation.

Senior managers live in a world which is dominated by the traditional materialistic approach to wealth creation which was associated with the growth of industrialisation. They operate within the framework of an economic theory which is obsolete and within the parameters set by a series of institutions sheltering behind the label 'market forces', and which virtually eliminate longer term strategic planning. Given the immediate and specific goals of the industrial enterprise, it is scarcely surprising that, until relatively recently, senior managers gave little consideration to the long term impact of their decisions on the environment. Even in cases where, as citizens, parents and enlightened individuals, senior managers were knowledgeable and concerned about environmental issues, they rarely felt able to relate such knowledge and concern effectively to their managerial roles.

Similarly, those outside the world of business who have been deeply concerned with environmental issues have failed to understand how business works and hence how formidable is the task of achieving real and lasting change.

The chances of our achieving timely and effective change will depend to a very considerable degree on the extent to which the two groups can be brought together, equipped with a common language and empowered to bring about change.

Colin Hutchinson has set himself this task and he is extremely well qualified to tackle it. His experience in industry in a senior management capacity is balanced by his later career experience as a consultant and change agent, working mainly in the field of organisation development. Since the 1970s he has been recognised as a leading figure in the environmental movement.

I hope this book will be adopted as a key text in MBA programmes and similar courses in business schools – not only in Britain but in other industrialised nations. The rapid growth of formal programmes of higher education for management gives us the opportunity to create a critical mass of men and women who have been educated for management. An educated manager is one who, as well as being equipped with the tools and techniques of management, has a mature understanding of the socio-economic context of business, is capable of thinking strategically, and is able and willing to challenge the conventional wisdom and break away from practices which, although they may have been effective in the past, are unlikely to serve the future well.

Foreword

Chris Baines

It's not so long since 'the environment' was seen by most people as the exclusive preserve of a few strange extremists on the lunatic fringe – quite unimportant to the rest of us, 'in the real world'. Now, quite suddenly, we're realising that the environment is the real world. It concerns every aspect of our lives, and every one of us affects it, for better or worse, with every single thing we do.

We are also discovering just how complex and interconnected the environment is. Seemingly innocent acts have surprising and alarming repercussions. On the global scale, who would have thought that the *pfff-ssss!!* in aerosols, might extend its influence beyond the Earth's atmosphere, weaken our protective layer of ozone, and increase the risk of skin cancer? Closer to home, the detergents that we use to improve hygiene in our homes are wiping out the natural cleansing systems in our streams and rivers and adding to pollution in the sea. We drive our children to school in cars for fear that they may be mown down by the traffic! This helps clog up the rush hour, fills the air with fumes, and boosts the asthma epidemic which is now affecting one child in seven.

We have a complicated, wasteful lifestyle in the West. There is nothing remotely resembling self-sufficiency here. Each one of us relies upon a tangled web of other people, for the food we eat, the homes we live in, the services we enjoy and the markets for the goods we manufacture. There is an urgent need to make that whole incomprehensible matrix more efficient in its use of the Earth's resources. It must become less wasteful, less damaging; perhaps even a little more sustainable in the long term. Obviously the changes that are needed can't be left to a few specialists called environmentalists. Every one of us is implicated in the crisis, and every one of us must start to make significant progress now.

The biggest challenge of all is to stop kidding ourselves that technological fixes will always save the day. The environment's complex interconnectedness should give the lie to that naive idea. Improved environmental performance depends above all else on thinking laterally and forging partnerships. Complementary players must combine their strengths to tackle issues in new ways, and many major organisations are at last acknowledging this. City councils are breaking down traditional interdepartmental barriers, and multinational companies are seeking out non-specialists to lead the way forward. We need to develop a whole new *culture* which builds environmental awareness into every activity and subconsciously assesses the environmental impact of every decision. In industry, people are equating this with 'health and safety', while in local government 'equal opportunities' is an easier parallel to use. Both are relatively recent philosophical revolutions which have been absorbed into the culture of the work place.

In business management terms, environmentalism requires a holistic approach to decision-making. That's quite a shock to a system traditionally built on predictable, narrow career ladders. In the past those ladders have almost inevitably turned into tunnels. No, we must find new management models which encourage greater sensitivity, broader vision and more sharing of solutions.

It would be comforting to think that we could follow an orderly step-by-step transition to a new age of environmentally sensitive management: first defining the practical meaning of sustainability, then designing the appropriate management structures that would favour innovative collaboration, and eventually tackling painful issues such as re-ordering orthodox economics to take account of true environmental costs and benefits. Unfortunately, time is running out too fast for that. We must move forward on all fronts, seizing inspiring examples when and where we can, experimenting as we go, and recruiting imaginative and influential colleagues at every opportunity. A few people are already ahead of the game – indeed some of them have successfully migrated from that self same lunatic fringe mentioned at the beginning of this foreword. A few organisations have always had an alert, adaptable style of management, and not surprisingly they are in the vanguard of environmental action. They all have a vital role to play in offering encouragement to the rest, in sharing their experiences, and in setting a more ambitious pace for change.

In this book, Colin Hutchinson manages to combine the wisdom of the seasoned pioneer, with the ambition of the explorer. Inevitably this is a book as rich in questions as it is in answers, but that's good. At this stage of the game what matters most is that we see a stimulating, challenging debate emerge. By the twenty-first century, we all need to find a far more sustainable way of living on the Earth. Since the way we manage our own small corner has an undeniable and unpredictable impact on the rest, there is an urgent need to make environmental managers of us all.

Acknowledgments

The origin of ideas is not always easy to trace. It is particularly difficult when extended timeframes are involved. The need for a book of this kind first occurred to me 20 years ago but did not take hold in a tangible form until the latter part of 1992 when the outline was written and the idea took shape.

I would like to thank all those who, sometimes unknowingly, helped with ideas, insights and encouragement. These include many friends and colleagues from my business world as well as those I know from several different environmental organisations. For over twenty years my voluntary environmental interest and my professional work in organisation and individual development have run on parallel paths, with few crossovers. In 1992 I realised that the time had come to integrate my own thoughts, and try out with others whether the links I was making made sense to them.

In this context I would like to pay tribute to friends and colleagues in Sheppard Moscow who, over fifteen years, provided both support and challenge while my ideas, models, processes and skills were developing. I would also like to thank my clients, because they helped me to learn more about the processes of organisational and individual change while working with them on live, practical issues.

Having drawn on material published elsewhere, I have endeavoured to attribute sources and to seek permission from the appropriate source when making use of copyright material. If any have been missed or incorrectly attributed please let me know.

I am very grateful for the cooperation provided by the following organisations and the permission they have granted to reproduce their material:

Sheppard Moscow for letting me use the following charts:

44   Influencing Skills
45   Management & Leadership
50   Giving Positive Support
65   Negotiating Skills

I would also like to acknowledge that the following charts are based on Sheppard Moscow materials which I have adapted and modified as a result of personal experience:

15   Values, Beliefs and Culture
17   Support & Challenge Groups
34   An Organisational Model (original model by Jay Galbraith)
39   Managing Meetings at Three Levels
40   An Organisational Change Model
57   Change Management Roles
60   Assessing the Capacity for Change
61   Enhancing the Capacity for Change
62   Learning and Change
64   Role Negotiation (adapted from Roger Harrison)
66   Action Planning
67   Communications Strategy
68   Human Reactions to Change

Many of the change management models are adaptations of the work of Richard Beckhard and are attributed in the text at appropriate points. Oxford University Press for letting me use material from *Global Warming* by Jeremy Leggett, in chart 7, and material from The World Development Report in the following charts:

2   World Population Growth
4   GNP per Capita 1990
10   GDP and Pollution
11   Reducing Emissions
12   Sources of Primary Energy

The Central Statistical Office for giving permission for some of their information to be incorporated with other material in the following charts:

14   Membership of Environmental Organisations
18   Perceptions of Problems
19   Actions in UK to Improve the Environment 1991/2

Banson for information from *WWF Atlas of the Environment*, Lean & Hinrichson, Helicon 1992, used in the following charts:

3   City Populations
6   Distribution of World Water

The Worldwatch Institute for permission to use their information in the following charts:

20   Costs of Renewable Electricity 1980–2030
27   Estimated Expenditure Required to Restore Environmental Security 1990–2000
36   Technology Sourcing

Alison Clark of Shandwick for permission to use her idea in chart 29: The JIMM Theory, which is explained in the text.

Human Synergistics-Verax for permission to reproduce their life style and culture inventory circumplex, and to describe their model for 'Life Styles and Organisation Culture Inventories', in chart 43: Organisation Culture and Life Styles.

The International Chamber of Commerce for permission to reproduce the Business Charter for Sustainable Development as Appendix 3.

I am particularly indebted to Shell UK Limited, Matt Whitelaw, of Lloyds Bank, and Roger Singleton and Mike Jarman, of Barnardos, all of whom were my clients, who have given permission for me to describe – in chapter 9: Managing Organisational Change – some of the work I did with them when I was working as a Sheppard Moscow consultant.

MORI for permission to use their information in chart 28: Britain's Green Consumers.

Holden Meehan for permission to reproduce figures from their 1994 Guide in chart 13: Ethical and Green Investments.

British Telecommunications for permission to use their figures in chart 35: Comparative Energy Consumption – Telecommunications.

The Centre for Exploitation of Science and Technology for permission to reproduce their figures in chart 26: Key Environmental Problems.

I am indebted to Alexander King and Bertrand Schneider, who developed the 'Problematique', published in *The First Global Revolution*, which provided me with a metaphorical springboard that resulted in the development of several charts which are a central part of the early chapters of this book.

Members of The Conservation Society, The Conservation Trust, The Environment Council, GAP UK, the Centre for Sustainable Industry, the Association for Management Education and Development, and the RSA, who helped shape my ideas.

My articles in *Long Range Planning* contained charts which have subsequently been developed while writing this book. This applies to the following charts, all of which appeared in *Long Range Planning* in an earlier form:

25   Reactive Environment Involvement

Abhay Bhushan of Xerox Corporation provided helpful information incorporated into Chapter 7: Strategic Approaches to the Challenge.

Chris Baines and Philip Sadler kindly contributed the forewords for which I am very grateful.

Roger Beavil helped me with the skills required to use my computer, without which this book could not have been written.

I am particularly indebted to Roger Harrison and Jim Watson who read and commented on the chapters as they developed. Many ideas they suggested have greatly improved the original text. Mary Moore helped with comments on the first five chapters and chapter 9. Michelle Corrado, David Evans, Ivan Hattingh, Suzanne Pollack, Richard Tapper and Bernard Taylor offered ideas and helpful advice on specific topics.

Jeremy Geelan of Adamantine Press had the courage to back me and Sheila Moorcroft, as my editor, has been very helpful with advice, suggestions, encouragement and support as the work developed. John MacMorland has compiled the Index and I am delighted that he was willing to do this for me.

My wife, Pat and my son Nick both read the drafts and made valuable contributions from their different perspectives, and provided strong support and great tolerance during the long hours spent writing the book.

To all these people I am deeply grateful.

Vita
Re

A Manager's Gu

CHAPTER 1

Executive Summary and Introduction

Never before has humanity possessed as it does today the knowledge and the skills, the resources and the cohesion to shape a better world. This should generate a resounding hope for all people......The tragedy of the human condition is that we have not yet reached a position to realise our potential.

Alexander King and Bertrand Schneider[1]

We are destroying the Earth's life support systems, depleting its resources, devastating some of the human communities around the world and relying on outdated economics as a guiding principle. We cannot tackle the issues piecemeal nor can one country do it alone. Emissions which cause climatic change and deplete the ozone layer do not respect national boundaries, and contain valuable chemicals which should be recovered and re-used. Global cooperation is essential and requires an unprecedented joint endeavour that will affect the lives of every one of us as well as future generations.

The environmental challenge is an integral part of the human predicament. In Africa, starvation and warfare destroy communities and leave millions of people devastated by unfolding tragedies. In developed countries our industrialised infrastructure needs to be changed from the linear processes which waste resources and produce toxic emissions to a cyclic regime which conserves resources, recycles emissions and contributes to healthy, sustainable development.

The Challenge

Although the environmental challenge and the search for sustainable development are central themes of this book they are not taken in isolation. Without cooperation between people and economic viability a sustainable society will remain an illusion. Maintaining peace while we search for harmony with nature is an even bigger challenge. We need a clear vision with effective leadership, creativity and innovation, learning at every level, sound communications, open-systems thinking and the ability to deal effectively with the conflict that will be generated by new and radical ideas. New economic thinking is also necessary to guide our pathway to a future that our children and their children can enjoy.

The role of business in this endeavour is central. The industrialised world provides for our material well-being and is, or is becoming, a crucial part of every community. It also helps to provide the way of life that many people in developing countries wish to emulate. However, this can never happen with our existing form of industrialisation – the Earth cannot cope. The nature of our industrialised world lies at the heart of much that is good about our world today. But it is also the unintentional cause of most of our problems. It is essential that business organisations of every kind play a major role in the search for new solutions. Business organisations have been a tremendous source of creativity and their energy and leadership are needed now to bring about change with new and appropriate solutions. Enlightened companies realise that effective environmental management requires changes in organisation culture and behaviour – right through the organisation. Integrated change management is becoming increasingly sophisticated and involves people at every level.

This does not imply that business alone must find the way ahead. There is a vital role for legislation and for fiscal measures to influence behaviour. However, laws are restricting and generate a great deal of energy to avoid their effects. We also need a clear vision of a desirable future which will release and stimulate positive creative energy from people everywhere.

With the right sort of leadership and an understandable vision people will respond. Many are confused by the mass of information that is available and disheartened because they believe that individual effort makes no impression on the enormity of the challenge. Inertia can be replaced by focused activity if the right ingredients are present. As a community, we do not lack the will, nor are we antagonistic, but we do need to believe in ourselves. The aim of this book is to make big issues understandable, to show that much is already being done and to indicate how more could be done. Simple but powerful processes and techniques are explained so that they can be more accessible to those who want to make a difference where they work and live.

Who Will Be Interested in This Book?

The book will be useful to senior and middle managers and, indeed, any manager who is keen to provide leadership within his or her sphere of influence. Managers do not look at environmental issues in isolation. They want to be able to see how to tackle the environmental challenge within an economic and social context. This book offers a framework for this wider context.

After an organisation has made some basic changes which typically save money, comply with the law, strengthen public relations and

The Worldwatch Institute for permission to use their information in the following charts:

20　Costs of Renewable Electricity 1980–2030
27　Estimated Expenditure Required to Restore Environmental Security 1990–2000
36　Technology Sourcing

Alison Clark of Shandwick for permission to use her idea in chart 29: The JIMM Theory, which is explained in the text.

Human Synergistics-Verax for permission to reproduce their life style and culture inventory circumplex, and to describe their model for 'Life Styles and Organisation Culture Inventories', in chart 43: Organisation Culture and Life Styles.

The International Chamber of Commerce for permission to reproduce the Business Charter for Sustainable Development as Appendix 3.

I am particularly indebted to Shell UK Limited, Matt Whitelaw, of Lloyds Bank, and Roger Singleton and Mike Jarman, of Barnardos, all of whom were my clients, who have given permission for me to describe – in chapter 9: Managing Organisational Change – some of the work I did with them when I was working as a Sheppard Moscow consultant.

MORI for permission to use their information in chart 28: Britain's Green Consumers.

Holden Meehan for permission to reproduce figures from their 1994 Guide in chart 13: Ethical and Green Investments.

British Telecommunications for permission to use their figures in chart 35: Comparative Energy Consumption – Telecommunications.

The Centre for Exploitation of Science and Technology for permission to reproduce their figures in chart 26: Key Environmental Problems.

I am indebted to Alexander King and Bertrand Schneider, who developed the 'Problematique', published in *The First Global Revolution*, which provided me with a metaphorical springboard that resulted in the development of several charts which are a central part of the early chapters of this book.

Members of The Conservation Society, The Conservation Trust, The Environment Council, GAP UK, the Centre for Sustainable Industry, the Association for Management Education and Development, and the RSA, who helped shape my ideas.

My articles in *Long Range Planning* contained charts which have subsequently been developed while writing this book. This applies to the following charts, all of which appeared in *Long Range Planning* in an earlier form:

25　Reactive Environment Involvement

Abhay Bhushan of Xerox Corporation provided helpful information incorporated into Chapter 7: Strategic Approaches to the Challenge.

Chris Baines and Philip Sadler kindly contributed the forewords for which I am very grateful.

Roger Beavil helped me with the skills required to use my computer, without which this book could not have been written.

I am particularly indebted to Roger Harrison and Jim Watson who read and commented on the chapters as they developed. Many ideas they suggested have greatly improved the original text. Mary Moore helped with comments on the first five chapters and chapter 9. Michelle Corrado, David Evans, Ivan Hattingh, Suzanne Pollack, Richard Tapper and Bernard Taylor offered ideas and helpful advice on specific topics.

Jeremy Geelan of Adamantine Press had the courage to back me and Sheila Moorcroft, as my editor, has been very helpful with advice, suggestions, encouragement and support as the work developed. John MacMorland has compiled the Index and I am delighted that he was willing to do this for me.

My wife, Pat and my son Nick both read the drafts and made valuable contributions from their different perspectives, and provided strong support and great tolerance during the long hours spent writing the book.

To all these people I am deeply grateful.

Vitality and Renewal

A Manager's Guide for the 21st Century

improve health and safety, the realisation dawns that the challenge has much greater depth. This book helps you to appreciate that strategic choices and cultural and organisational change are required. It enables you to identify strategies for involving your staff or selling the ideas to them. Many organisations face the need for radical and complex change. Proven methods for managing individual and organisational change are described in an accessible way. The cross-referencing provided means that the book can be used as a source of ideas, processes and techniques to tackle a wide range of situations.

Most managers are able to take more initiatives than they imagine. If you have the will to make things happen much can be achieved and your own career will be enhanced.

Specialists who provide services to senior and middle managers from within the organisation or outside it will find many useful ideas and approaches. This is true for both public and private sectors and any industry. It is sometimes helpful for both the client and the adviser to have access to methods and processes which can be used to tackle complex situations. Sharing an understanding of the processes facilitates progress towards desired goals.

Environmentalists will find this book helpful because it provides a synthesis of the issues in a way which places resource depletion and ecological damage in a social and economic context. Some environmental organisations are adjusting their approach from identifying the problems towards developing the solutions. This is not just a shift in emphasis. Carefully reasoned solutions are often resisted because of the inherent dislike most of us have for recommendations which are created and offered by others. What we really require is new ways of working together to establish solutions that move us towards a sustainable society. This is a joint endeavour. Sustainable development is a process not a prescription. This book helps the reader to understand how the processes can be developed and implemented with commitment.

Some campaigning organisations have their own internal change problems to face. The first signs of this are that their growth in membership slows down or stops, revenue comes in more slowly, environmental issues for campaigns are harder to find because the problems are better understood by the public and budgets have to be pruned. Some will regard this as a temporary phase and hope that as the economy improves previous trends will be re-established. Others will realise that as more companies, local authorities and households initiate their own environmental programmes the situation is no longer the same. How environmental organisations come to terms with these new realities will test their ability to cope with internal change. This book will help them understand better how to do this.

Environmental organisations will be able to use this book to gain a better understanding of the scale and nature of problems faced by business and other organisations. Armed with this enhanced understanding they will be able to make their contribution more helpful and relevant. They have the potential to earn respect as contributors to solutions if they can work effectively with others.

By bringing together both the business and the environmental perspective the reader can better appreciate how the daunting challenge is seen by different parties. With clearer appreciation of these perspectives both parties can search for new ways to work together, using change processes which are powerful and effective.

Talks given to various groups while writing this book have made it clear that the analysis, ideas and processes are relevant to:

- senior and middle managers;
- managers attending management development programmes;
- specialists in public and private sector organisations;
- facilitators, consultants, trainers and change agents;
- environmentalists searching for change management skills; and
- environmental organisations reviewing their own methods.

How Is the Book Organised?

It is unusual to find information about the environment, business opportunities and the processes for managing organisational change in the same book. Each of these topics is normally found in separate texts, thus leaving the reader with the task of integration.

Three distinct topics are dealt with in this book:

- the environment and sustainable development;
- business opportunities, strategy and tactics; and
- the management of individual and organisational change.

These three themes have been combined because there is already considerable evidence that businesses are responding to the environmental challenge partly in a piecemeal, reactive way but increasingly in a cohesive, strategic way. The few organisations which are more advanced in implementing their environmental policies now know that fundamental changes are often needed in staff education and organisation culture. This requires a high degree of skill in change management.

The three topics are brought together because they are increasingly linked in the practical world of enterprise. Scientific research is refining the nature of the environmental challenge and providing information from which the vision of a sustainable society can be developed. The turbulent world in which we live is constantly creating new challenges for business. As organisations of every kind respond to these challenges the management of individual and organisational change evolves and becomes more sophisticated.

The book is divided into four parts:

- the predicament and how people are responding (chapters 2, 3 & 4);
- sustainable development and opportunities for business (chapters 5, 6 & 7);
- personal development and organisational learning (chapters 8, 9 & 10); and
- managing individual and organisational change (chapters 11 & 12).

My own experience as a campaigning and educational environmentalist and first hand experience as a line manager, as well as my work as a management development specialist and latterly as a consultant specialising in change management, has convinced me that this book would be valuable to many of my colleagues. Rather than track down the relevant information and ideas from different sources it is helpful to find them in a single book. This enables the reader to move between the different perspectives and see how they relate to each other.

Information has been brought together from many sources, and tested against my own experience. Every effort has been made to present it in an accessible form. The aim is to provide summaries which convey the essence of important ideas in ways which have meaning for the reader. This inevitably means that no subject is explored in depth. Instead, to aid easy reference to key ideas, seventy-two charts are incorporated into the text. These complement the text and act as a quick reference to key ideas.

Examples of ideas in action are used to show how practical implementation is being handled by various organisations. The appendices, annotated bibliography and sources of help provide the reader with easy access to ideas and information which can be followed up as required.

The book emphasises that there are signs of hope. It dwells deliberately on successes and encourages the release of enthusiasm and energy so that work on these issues can become profitable and fun. The intention is to empower people to take informed action.

Chapter 2 describes the predicament, beginning with a model of the Earth reduced to the size of a house, so that we can better understand it as an entity. The key elements are identified in an introductory chart which highlights the need for, and shows the relationship between, peaceful human communities, viable economics, conservation of physical resources and respect for biodiversity. This basic model is then enlarged to include government, business, technology, materials, energy, water, ecology, food, population and values, and each of these topics is discussed.

This expanded model is used to introduce chapter 3 which describes the ways in which people all over the world are contributing to solutions. In this chapter we discuss the six main ways in which we need to respond to the challenge, namely: leadership, innovation, learning, communications, open systems and conflict resolution. Each of these initiatives is described and its relevance shown.

Part 1 concludes with chapter 4 and examines the underlying beliefs and values which provide the underpinnings of our ways of life and which will need to change as we grapple with the issues that have been described.

Part 2 outlines the opportunities for business and begins, in chapter 5, with the meaning of sustainable development. The model introduced in chapter 1 is now converted into a vision of a sustainable society, based on the available research, with references indicated. The challenge we face in bringing about this change is summarised at the end of this chapter and sets the scene for the task to which business is contributing and needs to contribute more – which it can do in profitable ways.

In chapter 6 we look at some of the ways in which business organisations have responded tactically to the challenge. Several notable achievements are interspersed with practical tips for the future. Many of the examples reveal how companies have been surprised by the speed at which they have recovered their investments.

Chapter 7 explores the strategic approach and argues that this is the appropriate response to meet the challenge, and is in the best interests of the organisation. Practical examples are used to illustrate what some companies are doing and how the strategic approach is more likely to identify with the latent interest of staff, who are often waiting for the opportunity to tackle environmental issues in a more determined way.

Part 3 begins with chapter 8 which poses the question: 'Who is in Charge?' The answer to this question provides an opportunity to describe how it is possible, with appropriate support and challenge, to develop mature groups which achieve consistently high standards of performance.

Chapter 9 takes this theme further and explores how to manage organisational change. Examples are given of organisations of different size and in different industries to illustrate some principles which work well. Key points from experience are summarised.

There is no doubt that many managers, and others, will need to learn a lot during the coming years about the topics discussed so far. Chapter 10 offers some guidance on areas of learning and how to pursue this interest in a variety of ways to meet individual needs. The areas for learning are related to the model introduced at the beginning of the book, namely: human communities, economics, physical resources and biodiversity.

Part 4 is about putting ideas into action. Chapter 11 contains practical information about several useful processes and techniques which will help the reader to manage change and bring influence to bear to get results. Every one of these approaches has been tried out in many different situations and can be learned by those seeking to enhance their ability to bring about change, sensitively and effectively.

The final chapter explores the relationship between social responsibility, environmental responsibility and environmental impact. The juxtaposition of these three concepts is explored and the reader is invited to consider which of eight categories apply to the organisation where he or she works. There are also several tips for both client organisations and consultants to help them work together effectively, especially on major projects involving organisation transformation. Process consulting is recommended and explained briefly.

The book contains four appendices which provide an environmental checklist, a list of organisations with environmental policies, a copy of *Business Charter for Sustainable Development*, and a summary of the Earth Summit Agreements. These amplify the text and provide practical guidelines for action or further research.

Readers who wish to extend their study of the themes covered in the book are offered an annotated bibliography which gives a brief review of each of the books mentioned as a reference. This covers 100 titles and is divided into three parts – the predicament, business opportunities and information, and individual and organisational learning. The final section on sources of help covers organisations, journals, bulletins, reports and directories which can be followed up as required.

In conclusion it is appropriate to reaffirm that the book brings together environmental and social issues as its context and advocates individual and organisational change as the primary driving forces to bring about the transitions that are needed.

Finally, this is a book which encourages you to believe in yourself – you *can* make a difference!

Note

1   King and Schneider, 1991, pp. XIX and XX.

CHAPTER 2

The Nature of the Predicament

*Man's conquest of Nature turns out, in the moment of its consummation,
to be nature's conquest of man. Every victory we seemed to win has led us,
step by step, to this conclusion.*

C. S. Lewis

Visualising the Earth

It is difficult to comprehend the global predicament because the Earth is
enormous, the issues are innumerable and the complexity is vast. We need
some way in which to see the whole, using a scale that is more familiar.

Imagine visiting a street in your neighbourhood and finding that
instead of a house, one of the plots was occupied by the Earth – a sus-
pended model about the size of a two-storey house, say twelve metres in
diameter. This would mean that it was a model of the Earth scaled down
to about one trillionth of its actual size. At this size it is possible to take a
good look at it – let's see what we find.

The first thing we notice is that about two-thirds of the Earth's surface
is covered by water. The land blocks are the familiar shape we have
become used to from maps and globes. Notice the size of Africa, North
and South America and the former Soviet Union, compared with
Europe. The area around the North and South Poles may seem bigger
than we expected. Of course the sun shines on only half the Earth at a
time so we will need to visit it at different times to be able to see it all
clearly. Take a look at the dark side and notice the concentration of artificial illumination across Europe and North America. Appreciate how
much less illumination there is in the Southern hemisphere and how it is
concentrated in just a few places.

Let us now take a closer look at some of the physical features. Everest is
only nine millimetres high and the depth of water, even in the deepest
oceans is about the same. The remarkable colours we have become used
to seeing in pictures of the Earth from space are right here before our eyes
– the blue water and the green forests are particularly striking. Notice the
size of the Sahara and other deserts in Africa, Asia and Australia.

Think of all the tiny forms of life which cover the Earth's surface – but
which will not be visible at this scale even with an extremely powerful
magnifying glass. However, all the various forms of animal, bird, insect,
plant and human life make a complex web. Together they sustain each
other. Of course they also depend on the energy and light from the sun
and the balance of the various gases which give Earth its atmosphere

and make life possible. All this teeming life depends for its existence on the Earth's topsoil and the shallower depths of the oceans – rather like the Earth's skin. On the model you are looking at, the depth of this skin is about one thirty thousandth of a millimetre!

Now let us take another imaginative leap to see the Earth as if we had turned the clock back 150 years. In this snapshot the overall appearance of the Earth is much the same as it is now. On closer examination, however, there are two big differences. The green, forested areas were much greater in 1850 while the deserts were significantly smaller. The second big difference is that in 1850 there were virtually no areas illuminated at night.

These changes have been brought about by the activities of one of the species occupying the Earth – humankind. Our numbers have increased from 1.2bn in 1850 to 5.3bn now. This growth in numbers has been accompanied by industrialisation, mostly in the Northern hemisphere, as indicated in broad terms by the illuminated areas. This development has been achieved by using energy derived mainly from fossil fuels – coal, oil and gas – extracted from beneath the Earth.

These broad perspectives give a general picture of the predicament of Earth and a very general idea of how industrialisation, as represented by the illuminated areas, has changed the world. Many people have benefitted but no one intended or expected the problems that have arisen. One important change, invisible in the model, is the profligate use of the Earth's resources since the beginning of industrialisation and the enormous quantities of waste that have been produced, much of it toxic, which are now adversely effecting the life support systems of the Earth.

The Key Elements

In this chapter the key elements of the predicament are explored in order to establish a broad understanding of the nature of the dilemma we face as a world community.

For many centuries the Earth has evolved without any concern for its viability. The many forms of life have coexisted in a complex and interdependent web. This biological variety is often referred to as biodiversity and is an essential element, together with the atmosphere, and the carbon, nitrogen and water cycles, in maintaining the Earth as a viable home for all its species. The energy source which makes life possible is, of course, the sun.

The physical resources such as water, forests, topsoil, fossil fuels, metals and minerals have always been there. Significant but gradual changes in such things as forest cover have taken place over time and metals and minerals have been mined and used for millennia. However, the Earth's resources have only been exploited by humans to a significant degree in the last hundred years.

The third key element is human communities. They too have existed for centuries and evolved slowly until recently. The pace of change has been increasing steadily since the advent of the industrial revolution. In recent years we have seen large scale urban development, increased mechanisation, changes in the global balance of power, the rise of transnational industries and the accelerating pace of technological development. The size of human communities has also increased rapidly and the resource base available to them has expanded.

These three elements – biodiversity, physical resources and human communities – have all been affected by the fourth key element, namely, economics as a method of resource allocation. In addition to the necessary role of economics in achieving this allocation of resources we have, as an industrial community, developed economic doctrine as a guiding principle for our societies. The way in which communities assess progress and development, the way in which physical resources are valued and their exploitation is judged to be appropriate, and the way in which the impact on the Earth's biological systems is ignored, all stem from the way in which economics as a discipline is applied. Even science is influenced by economics in that priorities are set partly as a result of economic judgements.

These four key elements interact with each other and are represented in chart 1.

CHART 1: THE KEY ELEMENTS

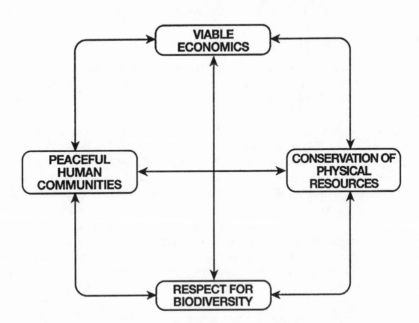

This framework is used to explore the inter-relating problems and this chapter will be concluded with a development of this basic model to summarise the points discussed below. The World Conservation Union (IUCN) advocates a sustainable society and recommends a strategy for attaining it. We shall look at this concept in more depth in chapter 5, but at present it is worth noting what they say and relating it to chart 1:

> "'A strategy for sustainability' is a process whereby a country, a group of countries, or a community works to balance and integrate economic, ecological and social objectives through sustainable use of natural resources."

Human Communities

We looked back to 1850 when examining the model of the Earth and saw that world population has doubled more than twice in the last 150 years – from 1.2–5.3 bn. During that time the Northern hemisphere has experienced rapid industrialisation which has continued to accelerate throughout the period. It is also a time which has been marked by two world wars and hundreds of lesser conflicts in many parts of the world. Despite this turmoil, material standards of living have improved dramatically for the richest billion people . In the Southern hemisphere, however, the effects of change have been largely confined to increasing life expectancy and thereby creating massive population increase. Poverty is rife while the benefits of industrialisation have been meagre and confined to elite groups within the developing countries.

Some remarkable changes have been taking place within world communities. In the mid-1980s it would have been inconceivable that the Soviet Union would break up, that the Berlin Wall would come down, that Germany would be unified, that South Africa would achieve majority government, that Yugoslavia would be torn apart by internal strife, that President Collor of Brazil would be forced out of office, that President Kaunda would be replaced in Zambia after a democratic election, that Kenya would have its first multi-party election and that Mrs Thatcher would resign as Prime Minister, with great reluctance, having never lost an election.

Understanding the nature of human communities and the varying pressures that exist within each is a prerequisite for finding solutions. There are about 170 countries in the world and many of these embrace a variety of ethnic groups. This gives rise to enormous tensions within countries; for example, the Kurds in Northern Iraq and the Shiites in the South, or the various elements now fighting each other in Yugoslavia. These internal tensions are further compounded by conflicts between nations which flare up from time to time.

As we shall see in chapter 3, solutions are dependent on understanding these conflicts. There is an urgent need to seek better more creative ways to resolve problems.

Population

Undoubtedly one of the most significant trends in the world is the rate of population growth. In 1900 the world population was estimated at 1.5bn. By 1960 it had reached 3bn, 4bn by 1974 and 5.3bn in 1992. Latest projections indicate that world population could rise to over 8.5bn by 2030.

This projected increase is speculative only in the sense that a substantial rise in numbers could only be averted by cataclysmic disasters. Within a timeframe of thirty to forty years, very little can be done but action taken now could begin to check the rise thereafter. The longer we delay, the more difficult the situation becomes and the higher the figure at which population is likely to stabilise. Each recent decade has shown a larger average annual increase than the preceding decade and at present 91 m people are added to the world's population every year.[1]

Chart 2 also indicates the proportion of the world's population living in low, middle and high income countries. This shows that the largest increase in numbers will come from low and middle income countries.

If we look at longer term projections of population growth up to the year 2160, by which time total numbers are expected to have levelled off, these reveal different figures depending on the rate of decline in fertility. The high figure, which will be the result of a slow decline in fertility, will produce a world population of 22bn. If there is a rapid decline in fertility, world population could level off at 10bn during the latter part of the twenty-first century. The 'base case', which is achieved by a reduction in fertility of about fifty per cent over the next forty years, produces a world population of around 12.5bn within the same timeframe.[2]

The main reason for this growth trend has been better hygiene and medicine which reduces infant mortality. No real change will occur until average family size starts coming down as a result of avoiding unwanted pregnancies and by making choices to have fewer children. A major reason why people want many children is to provide security in old age. This is an enormous challenge in most developing countries. Relief of poverty, provision of education, and appropriate development, which we shall examine more closely in chapters 3 and 4, are essential requirements in tackling population growth.

Population pressures aggravated by national or ethnic strife have been experienced for many centuries. In the past, the solution often chosen by the persecuted, and younger sons, was to move and start a new life elsewhere. It is no longer possible to move to empty spaces – there are none

Chart 2: World Population Growth

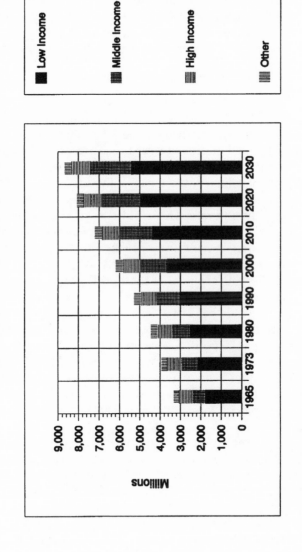

Based on World Development Report 1992
Income levels are for groups of countries

left. This results in continuing strife, local civil wars. and general unrest, in many parts of the world.

A consequence of the growth in numbers coupled with some industrialisation, is the movement of people into urban areas. Whereas the rapid growth of most cities in Europe and North America occurred prior to 1950, the growth of many of the newer cities of the developing world is taking place now, and many of these are already far bigger than London or New York. The quality of life in these cities as they grow ever larger will inevitably be hard to maintain let alone improve. Many of the inhabitants eke out an existence by scavenging or working part-time in low status jobs.

Values

It is estimated that 1bn of the world's 5.3bn population live in countries where the standard of living (health, housing, diet, education and material possessions) have improved over the last century. The remaining 4.3bn have not improved their standard of living significantly during this period and one billion of these people live in absolute poverty. They are too poor to grow or buy enough food to maintain their health. They are predominantly illiterate. This results in an absence of ideas and information which would enable them to escape from their plight – and the women, additionally, are disempowered by tradition and custom. The 1980s have been particularly difficult for the poor with not only the rich growing richer, but the poor of the world becoming poorer, in relative terms, than at the start of the decade.[3]

It is salutary to remember that at least 90 per cent of the world's population, not only those in developing countries, wish to improve their standard of living – the poor in developing countries for very good reasons. There is a universal wish among most people to do better, if at all possible. On the other hand, national governments, in developing countries, encourage their people to grow food to export, to raise foreign exchange and to pay off foreign debts, rather than to grow food to meet local needs.

During the current decade, with environment and development issues gaining more prominence, it will be necessary to re-examine our values, to review the policies which have failed to make any impression on the gulf between rich and poor, and to discover new solutions. The twenty-one countries which are members of the OECD account for two-thirds of the gross domestic product (GDP) of the world. The size of the gap between rich and poor can be appreciated by looking at some comparative figures for gross national product (GNP) for different regions of the world. Per capita GNP in OECD countries is over $21,000 whereas in sub-Saharan Africa it is only $340.

Chart 3: City Populations

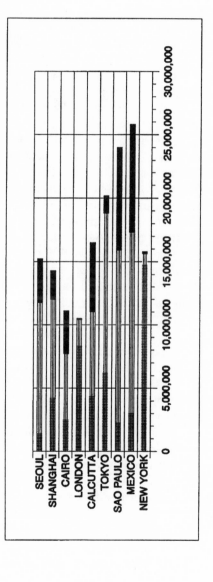

Legend: 1950, 1985, 2000

Cities: SEOUL, SHANGHAI, CAIRO, LONDON, CALCUTTA, TOKYO, SAO PAULO, MEXICO, NEW YORK

X-axis: 0, 5,000,000, 10,000,000, 15,000,000, 20,000,000, 25,000,000, 30,000,000

Source: Atlas of the Environment, 1990
Shading indicates population size for years shown

The figures shown in chart 4 make the situation look rather worse than it is because GNP does not include subsistence farming, energy derived from wood gathered locally and barter trade, but allowing for this still leaves enormous discrepancies in the distribution of wealth.

As we face the future and review our priorities work will be done to establish our values and declare those values which will have relevance for the next century. Facing up to this challenge and articulating appropriate values will be a key element in the future viability of the world community.

Although we inherited the Earth from our ancestors we behave as though we can do what we like to it. People everywhere are beginning to recognise, again, that we are custodians of the Earth and responsible for the condition it is in when our children inherit it from us. This was quite typical in the past among peasant communities. We do not have long, probably no more than forty years, to make dramatic changes to the way we think and behave. This process of change must be speeded up and business has a crucial role to play, as we shall see in later chapters.

Our priorities will be determined by our values. We shall need to review the way money is spent. For example the vast sums of money allocated to military expenditure needs to be reviewed urgently because there are so many other pressing priorities. With the ending of the Cold War global military expenditure by the major players has declined little, and it is questionable whether the scale and nature of the arms trade is still appropriate. The sale of arms to developing countries, even defensive weapons, is likely to result in further fighting. We may well find that we are fighting against people armed with weapons we ourselves have supplied – as happened in the Gulf War in early 1991. There appears to be no slowing down of the arms trade and military expenditure, because of short term fears that it will lead to further unemployment in one or more industrialised country.

The arms trade squanders resources and diverts scientific talent to weapons, many of which are stockpiled. Annual military expenditure worldwide is estimated at $900bn,[4] having reached a peak of US$1,000bn in 1987. Estimates suggest that this figure has grown dramatically from $400bn in 1960 and $600bn in 1970.[5] We shall return, in chapter 5, to ways in which this enormous drain on scientific talent and crucial resources could be better deployed.

Governments

Elected governments are inevitably influenced by their desire to continue in office. This focuses attention on short term issues. They give most attention to matters which win votes, and deal with them in ways which are broadly consistent with their stated philosophy. This phenomenon

Chart 4: GNP per Capita 1990

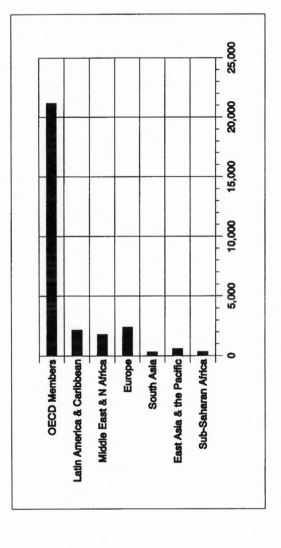

Source: World Development Report 1992
Figures in US $ Per Capita

has been prevalent for hundreds of years in the industrialised countries, which have acquired more and more influence in the world. Dictatorships are usually worse as they struggle to maintain control and achieve economic results to appease their people.

The desire for material well-being has been a common goal for most industrialised countries and they have collaborated with each other in a variety of ways to accomplish their aims. This has resulted in creating formal organisations such as the Organisation for Economic Cooperation and Development (OECD) which is made up of some twenty-one of the richest countries in the world. A smaller number of the richest countries have formed the Group of Seven (G7) and arrange periodic conferences to agree priority action, broadly in their own interests. The effectiveness of G7 has been under challenge for some time, especially from The Other Economic Summit (TOES). Many of the national leaders who attended the G7 meetings in July 1993 and 1994 were experiencing extreme difficulties with their own credibility at home.[6]

The ending of the Cold War and the break up of the Soviet Union has further strengthened the Western worldview. Since the collapse of Communism there is no obvious challenge to capitalism. This may be good for peace and for achieving industrial development but is not good for the relief of poverty nor for dealing with the environmental challenge which grows more pressing. Eastern Europe has many of the worst environmental problems, which are aggravated by social turmoil brought about by political upheavals and the desperate need to provide for the basic needs of large communities.

The USSR under the leadership of Gorbachev disengaged from the Cold War because of the need to devote attention to internal problems. Openness (*glasnost*) and restructuring (*perestroika*) became essential reforms requiring a strong internal focus.[7] Gorbachev's speeches indicated that he not only understood the internal issues but that he was also one of the first national leaders to articulate clearly many of the global problems. The task within the former USSR is enormous and no leader was going to find it easy. In fact Gorbachev became extremely unpopular within the USSR, and eventually lost his job because the people lost patience with him and with the time it was taking to improve living standards. It is, however, unlikely that anyone else could have done any better.

While in office, world leaders gain understanding of global issues which they are often unable to act on as effectively as they would wish. Short term, urgent, national, priorities take precedence over long term, international and more important issues.

This is illustrated by the number of prominent politicians who have devoted a considerable amount of their time to global issues once they have left office: Willy Brandt, Pierre Trudeau, Olaf Palme, Edward Heath, Shirley Williams and Frank Judd, all of whom played a significant part in raising awareness of global environment and development issues. Gro Harlem Brundtland, the Prime Minister of Norway, plays a significant international role in these matters while still in office.

A question was put to Shirley Williams at a public meeting, asking her to compare the influence she had when a cabinet minister, a member of Parliament or an out of office public speaker. Her reply was that as a cabinet minister you would be lucky to get one policy (perhaps two) agreed by your colleagues during a five year term in office. As a member of Parliament you would speak to an empty house unless the issue was topical. As a public speaker you were addressing a large number (200 at the meeting in question) of people who had an interest in the topic. She said it was a very close run thing which had most effect!

The industrial perspective, which has become the predominant guiding principle for most of the world, is under challenge. The nature of this challenge is not the same as that of the Cold War, which concentrated our minds on an identified 'enemy'. The era we are entering will inevitably be quite different from anything experienced in the past. The 'enemy' is ourselves, our values, the world view we have created and our behaviour. It requires very different thinking to discover ways of solving these problems.

The values of the majority determine the sort of government we have and, together with the legislative framework, define the role and function of business in our communities. Business is central to the problems that have been created and equally central to the search for solutions, as we shall see in later chapters.

The Significance of Communications

It is now possible for people all over the world to be informed about an event within minutes of it occurring. If an aircraft crashes, a tanker is shipwrecked, a political leader is assassinated or a sports star wins a major event the news is broadcast everywhere. Information of this kind used to be readily available within each village; as communications improved information was spread from the village to the town; the introduction of newspapers, radio and television increased information circulation to countries. Within a few decades the speed of travel and communication has increased to the point where instant world-wide communication is now possible.

Ideas and information can be exchanged across national boundaries with few formalities. Such information puts power in the hands of people. It can of course be used positively to enhance the lives of millions but it can also be abused and used to strengthen reactionary and criminal forces and to reinforce control by government.

People in many countries around the world now have access to information about the Earth's predicament. Armed with this information people can make judgements about how well governments are performing and in particular to take account of the major dilemmas we now face. Many people have become cynical about politicians because they seem to do so little to tackle the real issues. This cynicism coupled with high youth unemployment is a powerful force for social unrest. It is very easy for governments to lose credibility in today's world of rapid communications. There is now more pressure for openness and integrity in government than there has ever been.

Economics

Government Priorities

In the discussion of economics we are dealing with three distinct concepts:

- how the market operates and achieves resource allocation;
- economic theories which determine how this is done; and
- political ideology which determines the degree of freedom to allow the market to 'cut the cake'.

Economics grew as a discipline in order to find ways in which to cope with scarcity. In its simplest form it is a mechanism for dealing with the creation and distribution of material goods. However, now that many industrial economies have a large component of their economies based on knowledge, and the services which give access to that knowledge, the same situation no longer prevails. We need a new economics which is relevant to the twenty-first century.

It is very hard for national governments to depart from what they have always done, and easy to perpetuate the ways in which national economies are run. However, despite the difficulties it is now vital that the shortcomings of traditional approaches to managing the world's economies be recognised. Creative thinking about new approaches to economics is required, but will depend on acceptance of the belief that capitalism and communism are not the only options available.[8]

Economic measurements, especially GDP, do not take account of the damage inflicted on the environment. If the ozone layer is damaged this is not reflected in any economic analysis or performance measurement. If the Earth's forests, or oil reserves, are severely depleted this does not show up as a reduction in capital assets. If the natural ability of the Earth to absorb waste is depleted by over use this is not reflected in any economic statement. If fish stocks in the oceans are so depleted that the annual catch starts falling, this is only reflected in the value of the catch, which may well not decrease because prices rise as the shortages get more severe. The fact that over fishing is occurring is not reflected. The need to take account of such issues is now being developed and the search for new approaches is gathering momentum.

Materialism aided by traditional economics encourages competitiveness and the pursuit of higher living standards. This has been particularly dramatic in the industrialised countries. Despite this 'success' many wealthy countries have severe social problems. Many individuals suffer alienation and despite decades of effort, rich countries still have sizeable numbers of people living in poverty. In developing countries this is even more pronounced, and is compounded by the terms of trade set by the rich world to further their own ends.

The criticisms of traditional economics are countered by those who wish to perpetuate what already exists by saying that the damage to the Earth is exaggerated and that the evidence indicates that people prefer to have the benefits of industrialisation and put up with the problems it causes. They also believe that with adequate wealth, any problems that do arise will be overcome by ingenuity and technical solutions.

If an economist saw a country or a business running down its capital reserves, treating capital as if it was revenue, failing to maintain machinery in good working order and neglecting the declining morale of staff, these indicators of bad management would be quickly pointed out. However, these very same deficiencies exist in the way in which we manage the environment, but because they are not costed and valued they are ignored in economic performance measures.

It is increasingly necessary to recognise that exponential growth in throughput of materials is not possible indefinitely. The Earth cannot cope with indefinite growth in population, escalating resource depletion, and the consequent increase of damaging emissions. It is also hard to accept this fact when there still seem to be so many open spaces. However, the lily pond analogy aids understanding of this dilemma. Let us assume that a water lily is growing at a rate that will result in a pond being totally covered in thirty days. At the end of the 27th day only one eighth of the pond is covered. After twenty-eight days three quarters of the pond remains empty. After twenty-nine days it is half covered. When do we realise how close it is to complete coverage? Reverting to the issue of throughput of materials to fuel our economies, how close are we to the need to turn away from reliance on indefinite growth in materials consumption and how quickly will we be able to adjust? These are real and pressing challenges. The immediate challenge is to find ways to expand our economies without the same level of growth in throughput of materials; later we shall need to find new goals.

Business

The large number of business organisations which go bankrupt helps to reinforce the belief that the purpose of every business is to make a profit. Profit is the ultimate test of performance, but this is not the same thing as a statement of purpose. It is useful to think in terms of the costs of doing business and the costs of staying in business. The former covers salaries, raw materials, production processes, rents, rates etc. The latter covers dividends, research, innovation, new equipment and expansion. There is no doubt that profit is essential for business success and close attention has to be paid to managing cashflow. In fact most businesses fail as a result of running out of money rather than by becoming unprofitable.

However, it is unhelpful to state that the purpose of business is to make a profit. Peter Drucker has argued this point for many years.[9] He argues that the purpose of business is to create a customer. In today's world that might be broadened and it is more helpful to think in terms of satisfying stakeholders, which includes customers, shareholders and employees. This theme will be developed in chapter 3.

Business organisations have the resources and self-interest to examine the quality of their profits and will play a central role in the search for new solutions.

Technology

Northern and Western industrial countries have been remarkably inventive with their technological developments and there is no doubt that technology has an enormous role to play in coming decades. However, there are some significant shortcomings in much current technology which should be acknowledged.

Industrial countries follow a linear pattern of resource use. This means that resources are extracted, products are manufactured, they are used in various ways and in due course discarded. Such linear processes are often wasteful of resources and scant attention is paid to the consequences of discharging wastes, many of which are poisonous, into the environment. The challenge has been neatly summarised:

> We have been processing materials in a manner that is linear, wasteful and toxic, instead of cyclic, resource-conserving and healthy.[10]

There is also a marked tendency to prefer elaborate, high prestige technologies rather than significant but more mundane developments. Concorde, which benefits only a small minority, gets much more attention than a small scale innovation, such as a water pump, able to provide millions of people with clean water.

Physical Resources

Materials – Renewable and Non-renewable

Broadly speaking physical resources can be divided into two classes – renewable and non-renewable. Renewable resources include sunlight, air, soil, water, plants and animals all of which are continually renewed by natural processes. Provided that the rate of use does not exceed the rate of replenishment they remain available for the indefinite future.

Non-renewable resources, on the other hand, once used are gone for ever. They include metals, minerals and fossil fuels. The availability of metals and minerals can be enhanced by re-use and recycling, but they are eventually dispersed and become irrecoverable. Fossil fuels once burnt are necessarily gone for good, although the combustion product remains to pollute the environment.

The distinction between renewable and non-renewable resources is analogous to that between revenue and capital in business – with the important distinction that prudent managers (and individual investors) are very anxious to maintain, or preferably enhance, the value of their capital, but few people seem concerned that non-renewable resources are being used up at an increasing rate. People also want companies in which they work, or invest, to be competent at cash flow management and not to allow expenditure to exceed revenue.

Metals

Metals are vital for industrial production. It is not easy to estimate when shortages or costs would begin to create severe problems, because improved technology, new discoveries and substitution make accurate calculations difficult. However, one attempt calculated the average abundance of metals in the Earth's crust, and the cut-off grade beyond which the concentrations are too diffuse for mining to be economical. The result of this calculation is that aluminium, iron and titanium are found to be plentiful but most other metals are scarce. Those where the combination of abundance and the mineable cut-off indicate greatest scarcity are mercury, tungsten, lead, chromium and tin.[11]

These metals, like fossil fuels, were concentrated by powerful cosmological, geological forces working over aeons. Their exploitation has exploded in the last few hundred years.

Forests and Timber

It is estimated that all animal and plant life on Earth amounts to 830bn tonnes, 55 per cent of which (460bn tonnes) is in tropical forests and 21 per cent (175bn tonnes) in temperate forests.[12] Acid rain, over-logging for timber, and forest clearance for agriculture are reducing the Earth's forests, and the consequences, while causing concern, are not easy to predict. The loss of the green mantle is very serious.

The Earth's tropical forests are global assets of enormous importance. They help regulate our climate, maintain the oxygen balance, help to prevent soil erosion, protect water flow required for farming, contribute hardwood timber as well as wood for fuel, and are the source of untapped genetic diversity – in all a source of wealth that is incalculable. About half the tropical forests have already been destroyed, leaving some 800 million hectares of which about 11.4 million hectares are being felled annually, according to the Food and Agricultural Organisation (FAO) of the United Nations, whose figures are usually conservative. The *World Resources Report*, aided by aerial photographs, has estimated the annual rate of destruction at between 16.4 and 20.4 million hectares.[13]

As a forest is cleared, the valuable timber is sold and the rest is often burnt so that the land can be used for growing subsistence crops. After three or four years the soil is impoverished, insect plagues occur and yields drop. The cycle is then repeated in new areas. Sometimes the land is not used for subsistence agriculture but to grow cash crops or raise beef for sale to Europe or North America, in order to generate foreign exchange or provide profits to multinational companies. Wholesale clearance of tropical rain forests is likely to have drastic consequences for the Earth's climate, even in temperate regions, and anyway fails to provide a sustainable supply of timber. Slash and burn subsistence agriculture is sustainable and has been practised for ages. Problems arise when population pressure results in too much clearance at any one time with insufficient recovery periods. Forest clearance for permanent agriculture is much more serious because it is far too widespread and without any opportunity for recovery.

Wild Life and Loss of Species

All over the world, wildlife is under pressure from human activities, and very many animal and plant species are in danger of extinction. The main problem is the reduction and fragmentation of their habitats by human encroachment and forest clearance. Over-hunting (often by poaching) for food, furs/skins, tusks, etc. and sometimes for sport is partly to blame. Poisoning by agricultural residues also plays a part.

In the period 1700–1799 some 8,000 species of mammals and 25,000 species of birds became extinct. In the next 100 years, from 1800–1899, these figures rose to 30,000 and 60,000 respectively and in the period 1900–1987 over 50,000 species of mammals and 70,000 species of birds were lost.[14] This decline in species is being accelerated by forest clearance and is now quite frightening. Although the figures quoted are for mammals and birds, plants are similarly affected.

Extinction of species entails loss of genetic diversity. We do not know how many of the species at risk are potentially useful as food, or as sources of new medical treatments, for use in biological pest control or even as tourist attractions. By simplifying the environment and reducing the range of species we cripple our own self-interest.

Disruption of the balance of nature frequently leads to plagues of unwanted species whose natural predators have been eliminated. Once the complex web of life is disrupted whole ecosystems can collapse. The chemical control of pests often simplifies environments and usually leads in the end to resistances being built up and to the need for more powerful poisons. Loss of species diminishes the world for everyone and makes it less stable.

Fisheries

The United Nations Food and Agricultural Organisation (FAO) estimates that the maximum sustainable yield of fish caught world wide is 100 million metric tons per year. Since 1945 the recorded world catch of fish has increased from about 20 million metric tons to 92 million metric tons in 1987.[15] This is very close to the sustainable yield, which may have been exceeded already if fish catches by local fisherman are included in the official statistics. Some fish species are already severely depleted, so that quotas have been imposed on fishing fleets which are widely resented.

One of the more damaging practices is the use of drift nets, often several miles long, which catch everything. The fishermen only keep what is commercially significant, such as tuna, and discard everything else, which is by then dead – including species like dolphins. While this method is quick and provides edible fish, everything else is wasted. Supermarkets have been aware of this, and after adverse customer reaction many of them have changed their sources of supply to avoid handling tuna caught in this way.

Energy

Energy is the most critical resource: it is therefore vital to understand the types of energy available and what is happening to the Earth's energy reserves over a long period of time. Significant exploitation of fossil fuels began with the industrial revolution, and consumption has increased rapidly over the past 200 years. Growth in consumption cannot continue indefinitely. If the figures are plotted on a graph spanning seven hundred years the short era of fossil fuel consumption can be appreciated, and is illustrated in chart 5. Even if the peak shown in this graph is uncertain, this will only alter the situation by a decade or two. Discoveries of further reserves since the estimate was made in 1969 cannot alter the fact that consumption will peak some time in the next fifty years and thereafter decline as reserves are used up.

In addition to fossil fuels the developed world derives about 9 per cent of its energy from hydroelectric schemes (renewable) and nuclear power (non-renewable).[16] In developing countries, biomass (recently living bio-logical organisms) accounts for about one third of all energy used, but about half of this is timber used in ways which are not sustainable.[17] However, it may be possible to derive substantial amounts of energy from renewable biomass if appropriate methods are used.

Energy can be separated into primary and secondary sources. Oil, coal, gas, hydroelectric and nuclear are described as primary sources.[18] Another description of the energy for which statistics are readily avail-able is 'traded energy'. This is more informative because biomass, solar, wind, geothermal and tidal energy can all be classed as primary sources. However, they are not usually traded. A business selling units of energy (e.g. oil, coal, gas, electricity) is very different from a business that sells appliances which harness renewable, natural energy (e.g. sun and wind).

Solar energy, for example, is used increasingly in Mediterranean coun-tries to heat water, and is likely to become much more significant in the next few decades. This and other forms of renewable energy are obtained by purchasing equipment which gives access to the energy, but the energy itself is not purchased.

The abundance of coal, oil and gas has been sufficient to meet human needs up until now, but the situation is changing. There is no way in which the whole world can attain the material living standards of the industrialised countries using fossil fuels as their main source of energy. Work is being undertaken to harness renewable sources of energy such as wind, tide, solar and geothermal, and this will be discussed further in chapter 3.

One final point on energy is that two thirds of world consumption is accounted for by the industrialised countries, which have only one quar-ter of the world's population. While the problems associated with arrest-ing population growth are located mostly in Africa, Asia and Latin America, the problems of arresting current environmental damage are closely linked to energy consumption, and are therefore broadly located in North America, Europe and Japan.

Biodiversity

Water

One of the main constraining factors for social and industrial develop-ment especially in Africa and parts of Asia is the lack of fresh water. The Earth has an abundance of water but 97 per cent of it is in the oceans. Of the 3 per cent that is fresh water 79 per cent is in glaciers and the ice caps

Chart 5: Fossil Fuel Era

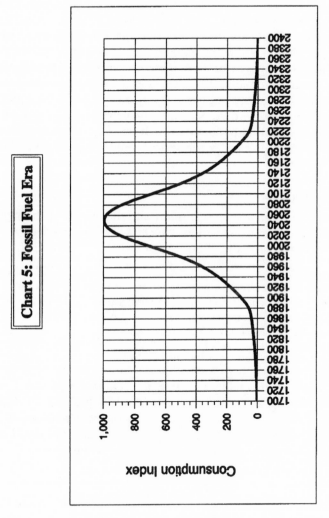

An estimate of the era of fossil fuel consumption based on Resources and Men published by the US National Academy of Sciences, 1969 and Ariadne's Thread by Mary E Clark, 1989, both using original work of Hubbert, 1962

and 20 per cent is ground water, leaving only 1 per cent as easily accessible fresh water. Of this 1 per cent, lakes account for 52 per cent, soil moisture 38 per cent and atmospheric water vapour 8 per cent. This leaves 2 per cent of which half is contained within living organisms and the rest in rivers.[19]

We do not destroy water. We make it dirty and in many places use underground water reservoirs faster than they are replenished. The problem with water is availability of fresh water where it is needed, and when it is required. There are four major strategic threats to water supplies. First redistribution, secondly rising sea levels and the effect on low lying areas, thirdly changes in land use patterns, especially deforestation, and fourthly the contamination of water systems with chemical pollutants. Many forms of intensive agriculture rely on underground aquifers without considering what would be a sustainable rate of use, and without regard for the chemical pollutants which have contaminated them. Water is often the limiting factor for agricultural, industrial and urban expansion.[20]

The Ecological Balance

Scientific opinion confirms that human activity on Earth has now reached proportions that cause serious concern. This was evident when for the first time ever, the Royal Society of Great Britain, and the US National Academy of Sciences, issued a joint press release saying:[21]

> If current predictions of population growth prove accurate and patterns of human activity on the planet remain unchanged, science and technology may not be able to prevent either irreversible degradation of the environment or continued poverty for much of the world.

The issues causing most concern include the greenhouse effect (global warming), stratospheric ozone depletion, acid rain and decline in species. The deteriorating quality of water, air and land in or near urban areas is very worrying. Pollution of various kinds is high on the list of concerns. Waste management and major spills and releases from biotechnology also cause great concern.[22] Lists of this kind have been confirmed by a succession of different authoritative statements.

Topsoil

An undisturbed ecosystem reaches an equilibrium between loss of topsoil, due to erosion by wind and water, and the very slow formation of fresh topsoil through weathering of rocks and deposition of decaying organic material. Deforestation, particularly in upland areas, drainage of wetlands, and agriculture all upset this equilibrium and lead to greatly increased loss of topsoil. When there are no trees, or bogs water runs off the hills much more rapidly, taking the soil (which is no longer stabilised

Chart 6: Distribution of World Water

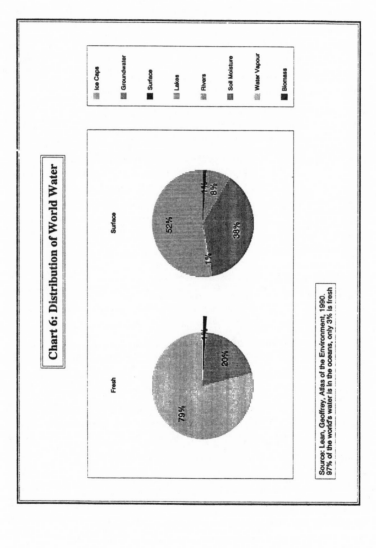

Fresh

Surface

- Ice Caps
- Groundwater
- Surface
- Lakes
- Rivers
- Soil Moisture
- Water Vapour
- Biomass

79%
20%

52%
38%
8%
1%

Source: Lean, Geoffrey, Atlas of the Environment, 1990.
97% of the world's water is in the oceans, only 3% is fresh

by the roots) with it and causing serious flooding downstream. Ploughing the land increases the rate of erosion, which is further increased by the widespread use of artificial fertilisers, because these suppress many soil organisms which help soil particles to stick together. Much topsoil is being lost by desperately poor people attempting to cultivate unsuitable land. All these processes are taking place at an alarming rate. Eventually a new equilibrium will be achieved with much less topsoil and correspondingly less agricultural potential.

The loss of topsoil has been studied in the USA through several surveys, mostly in the corn belt. The average depth of topsoil is 18 cm and the surveys reveal that for every inch of topsoil lost, yields fall by 6 per cent. The world farms about 61m hectares and if all this land lost one inch of topsoil it would mean the loss of 24bn tons of topsoil. This in turn would cause a drop in the world grain harvest of 9m tons. These are extrapolations from US data, but they indicate that some drastic corrective measures are needed to arrest the loss of topsoil.[23]

In Britain 95 per cent of lowlands grasses and 50 per cent of remaining fens have disappeared since 1930. 175,000 km of hedgerows have been removed since 1950. In the USA wetlands have declined from 870,000 sq km in 1800 to well under 40,000 sq km in 1990.[24]

Pollution

The cumulative effect of pollution has now reached such a stage that it is causing concern about global warming and depletion of ozone in the upper atmosphere. In 1800 carbon dioxide (CO_2) in the atmosphere had reached 280 parts per million (ppm). By 1990 this had risen to 350 ppm and it is estimated that if no action is taken there will be a further rise to 560 ppm by 2030.[25] Action *is* being taken and this will be discussed in chapter 3, but it is important to understand which gases are causing the problems and where they come from.

Most human activities affect the environment adversely on an increasingly global scale. Global warming is caused by gaseous emissions into the atmosphere, and if action is delayed flooding could occur in low lying areas, as well as ruin to crops in those parts of the world where rainfall could be dramatically altered.

The main cause of global warming is emissions of carbon dioxide, but other gases such as chlorofluorocarbons (CFCs), methane and nitrous oxide also contribute. Industrial and commercial activity accounts for significant quantities of 'greenhouse' gases through the burning of fossil fuels, many of which are used wastefully, by the use of motor vehicles, by generating wastes which release methane and CFCs and by deforestation.

Releases of CFCs (used in refrigerators and aerosols) make a contribution to global warming. Even greater concern about their use relates to the effect they have on the ozone layer, depletion of which results in increased penetration of ultra violet light, which is harmful to life and could cause a higher incidence of skin cancer.

Burning fossil fuels also releases sulphur dioxide and nitrogen oxides into the atmosphere, resulting in smog over industrial areas, and acid rain which is having a devastating effect on forests, rivers and lakes. In some large cities (such as Mexico City and Tokyo) the quality of the air is, at times, so bad that oxygen dispensers are made available on street corners.

Food

Various estimates have been made, using different assumptions, to assess the number of people the world could feed. Highly optimistic assumptions about crop yields lead to very large numbers, but they have been largely discredited. More balanced and better reasoned assessments are available. They point to the growing number of countries which were exporting food but are likely to need food imports in the near future. They also explore different scenarios for diets which consume grain, rather than meat derived from animals which have been fed grain, and make assessments of the likelihood of increasing the world's total food production and achieving more equitable distribution. The situation is reviewed continent by continent. The effect of variations in climate are considered and demands that might be made on fertilisers and water supplies.[26]

The outcome of these considerations is sombre. Every year farmers have to grow food for an extra 91 million people. With loss of topsoil this is increasingly difficult. Already there are signs that total food production is approaching the limits of what is possible as sustainable yields. Those countries which depend on grain imports from the USA face a very worrying future because there may not always be surpluses. Food shortage is so severe in parts of Africa, such as Somalia and Zambia, that food riots have occurred, and there is widespread famine in Somalia, Ethiopia and elsewhere.

An Overall Perspective

A detailed analysis of the global problem (`The Problematique') is contained in *The First Global Revolution* by Alexander King and Bertrand Schneider,[27] followed by recommendations for bringing about appropriate change (`The Resolutique'). A modification of their model is shown in chart 11. The modifications have been made to accommodate the perspectives discussed in this chapter and to provide the framework which will be developed in chapters 3 and 4.

Chart 7: Greenhouse Gases

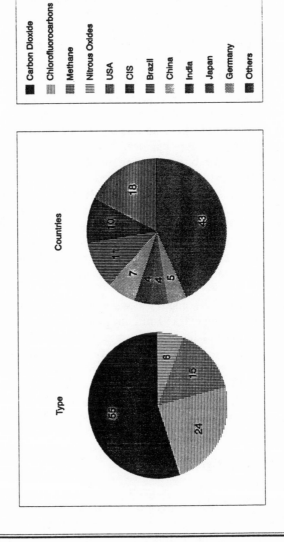

Type

Countries

- Carbon Dioxide
- Chlorofluorocarbons
- Methane
- Nitrous Oxides
- USA
- CIS
- Brazil
- China
- India
- Japan
- Germany
- Others

Sources: Leggett, J (Ed), Global Warming, 1990 & The Guardian November 8, 1990. All figures are in percentages.

CHART 8: THE HUMAN PREDICAMENT

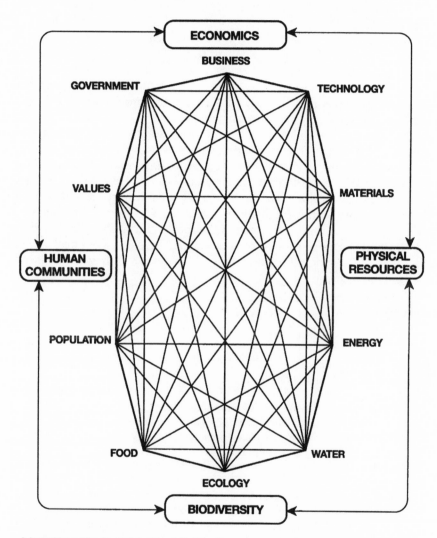

Adapted from "The First Global Revolution" by Alexander King & Bertrand Schneider, Simon & Schuster, 1991.

© Colin Hutchinson, *Vitality and Renewal*, Adamantine, 1994

There is little doubt that the world is moving towards a convergence of problems. The principal elements are growth in human numbers, and the ways in which communities are changing, with more people seeking a voice in matters which affect them. The way economic thinking now evolves is crucial. We can no longer ignore the effects of human activity on the Earth's life support systems. Physical resources, which include fossil fuels, are being depleted at rates which cannot continue for long, and yet so much of what people want from life seems directly related to their material well-being. The pressure on resources from developing countries with very large populations, such as China and India, is relentless. We are depleting the Earth's diversity of life, and by simplifying the living world making it increasingly vulnerable.

These environmental concerns need to be tackled by human communities, many of which are experiencing considerable internal tension. Internationally the tension between countries has eased with the ending of the Cold War, and there are signs that global cooperation is increasing. During the last decade or two better ways to deal with conflict have been developed both within and between countries. The use of these methods still makes little progress in some of the more difficult situations such as in Northern Ireland and in the Baltic states. There is a great deal still to be done and a strong likelihood that the issues which have to be faced will get more severe.

Notes

1   Brown et al., 1993.
2   The World Bank, 1992 p. 26.
3   Ehrlich and Ehrlich, 1990, p. 41.
4   Commoner, 1990 p. 173.
5   United Nations Development Programme, 1992 p. 85.
6   The New Economics Foundation (NEF) and The Observer July 4, 1993.
7   Gorbachev, Mikhail, Perestroika, Fontana Collins, 1987.
8   See especially Daly and Cobb, 1990.
9   Drucker, Peter, The Practice of Management, Mercury Books, 1955, reprinted 1990.
10 The Federation of Swedish Farmers Economic Policy Division, Energy Policy, abridged version of paper presented at IFAP Conference, Reykjavik, Iceland, 1992. This is part of the work of The Natural Step (see Sources of Help).
11 Meadows, Meadows and Randers, 1992, p. 85.
12 Myers, 1990, p. 29.
13 Lean et al., 1990, p. 65.
14 The World Bank, 1992, p. 58.
15 Lean et al., 1990, p. 157.
16 BP Statistical Review of World Energy, June 1992.

17 The World Bank, 1992.
18 BP Statistical Review of World Energy, 1992.
19 Lean et al., 1990, p. 59.
20 Gore, 1992 pp. 104–114.
21 Joint statement by The Royal Society and the United States National Academy of Sciences, 27 February, 1992.
22 Good, 1991.
23 Brown et al., 1990, p. 61.
24 Myers, 1990, p. 34.
25 Leggett, 1990.
26 Brown et al., 1990, and Ehrlich and Ehrlich, 1990.
27 King and Schneider, 1991.

CHAPTER 3

How People Are Responding

*Our common future is being shaped in literally countless ways by people
all over the world. Some of them make headlines. But the overwhelming
majority are people who do not make the news. They make the difference.*

Linda Starke[1]

Many people believe that the interest in the global predicament – the
parlous state of many human communities, inappropriate economics,
depletion of resources and destruction of biodiversity – can be judged by
the amount of attention these topics are given by the media. This is a
very poor way to judge the real work being done to respond to the
issues and seek solutions.

In recent years, as awareness of the issues has become more widespread and been understood at deeper levels by growing numbers of
people, the scale and nature of the response to the challenge has grown
rapidly. It is not possible to do justice to all the varied initiatives that are
being taken, many of them since the Earth Summit in June 1992.
However, it is possible to indicate how widespread the search for solutions has become. This shift from creating awareness to seeking solutions
is very significant, and more attention is now focused on what can be
done.

For some readers it will be important to know what sort of initiatives
are being and can be taken, others will want to get on with what is proposed and how this book might help. This chapter is for those who
would like to know what others are doing.

Al Gore, before he became Vice President of the USA, wrote a remarkable book entitled *Earth in the Balance*.[2] It contains a powerful analysis of
the situation we face as a global community, and much relevant information gleaned from discussions with many people, overseas visits and
through serving on Congressional committees. This foundation leads to
thoughts about the future and how important it is to recognise the
power of the people. He is a staunch advocate of democratic government
and (modified) free markets and proposes a 'Global Marshall Plan'. This
plan emphasises five specific goals:

- stabilising world population;
- developing and sharing appropriate technologies;
- a new global economics;

- a new generation of treaties and agreements; and
- a new global environmental consensus.

Gore is, quite rightly, recommending important goals in a global context, including international agreements and treaties which commit countries to collective action. He recommends that 'the agendas of the environment movement and the democracy movement must become intertwined. The future of human civilisation depends on our stewardship of the environment and – just as urgently – our stewardship of freedom.' He also values the power of people and states that 'strategic thinking is useless without consensus'.

In order to achieve the kind of initiative that Gore has in mind action has to be taken by people all over the world, operating at every level of our community. We need clear understanding of the ideas and processes which will strengthen appropriate action, because so much has to be done and time is limited. Many people are already working on this task and it is helpful to acknowledge their efforts and realise that we are not alone in our endeavours.

Activating the Global Perspective

The slogan 'think global, act local' has been around for some years and has been challenged by some because it is hard to think globally. However, we do need to understand global issues and relate them to our own sphere of influence. In chapter 2 the scale of the global predicament was described, and summarised in chart 8.

We now ask: 'What sort of action makes a difference?' We shall soon be considering action taken by very different people within their own spheres of influence. However, a framework for considering the sort of things they have done is helpful. This is provided in chart 9, which contains six different sorts of initiative, summarised as an acronym – LIL-COC:

Leadership – required at every level.
Innovation – in harmony with Nature.
Learning – for us all.
Communications – two way – especially listening to others.
Open systems – recognising the boundaries of different systems.
Conflict resolution – how to deal with and resolve disagreements.

These six sorts of initiative are each described briefly below.

Empowered people working at every level are demonstrating how *leadership* can achieve positive results. They did not wait for others to act or give permission but provided leadership themselves in their own sphere.

There is no limit to the creative ideas that can be harnessed. The scope for *innovation* has never been greater and the scale of the initiatives is growing all the time. A fundamental requirement for innovative thinking is easy access to good information.

Through involvement more people are *learning* about ecology, biodiversity, physical resources, conservation and how all this affects human communities. They are learning about the inter-relationship between these parts and how networking helps to provide both the support and the challenge required to make a real difference. Working with others it is possible to identify new visions of how things might be, and then to find ways to take action together.

The strength and value of *communications* is growing all the time, aided by new technology and the ability of people to use it. This places a heavy responsibility on those who have the ability to influence the media, the channels of communication and the access to information.

As more people get involved and communicate with others it becomes more obvious that we live in '*open systems*'. We interact with so many people in other organisations and have the scope to influence and be influenced by those with whom we come into contact. Open systems also apply to the boundaries of the living world, and to the unintended side effects of our actions.

We encounter people who do not always agree with our views and the things we want to do. As we strive for the solutions we discover that disputes and conflict arise, probably more often than we would like. Our search for new ways to deal with these situations leads us towards better ways to resolve *conflict*.

We shall now consider some examples of ways in which people are responding, under the headings: leadership, innovation, learning, communications, open systems and conflict resolution.

Leadership

The United Nations and the Earth Summit

The United Nations Conference on Environment and Development (UNCED) – The Earth Summit – attracted 178 nations of the world – 120 Heads of State attended in person. Never before has there been a conference attended by so many of the national leaders. Five years earlier a gathering of this kind would have been dismissed as extremely unlikely. The fact that it happened at all is heartening and there were some notable achievements.

UNCED agreed the following:[3]

(1) A global convention on climate change.

CHART 9: SEEKING SOLUTIONS

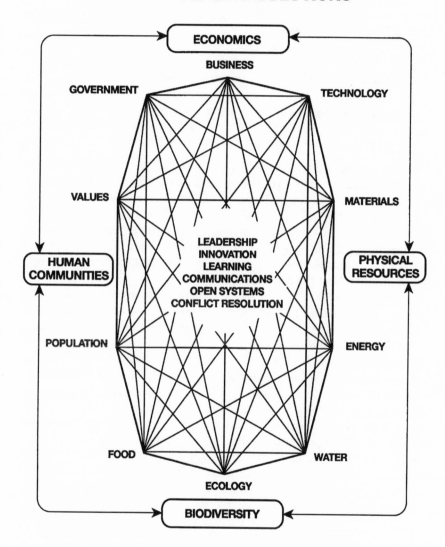

© Colin Hutchinson, *Vitality and Renewal*, Adamantine, 1994

(2) A global convention on biological diversity.
(3) A global convention on forests.
(4) The Rio Declaration was signed as the basis for governing the relationships of people and nations with each other and the Earth.
(5) A programme of action called 'Agenda 21' was developed for implementing the proposals.
(6) The Earth Charter was signed.
(7) New financial resources were committed to underwrite Agenda 21, even though this fell short of the stated need.
(8) A programme of technology transfer from rich to poor nations of 'environmentally sound technologies' was created.
(9) The international institutional machinery, through the UN was strengthened to carry out the agreed commitments.[4]

This positive picture of the achievements of Rio was not how many of environmental groups saw the results of the Earth Summit. Even Maurice Strong, Secretary General of UNCED, recognised that the results fell far short of his stated intentions. The main criticisms were concerned with the extent to which the conventions had been diluted. Furthermore, the undertakings were intentions rather than firm commitments. In part, this was attributed to the insistence of the UN that all outcomes should reflect the consensus view.

The USA refused to allow the treaty on climate change to include specific targets and timetables for reducing greenhouse gas emissions. Having weakened the biodiversity treaty, the USA then refused to sign it because of fears that it would adversely affect its own biotechnology industry. However, it has now been signed by President Clinton. The principles of forest management, although sound, contain no binding agreements.

Agenda 21 covers every conceivable aspect of sustainable development, but still requires financing and needs to be broken down into plans that can be implemented within countries, right down to local government level, with priorities identified. This is already happening in some places.

The overall responsibility for supervising the follow-up to Agenda 21 lies with the UN Commission on Sustainable Development (UNCSD). The Commission has divided the chapters of Agenda 21 into clusters, in order to create a more manageable work programme with regular reviews. For example they have clustered the elements of sustainability, financial matters, education, science and technology, and decision-making structures, into separate groupings.

All this is very encouraging, but the acid test is whether it will be sufficient; many people fear that current efforts fall far short of what is required. However, as a strategy for encouraging more people to take initiatives, there is much to be said for building on what is already being done and giving praise where it is due.

The real achievements of Rio will be seen in what people do, rather than in the written agreements or in what was said. Tough, binding agreements do not necessarily guarantee that effective implementation will follow: commitment is essential. Even when sanctions are written into the agreements there is no guarantee that they will be used against those who fail to do what is required. One undeniable achievement is that the preparations for the conference, which began in 1990, involved an enormous number of people from all around the world. This process raised the awareness of millions of people from virtually every nation of the world, that there are real problems and we are all affected. It provided the foundation for countless thousands of initiatives which continue to this day and which will contribute to eventual environmental solutions.

The momentum must be maintained and strengthened as more people of all ages from every corner of the Earth take part in the process of learning, adjusting their attitudes, modifying their behaviour, influencing others, creating solutions, implementing new initiatives and reviewing results. How this can be done with more vigour and effect will be explored in later chapters with particular reference to the contribution of business. But first it is important to recognise the scope of other initiatives that are taking place. Chart 9 shows how everything is connected and that, with collective action, progress towards a sustainable future can be accomplished. Business has a major role to play because it influences every one of the ten dimensions of the model directly or indirectly. However, there are others who must also play their part and the work has started.

The US Government

President Clinton's approach to the environment, aided by Al Gore, his Vice President, is very different from the attitude and approach adopted by the two previous presidents of the USA. Al Gore has been associated with environmental issues for many years and reference has already been made to his book (*Earth in the Balance*).

President Clinton has brought the head of the Environmental Protection Agency into the Cabinet and made Vice-President Gore responsible for ecological coordination. This should enable environmental issues to be considered at an early stage in every aspect of government policy. Time alone will be the judge of the extent to which this is achieved and the degree to which it is beneficial but some indications look promising.[5]

Many US companies such as Du Pont, 3M, IBM, Procter and Gamble and Dow Chemicals have been at the forefront of environmental management for many years. They have also been at the leading edge of new technology which contributes to environmental solutions. This leadership position slipped during the Bush administration because the environment was given so little attention, but a revival seems likely with new thinking emanating from the White House.

One of the areas in which the USA does provide a lead is satellite technology to monitor the condition of the Earth. A US space operator has launched a $20 million Brazilian satellite which will survey the Amazon forests and the surrounding area, and feed back information about levels of carbon dioxide and carbon monoxide in the atmosphere[6]

The Business Council for Sustainable Development

In order to have an authoritative contribution from industry to the Earth Summit, Maurice Strong appointed Dr Stephan Schmidheiny, a prominent Swiss industrialist with trading interests in several countries, to be his industrial adviser. Schmidheiny formed the Business Council for Sustainable Development by inviting fifty chief executives of major companies from all over the world to join him. They came from every continent and included representatives of companies such as Norsk Hydro (Norway), Volkswagen (Germany), 3M (USA), Ciba Geigy (Switzerland), Mitsubishi (Japan), John Laing (UK), Antah Holdings Berhard (Malaysia), Northern Telecom (Canada), First Chartered Securities Ltd (Kenya), Salim Group (Netherlands), Oji Paper Ltd (Japan) and Mount Isa Mines Pty (Australia). Their contribution was presented as a book entitled *Changing Course*.[7] The first part of the book consisted of an analysis of the challenge we face as a world community, much of which is covered here in chapter 2. The second part consisted of a series of case studies, some of which are described here in later chapters.

This initiative provides an example of how important it is for chief executives of large commercial and industrial enterprises to demonstrate their leadership in tackling the global predicament. Phase 1 of their work was to provide the contribution to UNCED and they have now embarked on Phase 2 which involves widescale implementation of their recommendations, with a re-formed organisation.

Tomorrow's Company

The Royal Society for the Encouragement of Arts, Manufactures and Commerce (RSA)[8] has initiated an Inquiry entitled 'Tomorrow's Company: the Role of Business in a Changing World'. This was stimulated, in particular, by Charles Handy when he gave the Shank Memorial Lecture in December 1991, to some 200 RSA Fellows under the title 'What is a Company for?'. The outcome has been a leadership initiative and the formation of an inquiry team.

The inquiry team consists of representatives from several leading organisations, some of whom are chief executives of major organisations. The concern expressed by some members of the team is that the philosophical rationale for business is now in question. They support a wide ranging inquiry which they believe could lead to a restatement of the underlying role of business in society. The outcome of this inquiry is expected in 1995, following the Interim Report in 1994.

The inquiry team has established a number of task forces focusing on different aspects of the broad topic. To enable RSA members to contribute to the inquiry process an inquiry network has been established and a number of network workgroups have been formed.

International Chamber of Commerce

The Institute for Business Ethics (IBE) conducted a survey among 500 of the top 1,000 UK companies on the management of environmental issues. The report highlighted the crucial role of organisations such as the Confederation of British Industry (CBI) and the International Chamber of Commerce (ICC) in fostering corporate responsibility on environmental matters. The main findings were that leadership from the top is vital, staff at all levels should be involved, policies should be comprehensive, clear objectives should be set with measurable goals, internal and external communication should be effective and procedures for monitoring and review should be established.[9]

ICC has published the *Business Charter for Sustainable Development* which has been signed by 1,200 companies from 50 different countries around the world.[10] The signatories encompass very large industrial corporations, very small service companies, major financial institutions, and business schools. Over 100 of the top 500 corporations in Europe had signed the charter by October 1992 and the numbers are rising steadily. The Charter consists of sixteen clauses and is reproduced in Appendix 3 of this book. It is a voluntary commitment but the final clause declares the intention to report progress on meeting the requirements of the other fifteen clauses. A summary of the initial reports has been published in an ICC book.[11]

The ICC formed the World Industry Council for the Environment (WICE) in 1993 to establish close links with governments and inter-governmental organisations. It will also give publicity to business achievements in environmental matters, report progress on implementing the Charter, provide a network for the exchange of company experience, promote technology cooperation and foster partnership projects.

Union Carbide

Sometimes it takes a disaster to awaken interest in environmental issues; for example Union Carbide in Bhopal and Exxon in Alaska. In both cases mismanagement after the disaster harmed the organisations as much as the adverse publicity about the incidents themselves. Both organisations have since become deeply involved not only in their own interests but also in the interest of environmental management.

Robert Kennedy, Chief Executive of Union Carbide, speaking in London in October 1992, said that the greatest barrier to effective environmental management is the need to change organisational culture and behaviour. He went on to say that it is necessary to cultivate a feeling of dissatisfaction with current practices, to build a vision of a future desired state and to take practical action to achieve the desired outcomes. Robert Kennedy's remarks paraphrase the reason why this book has been written. These ideas will be enlarged in chapter 9, where these and other ways of managing organisational change are described.

Buying Behaviour

The influence of environmental criteria on buying behaviour has become sufficiently strong for market research to identify a new class of consumer. In January and June 1989 two major conferences were held in London on the theme of attracting and keeping the green consumer.[12] The fact that general conferences of this kind have not been repeated is an indication of the speed at which things are changing. Conferences and seminars with broad, generalised themes have given way to more focused events tailored to specific audiences.

A survey carried out in 1992 among UK marketing directors showed that environmental affairs were considered one of the top three communications concerns for the 1990s. The other two were corporate reputation and consumer marketing. The report made it clear that adopting green policies would require changes in corporate culture – not just minor adjustments to the Mission Statement.[13] The overt evidence during the 1980s was that yuppies (young upwardly mobile people) were making all the running, and they overshadowed those who felt deep concern about how the world was evolving. This latter group, not yet named, could well become a powerful force during the 1990s.

There is little doubt that social development and environmental management are the challenges for the twenty-first century. These will also be the areas in which business organisations will gain competitive advantage by seeking new opportunities and contributing to solutions which tackle the global predicament.

Innovation

In this section we look at some significant innovations which have been introduced in recent years and which have particular relevance to the global predicament and to business.

Advisory Committee for Business and the Environment[14]

In May 1991 the Advisory Committee on Business and the Environment (ACBE) was set up to strengthen the dialogue between leaders in industry and government. ACBE was jointly sponsored by the Department of Trade and Industry (DTI) and the Department of the Environment (DOE), and soon established four working groups on global warming, environmental management, recycling and commercial and export opportunities. They publish regular reports[15] to put forward their recommendations to government and others.

The *Report of the Financial Sector Working Group* arose from the first joint consideration by the financial sector of its response to environmental problems. It recommends that information already disclosed should be made more easily understandable and accessible, and that all companies should be encouraged to publish environmental reports. The report also acknowledges that all businesses have an impact on the environment and proposes that every business in the financial sector should publish its environmental policy. In particular it recommends that 'the London Stock Exchange should consider adopting standards of environmental disclosure as one of the requirements of its listing particulars.'[16]

Confederation of British Industry

The Confederation of British Industry (CBI) has had an active Environment Unit for many years and publishes guidelines for business, including a popular booklet on environmental audits. It has established the Environment Business Forum which holds regular meetings and now has 250 members.[17] The aims of the Forum include:

• helping members to pursue environmental excellence;
• providing environmental information;
• demonstrating the effectiveness of voluntary action; and
• encouraging partnership arrangements to assist smaller companies to improve their environmental performance.

Rocky Mountain Institute (RMI)

Amory and Hunter Lovins of the Rocky Mountain Institute have established a worldwide reputation for creative work on energy, global security, water, agriculture, transportation and economic renewal.[18]

Whereas most official approaches to energy policy are based on projecting trends and estimating broad future requirements the Rocky Mountain Institute starts from the requirements for energy. They begin with the jobs for which energy is required, how much is needed for each task and what is the cheapest way to get it. This approach led Lovins to estimate in 1972, when actual consumption was 75 quads (quadrillion

BTUs) per annum, that the USA energy requirement for the year 2000 would be 125 quads. At that time official estimates ranged from 160 quads to 230 quads. Current predictions have come down to 60 to 70 quads and Lovins now believes that by 2080 the USA could get by on 15 quads.

The RMI estimates are based on the strict application of a host of energy saving measures, including weatherisation, efficient technology and improved insulation, and the development of renewable energy sources. The importance of reasonably accurate estimates, based on the use for which different sorts of energy are required, is vitally important. Increasing production of energy is very expensive, and if the energy cannot be sold the utilities that provide it are liable to go bankrupt. Rather than face this, the utilities try to influence government to help stimulate demand for their product, even if there are other less damaging, cheaper ways in which appropriate energy can be provided.

The RMI have done some remarkable work and the Lovins's book *Energy Unbound*[19] is well worth reading even if it is written primarily for the USA.

Technology Exchange

One of the recommendations from the Earth Summit was that appropriate technology should be more readily available around the world and that this would make a considerable contribution to achieving sustainable development. The Technology Exchange Ltd, established in 1985, is a non-profit making company controlled by a voluntary Board comprising people who have made significant contributions to technology transfer. It enables manufacturers to locate new product and process developments which can be purchased, directly or through joint venture arrangements, to strengthen and improve their product range.

The Exchange owes its origin to the Intermediate Technology Development Group[20] and the Local Enterprise Trust Movement. It links business organisations, universities, development authorities and information services in over seventy countries and handles 500 business to business introductions per month. It works closely with the United Nations Industrial Development Organisation (UNIDO), through which the Exchange Catalogues are published. These catalogues describe products, materials and processes for which firms can provide equipment, training and support services for sale, licensing or joint venture arrangements. Techmart events have taken place, or will do so in the near future, in India, Brazil, Costa Rica, Mexico, Vietnam and Zambia. Published in two volumes, the catalogues describe technology under twenty-nine categories including agriculture, mining, organic chemicals, electronics, medicine, communications, transport, energy and water.

Learning

Another key area for initiatives is learning. Because time is short for devising and implementing solutions to the Earth predicament we cannot afford to rely solely on children growing up, eventually occupying leadership roles and then applying their knowledge. Initiatives are needed in adult education so that those in the thirty-plus age group can learn quickly and effectively, integrate their experience and apply their knowledge and skills wisely and appropriately in their own sphere of influence. Several initiatives in this area are worth noting.

The World Bank

Large global institutions have shifted the emphasis of their work. For example the World Development Report is published annually by the World Bank. The 1990 Report focused on poverty, in 1991 the theme was development strategies, and in 1992 it was development and the environment.[21]

Three examples of potential solutions to environmental pollution, from The World Bank Report 1992, are described here in general terms:

- separating the direct link between growth in gross domestic product (GDP) and polluting emissions;
- a combined approach to reducing emissions; and
- in the sources of primary energy.

The potential for separating the direct link between growth in GDP from polluting emissions is illustrated in chart 10:

Achieving this will depend on several factors including more efficient combustion of fuel so that emissions are reduced, making better use of each unit of energy consumed, and replacing fossil fuels with renewable sources of energy where this is possible. All these changes can be encouraged by stricter regulation of inefficient energy use, and by financial incentives which encourage appropriate changes, and penalties to discourage wasteful practices. The findings of the RMI strongly endorse this approach and describe many examples of successful applications.

Reducing Emissions

The World Bank cites efficiency reforms to encourage more efficient use of resources and abatement measures which involve adopting cleaner technologies, as the main techniques for reducing emissions. Efficiency reforms alone achieve some improvement, but together with abatement measures could reduce emissions below 1990 levels.

In temperate climates, where 30 to 50 per cent of energy is used for heating purposes, it is possible to make much greater use of wasted heat.

Chart 10: GDP and Pollution

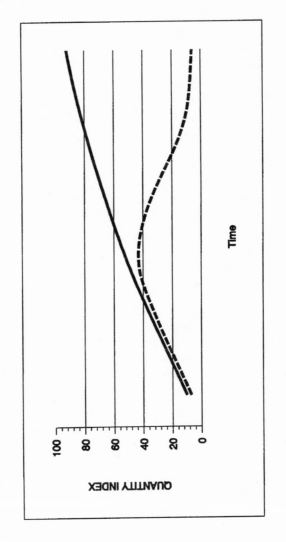

With appropriate incentives and cleaner, more efficient technologies, the link between GDP (solid line) and pollution (dotted line) is being broken.
Source: World Development Report 1992.

Chart 11: Reducing Emissions

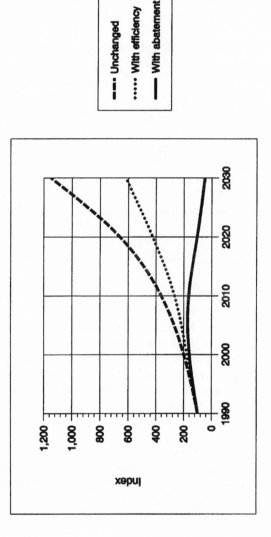

Legend:
- – – Unchanged
- ⋯⋯ With efficiency
- —— With abatement

Source: World Development Report 1992. Index (1990 + 100)
Unchanged scenario assumes current policies and practices. Efficiency means more
efficient use of resources. Abatement means efficiency and cleaner technology.

Combined heat and power (CHP) schemes, which are now receiving more attention, are designed to do this. More efficient combustion of fossil fuels can also be achieved in engines and boilers. Renewable-source energy from wind generators, tidal barrages and solar panels can be introduced as costs come down. Financial incentives could be used more widely to speed up these changes. Finally more effective information and education, explaining the environmental benefits, could also be used to demonstrate cost-effectiveness.

Changes in the Sources of Primary Energy

The third example from the World Bank report on potential solutions to environmental pollution, concerns the types of energy used, and shows the different proportions of world primary energy consumption. Fossil fuel sources are shown as declining dramatically over the next sixty years, while hydroelectric and nuclear sources decline slightly. The compensating factor which shows significant growth is energy from renewable sources. This would not only reduce emissions but would also achieve a significant move towards a sustainable world. The forms of renewable energy would vary from country to country depending on what is available: geothermal energy in Iceland and the Philippines, wind and tidal energy in Northern Europe, and solar energy in tropical countries. The business opportunities associated with developments of this kind will be explored in chapter 7.

New Economics Foundation

More attention is now being paid to alternative ways in which to measure economic progress. The conventional yardsticks of gross national product (GNP) and gross domestic product (GDP) are recognised as unsatisfactory even by institutions such as the World Bank.[22] Meanwhile people like Herman Daly and John Cobb have worked out in some detail how to redirect economics towards community, environmental and sustainable development priorities.[23]

The New Economics Foundation and other organisations are working on formulating alternative indicators for measuring economic success.[24] They also organise The Other Economic Summits (TOES) which are held at the same time and in the same place as the Economic Summit conferences of the seven leading world economies (G7), and which offer a very different perspective on how things might be.

New economic thinking gives emphasis to:

• enabling people to make wise choices;
• conserving resources;
• recognising that the environment is not separate from nor secondary to the economy;

Chart 12: Sources of Primary Energy

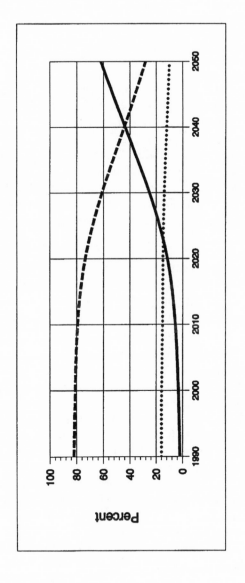

--- Fossil Fuels   ····· Hydroelectric & Nuclear   —— Renewables

Source: World Development Report 1992

- recognising that environmental changes which threaten peace and security stem from economic and physical realities;
- treating the world economy as an integrated entity, with several autonomous levels which are interdependent; and
- protecting values which are important but which it is difficult or impossible to protect in the market.

The Environment Council

The Environment Council, first formed in the early 1970s as The Council for Environmental Conservation, has become a powerful forum for organisations and individuals. In 1989 the Council launched its Business and Environment Programme. In the first year the Programme attracted over 500 companies including 61 of *The Times* 'Top 100 companies in the UK'. Nearly 10,000 delegates attended 37 programmes and briefings. The Programme continues to flourish and in early 1993 had 800 members, which is believed to be the largest group of environmental managers anywhere in the world.[25] Members receive a handbook which is updated monthly, and can take part in a wide range of seminars, conferences and briefings.

In 1994 The Environment Council introduced 'Conservers at Work', which is a scheme requested by members of the Business and Environment Programme to encourage staff at every level to get involved in the practical implementation of corporate policy and to gain an understanding of environmental issues.

Global Action Plan for the Earth

The Global Action Plan for the Earth (GAP) is an international initiative, started in the USA by David Gershon,[26] to enable individuals to take effective environmental action in their households, workplace and communities. GAP is designed to help people reduce their impact on the environment and is particularly relevant to those living in industrialised countries. The scheme enables participants to measure and record their household's current impact on the environment. Ideally they work in EcoTeams, typically made up of six households living near to each other. They use the Action Packs to guide themselves through a six-month programme. In the first month they concentrate on household waste. Having classified, weighed and measured their waste they are guided by the Action Pack to find ways in which to reduce it. The guidance includes suggestions for avoiding waste in the first place, re-using some articles and recycling others. The teams send in their starting and finishing figures to their national office and receive back data on the total savings achieved by all those who are taking part in the scheme.

In the second month the teams move on to the use of energy in the home and follow the same procedure of measuring their starting points, finding ways to reduce energy consumption and measuring again.

In the third month they move on to water consumption, the fourth month looks at transport and ways of getting around, the fifth month at shopping and eco-wise buying and the final month considers how the GAP idea can be taken to others. This might be to get other EcoTeams into action, to influence people they work with, or to lobby local or national government.

By the end of the six month programme the average EcoTeam in the UK has been able to reduce their waste by 36%, carbon dioxide emissions by 635 kg per year and petrol consumption by 15%. GAP is now active in the USA, Canada, the UK, Germany, Holland, Sweden and Norway and is expected to extend to Finland, Switzerland and Australasia by 1994.

Communications

The media have a vital role to play in keeping people informed about environmental and community issues, explaining what they are and in describing ways in which progress is being made.

Television, Radio, Magazines and Newspapers

Every TV channel has developed its own environmental programmes – many of them quite excellent. The standard of photography and commentary is very high and many of these programmes are broadcast during peak viewing times and attract large audiences. This is one of the most important ways in which people of all ages gain environmental understanding. Many excellent radio programmes are also broadcast and incorporate environmental themes into other programmes such as those on farming.

Many magazines now have their own environmental sections and leading environmentalists contribute regular columns. Newspapers also devote more attention to the environment than before and some have special weekly sections, articles on particular topics and/or periodic supplements.

These are all useful developments and help to communicate vital messages. There are two areas where more could be done. First the juxtaposition of contradictory messages, such as a story or advertisement which flouts environmental responsibility placed alongside an important development initiative, should be avoided. Secondly more can be done to bring home more clearly how individual behaviour has a direct impact on the environment or the community; for example, how replacing light bulbs with low energy, long life, bulbs not only saves money, but the cumulative effect, if enough people do it, can obviate the need for a new power station. This helps to bridge the gap between concerns that are felt and actions that can be taken.

Compact Disc Interactive

There is no doubt that compact discs have improved the quality of sound recordings and the rapid growth of this market has been helped significantly by manufacturers' agreements on technology standards. A similar innovation is now taking place with compact disc interactive (Cdi) which enables people to change their television set into a communication and learning medium with which they can interact. This sort of participative experience is not only more interesting but also provides scope for deeper learning. As the technology improves, more programmes become available and the price comes down, more people will be able to afford to purchase Cdi.

There are already some very interesting Cdi products which leading-edge companies such as Sony and Philips are marketing, and which provide scope for business growth. As they develop many organisations will want to consider the use of this and related technology for communicating to their staff, their customers, and their suppliers.

Waste Management and Life Cycle Analysis

Waste management and recycling is another topic which is receiving increased attention from local authorities and some industrial organisations. The UK target is to achieve 25 per cent recycling by 1995. To keep up with this topic funds have been provided (by undeclared benefactors) to publish and distribute an excellent publication, the *WARMER* bulletin (World Action for Recycling Materials and Energy from Rubbish) which is available free to anyone who wishes to receive a copy on a regular basis.[27]

Life cycle analysis, which is a way of assessing the environmental impact of products at every stage of their life cycle, is growing in importance. The Society of Environmental Toxicology and Chemistry – Europe (SETAC) is an organisation which brings together different interests concerned with this subject. SETAC publish a bi-monthly newsletter available free to those who wish to receive a copy.[28]

Open Systems

As the art and science of environmental management develops, the significance of open-systems thinking grows with it. The term 'open systems' is applied to computer systems and networks, to the development of systems thinking generally, to the ways in which human organisations work and to the way in which the boundaries between different systems are defined.

Environmental Management

The Global Environmental Management Initiative (GEMI) was inaugurated in 1991 and established links between total quality management (TQM) and environmental management. The proceedings of the first GEMI conference, held in January 1991, have been published.[29] The links between TQM and environmental management have grown stronger and some now talk of TQEM – total quality environmental management. This concept is very helpful to organisations which have adopted quality programmes because they can use most of the procedures used in TQM to manage environmental issues. The main additional factor for environmental management is to understand and measure the ways in which a particular firm, or operation, impacts on the environment. Quality management and environmental management systems are both powerful approaches to developing sound processes but they also focus on how to do things better in general. They assume that effective implementation of these processes will produce improved results. This does not always follow.

The British Standards Institute (BSI) have developed two British Standards in recent years which are relevant to the theme of this book, namely BS5750 (Quality) and BS7750 (Environmental Management Systems). There is also an international quality standard which is being developed for environmental management.

An Integrated Approach to Waste Reduction

The European Recovery and Recycling Association (ERRA) has various schemes in operation. One of these, in Adur in West Sussex, involves the weekly collection of household waste which has been sorted by householders into separate containers for aluminium, other metals, glass, plastic and paper. The pilot project is investigating the possibility of achieving integrated waste management at no extra cost. Procter and Gamble is a founder member of ERRA and is actively involved in this scheme.

One of the main reasons for initiating the scheme is that household waste management is an issue that affects many different interests. Manufacturers of food and household goods, product designers, distributors, retailers, and local authorities are all involved. Such interested parties increasingly appreciate that their own systems interact with others to create the problems of waste management and that they need to work together to find solutions.

Jonathan Williams has established a Group for Environmental Manufacturing (GEM) to provide a service which facilitates the search for solutions to this kind of complex problem involving different people and organisations with different interests.[30]

Reviewing Paper Usage

London Electricity gave a presentation to an Environment Council seminar on their review of paper usage. They undertook a project to find out how much paper they used, all the different kinds of paper that were involved and what they could do to reduce consumption and recycle waste paper. An additional goal was to achieve significant improvements in environmental impact without increasing their costs. They achieved their goals but also identified one particular problem which they could not tackle alone.

The company's invoices have to comply with standards laid down by the banks because part of the invoice is processed mechanically on equipment purchased and run by the banks. This equipment works well only if the quality of paper that goes through the machines meets exacting standards. London Electricity could not change the quality of paper they use for their printed invoices without the agreement of the banks. This problem is a very good illustration of open systems in action and the need for cooperation to set and achieve new standards.

Similar issues of multiple involvement arise when considering the packaging of all household and other goods.

Conflict Resolution

The final area we consider here is concerned with how disputes, disagreements and conflict are managed. An increasing number of issues involve people and organisations with different interests and perspectives. They do not always see eye to eye. The manner in which issues are tackled has a profound effect on whether escalation into serious conflict can be avoided and how an amicable solution which deals with the real issues can be found.

Avoiding Deadlock

There is increasing interest around the world in new ways of dealing with disputes and conflict. The art of negotiating has changed from achieving an outcome favourable to oneself (win/lose) to seeking outcomes where both, or all, parties have a favourable result (win/win). Win/lose is concerned with coming out on top whatever the consequences: win/win seeks solutions acceptable to both, or all, parties. The latter is also much more appropriate to companies which rely on repeat business from the customers. Most training in negotiation now focuses on 'win/win' concept, and is supported by a growing range of management literature on this subject.[31]

The Harvard Law School has been running a programme on negotiation, and Larry Susskind has been one of the most prominent advocates of their findings.[32] There have been some notable achievements, particularly in the USA, in applying the methods described. The preconditions for successful outcomes are now much better understood, and include:

- how the start up phase is progressed;
- ways in which 'representatives' are selected and their role defined;
- how the agenda is set;
- how facts and information are gathered;
- the way in which negotiations are handled;
- how the draft agreements are drawn up; how decisions are made; and
- what happens during implementation.

IDR Europe was founded in 1989 by a group of lawyers, businessmen and professional mediators to provide an alternative, cheaper means of resolving disputes.[33] IDR Europe provides the following services:

- dispute analysis;
- dispute prevention strategies;
- conflict management audits;
- intra-organisational mediation;
- training in negotiation and mediation skills; and
- on-line advice services.

In the UK the Centre for Dispute Resolution (CEDR) was formed with the backing of the Confederation of British Industry to develop alternative dispute resolution as a way of avoiding expensive litigation.[34]

Environmental Resolve is an initiative of the Environment Council which extends the Council's long established 'bridge-building' role by offering a service which can facilitate and mediate in avoiding and resolving environmental disputes.

Participatory Management

Many large firms have been working for some years on ways in which their management styles can become more participatory. This has been a growing area of personal development for managers and much has been achieved in several large organisations. There is considerable common ground between the skills involved in conflict resolution and those required for participatory management. Wider sharing of experience would help both the public and private sectors and could lead to further innovative steps in developing the art of participatory management and conflict resolution.

Other Initiatives

The examples described are by no means the whole story. A number of initiatives have been taken and a few of these are worth a brief mention to illustrate how widespread the search for ethical and environmental solutions has become.

One of the interesting trends in society has been the growth in ethical investments. Holden Meehan published their fifth report on this subject in July 1994.[35] They estimate that in the USA ten per cent of all investments are now screened to test their ethical credentials, and that in the UK the total scale of screened investments is growing fast. Green and ethical funds in the UK still represent a very small share of the market, but throughout the recession it was a sector that continued to grow. This growth is reflected in chart 13, which gives figures for some of the major funds. The good funds perform above the market average.

The military, too, have been reviewing their traditional role. Proper soldiering in today's world has been written up in a recent report.[36] The case is made for soldiers to be involved in peace keeping, peace building, disaster relief and environmental security. The research for this report covered over twenty countries and illustrated, with examples, how these changes have already taken place in many instances.

Some remarkable changes have also taken place in the size of membership of environmental organisations, including pressure groups, over the past twenty years. In the early 1970s Greenpeace and Friends of the Earth were just forming. They were regarded as fringe organisations with particular interests which were of little concern to most people. During the period 1971 to 1991 the number of members of various environmental groups grew dramatically, as can be seen in chart 14.

Chart 13: Ethical and Green Investments

Fund: £ millions	May'90	Oct'91	Feb'93	Jun'94	Stars for Screening
Friends Provident	158	200	244	414	*****
Abbey Life Ethical	7	7	11	22	****
Merlin Ecology	33	34	34	62	*****
Scottish Equitable Ethical	4	5	6	26	*****
Clerical Medical Evergreen	4	9	7	16	*****
NPI Global Care		New	2	7	*****
Eagle Star Env Opportunities	6	7	8	14	*
Commercial Union Env'al Pens	5		10	33	**
Number of Funds	17		31	30+	
Number of Fund Managers			20	22	
Total Invested	280		400	750	

Source: Holden Meehan, "An Independent Guide to Ethical and Green Investment, 4th and 5th editions, 1993 & 1994.

Notes: "Stars for screening" are given to reflect the rigour with which ethical considerations were judged in 1994.

Chart 14: Membership of Environmental Organisations

UK

Organisation	1971	Thousands 1981	1991
Civic Trust	214		222
CPRE	21	29	45
Friends of the Earth (England)	1	18	111
National Trust (England)	278	1,046	2,152
National Trust (Scotland)	37	110	234
Ramblers Association	22	37	87
RSNC	64	143	250
RSPB	98	441	852
Woodland Trust		20	150
Worldwide Fund for Nature	12	60	227
Greenpeace *			387

Source: Social Trends 1993, HMSO
* WARMER Bulletin No 37 May 1993, P 20

USA	Thousands 1970	1990
National Wildlife Federation	2,600	5,800
Greenpeace		2,000
Sierra Club	114	566
National Audubon Society	105	515
Wilderness Society	66	363
Environmental Defence Fund	10	150
National Resources Defence Council		140

Source: WARMER Bulletin No 37 May 1993, P 20
Quoting from The World Environment 1972-1992 by
Mustafa K Tolba & Osama El-Kholy, Chapman & Hall.

The 1970s and 1980s saw the transition of environmental organisations from fringe to mainstream. During the 1980s growing numbers of people were searching for environmentally appropriate products. They were also joining environmental groups which were gaining strength all the time.[37] This buoyant trend in membership took a dip in 1992/93 in some of the largest environmental groups with a consequent reduction in their finances; but it is too early to say whether this is a temporary set back or a more permanent change. At least one of the largest environmental organisations was also undertaking a change of role in 1993 and placing more emphasis on seeking solutions.

Local Exchange Trading Schemes (LETS) have been in existence for several years and are growing rapidly around the world. During 1992 the number of schemes in Britain grew from 10 to 40 and a further growth to over 200 was achieved by 1994. These schemes enable people to give and receive services from other registered users through a barter system. In each place where a scheme operates, the 'currency' is given an appropriate name. In Stroud, Gloucestershire it is 'Strouds', in Brighton they are 'Brights'. People joining the scheme are expected to identify and place a value on some service they can offer. They are also encouraged to use services already on offer from others. By getting into debt they are stimulated to find the market and correct price for the service they offer.

During the recession many people have found that these arrangements have enabled them to benefit from services provided by others, without having to find the cash to pay. Those who are unemployed have found this to be a way in which they can get back into action and recover self-respect. Payments are made by special cheque books in the local currency at the agreed rate per hour. The range of services is enormous and includes such things as window cleaning, plumbing, financial advice, baby sitting and legal advice. Those who have experienced the schemes in action find that they make money a more useful commodity for those things that they cannot buy through their local LETS.

LETS operate in North America, Japan, East and West Europe, Australia and New Zealand. So far most arrangements are local but work is in hand to see how trading between schemes could be developed.

One of the consequences of schemes like LETS and GAP is that consumer pressure builds up and exerts influence on buying decisions. This in turn influences businesses, and empowered people find new ways to make their voice heard while their actions demonstrate their interest and commitment.

In the educational sector, environment is now a cross-curricular subject in schools, probably throughout the world. Children are learning fast and taking part in many projects involving practical field work. As a result, parents, especially if their children are in the five to fifteen age bracket, are being confronted by an increasingly demanding set of questions. They are being asked what work they do, how the organisations for which they work are damaging the environment, and what they are doing about it. The comments from children are a very strong influence on managers and have stimulated more action than many other sources of influence.

This influence from children is likely to strengthen as more of them become involved not only in environmental initiatives but also in such things as youth parliaments (established in Sweden by The Natural Step.) It is easy to forget that children have access to the same information that is available to adults. Armed with a few facts they have an ability to ask simple questions in a direct way, to shame their parents, to draw attention to the generation gap and to reveal a sense of innocent justice, all of which pose demanding challenges requiring increasingly pressing answers.

Legislation

The European Community has been adopting laws on environmental matters since 1967. By 1970, six such laws had been adopted, and this rose to 55 by 1980. During the 1980s a further 200 laws were passed. In 1990 an additional 18 were added, and 38 in the following year. At the time of writing, many more laws are being prepared. This upsurge in legislation is a good indication of the strength of feeling that exists about environmental matters, and the confidence that laws are an effective way to help reduce and prevent environmental damage.

This confidence in legislation is not always appropriate. The sheer number of new laws makes it very difficult for people to find out about the regulations, let alone comply with them. Furthermore, legislation often stimulates an enormous amount of creative energy to find ways round it. These are not arguments for having no legislation but they do strengthen the case for trying to keep it simple and for using legislation in those areas where it is a real priority and where it works well.

In addition to legislation, governments use fiscal measures to penalise practices which damage the environment, and provide incentives for technology and policies which reduce environmental damage. A very successful example of this was the use of different rates of taxation to stimulate the market for unleaded petrol. Once the price difference became significant the demand for unleaded petrol increased rapidly.

The richness and variety of measures that could be adopted are described in *Costing the Earth* by Frances Cairncross.[38] One widely discussed measure is the carbon tax which would penalise the use of fossil fuels. This is a controversial issue and is likely to remain contentious. If incentives for renewable energy were also provided this could bring about a very healthy adjustment in the types of fuel used and the amount of carbon dioxide released into the environment.

Legislation has proved to be one of the most significant ways in which companies are influenced to take action on their environmental policies, and is probably the only effective way in which to get action on those issues which do not directly benefit corporate results.

Notes

1   Starke, 1990, p. 11.
2   Gore, 1992.
3   See Appendix 4 for a summary of the Earth Summit Agreements.
4   Johnson (ed.), 1992, and Quarrie (ed.), 1992.
5   The Guardian, 9 February 1992, p. 10.
6   Radford, Tim, 'B-52 Launches Eco-satellite', in the Guardian, 11 February 1993.
7   Schmidheiny, 1992, p. 11, 1993. The BCSD was reformed in 1994.
8   RSA, London.
9   Institute of Business Ethics, London.
10   International Chamber of Commerce, Paris, France and London.
11   Willums and Goluke, 1992, (see also Appendix 2).

12 Attracting the Green Consumer and Attracting and Keeping the Green
    Consumer, proceedings of a conference run by Marketing and Media
    Conferences in association with Marketing Week.
13 News from Paragon Communications Plc Group, Issue no. 12.
14 See Sources of Help.
15 Department of Trade and Industry (see Annotated Bibliography).
16 Report of the Financial Sector Working Group, ACBE, 1993, p. 12.
17 Confederation of British Industry, London.
18 See Rocky Mountain Institute in Sources of Help.
19 Lovins and Lovins, 1986.
20 See Sources of Help.
21 The World Bank, 1992.
22 The World Bank, 1992, p. 35.
23 Daly and Cobb, 1990.
24 New Economics Foundation, London.
25 The Environment Council, London.
26 Global Action Plan (see Sources of Help).
27 World Action for Recycling Materials, and Energy from Rubbish, UK,
    Quarterly.
28 SETAC, Europe Publication, Brussels.
29 GEMI (see Sources of Help).
30 See Sources of Help.
31 Fisher and Ury, 1981.
32 Susskind and Cruickshank, 1987.
33 See Sources of Help.
34 See Sources of Help.
35 Holden Meehan, An Independent Guide to Ethical and Green Investment
    Funds, Holden Meehan, 40 Park Street, Bristol BS1 5JG, February 1993 and
    July 1994.
36 Harbottle, Brigadier Michael (Retired), What is Proper Soldiering? published
    by The Centre for International Peace Building, 9 West Street, Chipping
    Norton, Oxon OX7 5LH.
37 Porritt, 1988.
38 Cairncross, 1991.

4

Beliefs and Values

*We shall not cease from exploration
and the end of all our exploring
will be to arrive where we started
and know the place for the first time.*

T. S. Eliot

The predicament we now face is not the result of some devious plot to create a mess. Nobody wanted to make a hole in the ozone layer, to disturb the Earth's climate, to create acid rain, to destroy topsoil, to diminish fresh water supplies, to over-fish the oceans or to cause excessive population growth. These consequences of industrial development were never desired. They are the unintended side effects resulting from the pursuit of other goals.

Decision-making has been based, most of the time, on best endeavours and good intentions. Things might have been very different if only the decisions taken all over the world had been wiser, if those taking them had been better informed and if the side effects had been properly assessed first. However, there is nothing to be gained by trying to rewrite history. We need to accept the situation as we find it and concentrate on influencing today's and tomorrow's decisions.

The environmental predicament is inextricably interwoven with the ways in which societies function, are managed, institutions are established and indeed how we all lead our lives in the communities in which we live. The only avenue for solutions is through the actions of people and the influences on them.

To do this it is helpful to look at what guides our behaviour and our judgements. If we understand better the basis for the decisions we make then we can test their validity more easily. The influences on our behaviour, and our decisions, can be represented diagrammatically to show that for each one of us our behaviour is influenced by our beliefs, by our values and by the culture of the community in which we live. Our values are at the centre of our being, then there are the beliefs we hold most strongly and both are influenced by the culture in which we live. All three influence the way we behave.

The terms behaviour, culture, beliefs, values, have various meanings, so it is important to identify the sense in which they are used here:

Chart 15
VALUES, BELIEFS AND CULTURE

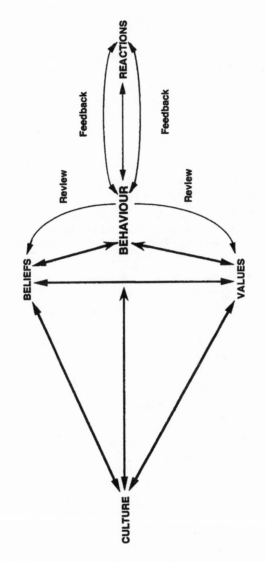

Notes:

1. Our *behaviour* is influenced by our *values* and *beliefs* and by the culture within which we live and work.

2. We can observe the reactions of others to our *behaviour* and receive **feedback** which enables us to examine and change our *behaviour*. We can then review our *beliefs* and *values* and modify them as appropriate.

3. Our *beliefs, values* and *culture* can be influenced by our *behaviour*, but it is a gradual process, requiring the combined influence of like-minded people to effect a change.

© Colin Hutchinson, *Vitality and Renewal*, Adamantine, 1994

(1) Behaviour means actions; what people do and say.
(2) Culture means the customs, traditions, thought processes and ways of doing things that have become the accepted norm – in an organisation or in a society.
(3) Beliefs are views and opinions which take two forms:
    (a) objective, scientific, demonstrable, widely accepted facts; and
    (b) subjective, unproven, personal convictions.
(4) Values are underlying principles that guide how we live.
    (a) moral values about how the world should be for everyone; and
    (b) personal interests which improve things for 'us'.

In this chapter we shall explore the sorts of beliefs that are generally accepted and conclude with a brief look at values. The purpose of doing this is to appreciate some underlying forces in our society and how they influence our pathway towards a sustainable future.

Before embarking on that exploration it is important to appreciate that we live in a turbulent era, at a very delicate point in time when the convergence of pressures discussed in chapter 2 could result in cataclysmic disaster, or a breakthrough to a sustainable society. The situation in the former USSR/Russia, the former Yugoslavia and Ethiopia would suggest that disaster is more likely than a breakthrough. It is not the purpose of this book to try to predict which is more likely, nor to paint a picture of innocent optimism. However, it is the purpose of the book to indicate the conditions which are more likely to prove helpful during the transition to a sustainable society and relevant when it has been achieved. It is also the aim of the book to identify some of the trends which can help the process.

Beliefs

The nature of our beliefs is a productive area for exploration. For example we behave as if the following beliefs – mostly subjective – have been widely accepted, implicitly or explicitly, for many years:

- the Earth is so large that humans cannot harm its life support systems;
- the Earth's resources are inexhaustible;
- the atmosphere and oceans can absorb any amount of pollution without lasting harm;
- population should be left to find its own level;
- strong government and tough legislation is the best way to control the irresponsible behaviour of the masses;
- if the rich get richer the poor will benefit, through 'trickle down' processes;
- justice is a matter for the courts;
- we have little or no obligation to posterity and future generations.

These and similar beliefs are now being re-examined in many countries around the world. They are increasingly recognised as inappropriate for the twenty-first century, and in many countries the search has begun to articulate beliefs which will provide more relevant guidelines for the future. In part this is a result of objective, scientific evidence and in part a result of evolution in personal, subjective beliefs.

First it is helpful to recognise some of the characteristics of the times in which we live.

The Third Wave

In the early nineteenth century when dramatic change was taking place in Britain no one described it as the industrial revolution. It was not until 1884, when Arnold Toynbee's book *The Industrial Revolution* appeared, that the term came into popular use. However, many writers and artists of the time were making predictions from some of the characteristics that they could see clearly. Many of them predicted that industrialisation would mean bigger cities, faster transport, more powerful technologies, and education available to the whole population.

The transition we are experiencing now is comparable in magnitude to the agricultural and industrial revolutions, but has no accepted description. Some people talk of the post-industrial age, but that is descriptive of where we have been rather than where we are going. Others speak of the information revolution, a social transition, the age of communications or the global village. These terms identify some important characteristics but do not quite capture the essence of the transition that is taking place.

Alvin Toffler's book *The Third Wave* is based on the belief that the phase we are in is a transition that is as great as the agricultural and industrial revolutions.[1] He describes many facets of the modern era to support his case and stresses the psychological importance of recognising that our belief systems also need to be modified if we are to cope with the changes, and with the era we are entering.

In transitions of this kind it is inevitable that people will see things differently, and this will often lead to dispute. Some of these disagreements will be the source of creative energy and ideas, while others will lead to long lasting feuds and, in their extreme form, will cause wars. How such conflict is managed will play a large part in the outcome, and we shall return to this later in the chapter.

The Emergence of the Western World View

Children acquire a view of the world from their parents, teachers peers and the media, especially television. This is their world view and it comes to influence strongly how each person regards others, the perspectives and priorities which guide that individual through life. In a similar way societies gain their perceptions of the world, often influenced quite strongly by a few prominent people whose ideas are regarded as particularly valid. A few thoughtful people have been especially influential in establishing a Western world view.

An interesting initiative was taken at San Diego State University by Mary Clark, Professor of Biology, when she inaugurated a course entitled 'Our Global Future'. The six month course brought together some fifteen faculty members to examine the modern world in a holistic way. This initiative provided the basis for her book entitled *Ariadne's Thread*.[2]

A brief digression is appropriate as a reminder about the Greek myth. Ariadne gave a skein of thread to Theseus to enable him to enter the Labyrinth, slay the monster (the Minotaur) and find his way out again. The parallel with our predicament is obvious. We badly need a continuous thread to help us understand the world we have created, find the 'monster' in our midst and then find our way out of the maze so that we can embark on the twenty-first century with greater confidence and be able to create a sustainable world.

A useful step in this process is to use Ariadne's Thread to understand how world views develop. Mary Clark's book traces the emergence of human nature from the origins of life through the development of emotion and instinct to the creation of society and cultures. Groups of people and societies develop shared beliefs and values which give meaning to their lives and provide a framework for survival skills – their national cultures. The world views that result are passionately defended. Because this happens in several different communities the communication between people holding different beliefs is often strained or hostile. It is a real challenge to cooperate with a community with a different view of the world without either overwhelming them or giving up your own treasured beliefs which give meaning to your life.

There are many examples of this, some of which are recent and striking. For example the fighting in Bosnia between Croats, Muslims and Serbs; the problems in Northern Ireland between Protestants and Catholics; and various long-standing tensions in the Middle East.

Mary Clark explores how ideology emerges. She describes the work of anthropologists and discusses the cultural traditions of several tribes from different parts of the world. Attempts have been made to change the culture of some tribes with disastrous results. Their fundamental beliefs were damaged by introducing alien influences with no appreciation of the consequences of what was being imposed.

Religion, which is part of culture, is a powerful influence on society and history is littered with the antipathies that have grown up between people holding different religious beliefs. There are now many initiatives being taken to explore the underlying philosophies of the world's leading religions and to relate them to the predicament we face.

Another important source of influence is the way we learn to think at school. More attention is given to cognitive development and rational thinking than to the exploration of values and beliefs. The result is that education at school is an affirmation of the prevailing culture, but is challenged by some people during further education. The alternative to cognitive development Mary Clark calls 'critique/create', which is a way of penetrating the distortions derived from education, the media and politicians, and cutting through to real understanding, and to the values which provide the foundation for a sustainable future.

The evolution through time of the Western world view is examined from its medieval beginnings through to the emergence of capitalism. The work of people like Thomas Hobbes, John Locke and Adam Smith is discussed and their influence analysed. Their views helped to produce individuals who wanted improved material standards of living, relished competition and sought independence which released them from drudgery and the constraints of socialism.

These views have often resulted in the emergence of small, rich and powerful minorities who dominate the decisions which affect the whole population – South Africa is a classic example. Capitalism reinforces this trend and the emphasis on efficiency becomes a strong influence. So long as the public are willing to accept this situation life is reasonably peaceful, but once there is some successful challenge turmoil can easily result. A less than satisfactory situation can prevail for years with many people feeling alienated, violence being prevalent and cynicism being rife, especially among the young. Growing numbers of people are recognising this scenario and re-examining their own beliefs and the options for change in their own lives.

There has been a parallel development in the communist world with even more dominance, alienation, injustice and damage to the environment. However, with the demise of communism in the early 1990s it is necessary to examine capitalism because it is too easy to believe that the battle has been won and the way ahead is clear. It is not. There are many positive aspects of capitalism but it also has weaknesses which must be understood and changed as we approach the twenty-first century. For example capitalism is an effective way to finance industry, allocate resources, produce goods, effect distribution and achieve wealth and, within a democratic system, it encourages enterprise, personal growth and self-development to improve the quality of life. However, precisely because it has proved superior to communism it is vital that its shortcomings should be recognised and changed. These include the way in which it is blind to such things as clean air, fresh water, healthy trees, integrity of the climate, and the diversity of species – none of which are commodities to be bought and sold.

Mary Clark is not alone in her analysis of the situation and her conviction of how important it is for our values to change. Peter Russell in his book *The White Hole in Time*[3] expresses a concern which reinforces the argument. He makes the point that we did not set out to create the problems. Our behaviour was aimed at creating a better world where food would be plentiful, where there would be protection from wind and rain, disease would be kept within bounds and people could live long and satisfying lives. However, our cultural conditioning is so powerful that we become ensnared by over emphasis on the materialistic world we have created. He adds:

> Humanity already has most of the understanding and technology necessary to avert environmental catastrophe. And we have the money. What we do not have is the will to do what we know is needed.

Can We Summon the Will?

While Peter Russell questions whether we can summon the will, Ronald Higgins, in 1978, wondered whether we could overcome 'the seventh enemy', which he described as the combined effect of political inertia and individual blindness.[4] However, Mary Clark concludes her book with ideas about new modes of thinking, and this is the theme we shall now develop.

The areas in which new modes of thinking are required embrace many important topics including:

- movement towards steady-state economics;
- better measuring devices to supplement gross national product;
- restating underlying moral principles;
- dismantling the remains of colonialism;
- partnership arrangements for appropriate development;
- relating population growth and consumption to the Earth's capacity;
- democratic governance;
- international political integration;
- tolerance of cultural diversity; and
- new approaches to conflict resolution.

Every one of these areas is a vast subject in its own right, but the overlap with Al Gore's priorities in his Global Marshall Plan (chapter 3) is striking. However, two ideas, which are linked, stand out as supremely important. They are the degree to which we can develop cultural tolerance and the way in which we deal with conflict. As Mary Clark puts it:

> There are two requirements for the process of 'critiquing' and creating a world view: a tolerance of diversity among cultures, and a tolerance of criticism and change within one's own.... The greatest challenge before us –

perhaps the greatest challenge humankind has ever faced – is learning
how to eliminate the rigidity of dogma without losing the sense of shared
meaning....we can all learn from one another the skills needed for the task.[5]

Undue reliance is often placed on legislation as the best way to stimulate
the necessary changes. While there is undoubtedly a role for legislation,
and it is probably the single most powerful reason why many companies
have adopted environmental policies, it is essentially a constraining
influence. By contrast, clearly stated values supported by a culture which
reflects those values in action, are a force for positive action. We can harness this force much more effectively than we do. This will require sensitive, well planned and practical initiatives because it is a notoriously difficult area which will be explored further in chapter 10.

Social Trends

Some interesting research on social trends has been carried out in recent
years in the UK and other countries by Applied Futures.[6] Their research
findings were used by Francis Kinsman as the basis for his book
Millennium.[7] He developed the findings and related them to his own consulting experience.

The findings suggest that society is made up of three basic types of
people: the sustenance-driven people, the outer-directed and the inner-
directed. These three categories have different reactions to material circumstances.

Sustenance-driven people are mostly motivated by their need to survive and belong. Although this group includes those people who struggle to survive it also includes many people who are comfortably off.
They fall into this category because they have a strong wish to preserve
their position in life, to belong to one or more groups with whom they
can associate with ease. They tend to be conservative and resist change.
Even when they can afford to widen their interests they are inclined to
stay within the confines of the world that is familiar to them. This is
often reinforced by class consciousness.

The outer-directed people, by contrast, are strongly motivated by their
desire to demonstrate their success. They are keen to show this by displaying status symbols which are recognisable to those they wish to
impress. This is shown by such things as their choice of partner, their
house and its location, the car they drive and the schools they choose for
their children. They seek steady progress in materialistic and financial
terms as each year passes. In pursuit of their chosen goals they are energetic and enthusiastic and often achieve a great deal. Mostly they are
intelligent and well educated in conventional ways. They tend to support the status quo but they can change if this seems likely to enhance
their status.

The inner-directed people are interested in self-fulfilment. The criteria by which they judge their own progress are determined by themselves rather than by a desire to impress others. Many of them have wide-ranging interests, a good understanding of the world around them and considerable tolerance for others with differing outlooks. They are less materialistic than sustenance-driven and outer-directed people. They are more interested in ethics, personal growth, spiritual satisfaction, the environment and the quality of life. They make considerable efforts to continue their education in adult life, often experimenting with unconventional ways of learning.

These three basic types break down into seven sub-categories which are discussed in Kinsman's book. For our purposes it is sufficient to consider the values which are the foundation for the outlook and behaviour of these three categories of people.

The sustenance-driven look nervously to see if their fragile support systems are withstanding the turbulence of the world around them. The outer-directed keep a sharp eye open for how they are perceived and whether anybody else is getting ahead with more ostentatious material status symbols; in which case they need to catch up quickly. The inner-directed seek wholeness and satisfaction from their lives. They are tolerant of others while they seek self-fulfilment for themselves. This self-fulfilment is often combined with a desire to work on new initiatives that are at the frontiers of understanding.

In 1987, when the research was carried out, the three categories were fairly evenly balanced in Britain: 29 per cent were sustenance-driven, 36 per cent outer-directed and 35 per cent inner-directed. Of all the countries in Europe only the Netherlands had more inner-directed people (42 per cent). Scandinavia had fewer sustenance-driven people than other parts of Europe – which is hardly surprising considering the high standard of living and prevailing social structures in Scandinavia. France and Italy had few inner-directed but a higher proportion of sustenance-driven people. Germany had a higher proportion of outer-directed people than any other country in Europe, which places it close to Japan in this category. In the USA, outside the New England States on the East Coast, there is a high concentration of outer-directed people.

This means that the three countries with the strongest economies – the USA, Japan and Germany – have the highest figures for outer directed-people who are strongly driven by materialistic considerations – a conclusion which is unlikely to cause surprise but which does not augur well for finding appropriate leadership as we approach the next century. This may change in the USA as President Clinton and Vice President Gore develop their priorities and the action plans which give them meaning.

In 1990, the UK had the fastest growing proportion of inner-directed people. This was before the full effects of the recession had been felt. The trend may well have been arrested or even reversed, but it might resume when, and if, the economy picks up. One indicator of the trend is the growing proportion of people in Britain who are self-employed or starting new small businesses and avoiding large bureaucratic organisations as a place to work, if they can.

Applied Futures had plans to follow up this research in 1991 and monitor the trends regularly but, as a result of the recession, they failed to get the necessary funding. The rights to pursue this area of research have been purchased by Synergy Brand Values,[8] who conduct values-related research, and the survey is being repeated in 1993. Applied Futures, on the other hand, have moved their headquarters to the USA, to place more emphasis on their strategic consulting. As they point out, there is an obvious link between social trends and strategic corporate planning.

Can We Manage the Conflict?

The pressures on the environment will increase during the coming decades because there is no way in which population growth can be slowed down quickly. The material aspirations of those in developing countries will place heavier demands on resources and on the biosphere. In the short term the emphasis must be on mitigating the adverse effects, by changing from linear, wasteful and toxic industrial processes to those that are cyclic, resource-conserving and more healthy. This will inevitably provoke resistance especially from those industries which are already past their evolutionary peak and are reluctant or unable to change. Newer, relevant industries using more benign technology should be at the forefront of industrial development, but even here there is unlikely to be a smooth passage because there will be dispute about the choice of technology and how to make it widely available in ways that remain profitable.

In the political sphere there will be tensions between the Treasury and other departments. The areas in which budgets could be reduced are military spending and agricultural subsidies: military spending because there is less need now that the Cold War has ended, and agriculture because it is absurd to build up mountains of surplus food. A 20 to 30 per cent reduction in both these areas would generate enough funds to make a profound difference. The incentives which could then be provided would encourage appropriate development of agricultural practices, such as organic farming, and appropriate industrial development. If the budgets of the two targeted areas were cut by as much as 50 per cent, which is perfectly feasible, capital investment in renewable energy sources could also be provided and public transport could be improved.

Of course this will not be easy, as there are very powerful lobbies which would strongly resist such moves. Again the skills to manage such conflict will need to be robust, original and effective.

Within communities there will be increasing tension between short-term requirements, for example the preservation of employment in outdated, polluting and wasteful industries, and the longer-term requirement to reduce the threats of global warming, ozone depletion and acid rain. How we strike the right balance between meeting the needs of today's generation and providing a habitable world for our children and their children will also be a source of great contention.

In all these areas, and many others, we need to experiment with new approaches to managing disagreement. This requires great skill and a clearly articulated values base which will guide our actions. One thing that will help enormously is to recognise that all of us, in every country of the world, face an interwoven set of problems that we cannot solve alone. In effect we share a common problem which can only be tackled effectively if we find new ways to work together. Past methods of dealing with disagreement, such as suppressing it, trying to smooth things over, compromising and abdicating responsibility, will not be adequate. We shall have to find ways in which the underlying causes can be appreciated, and learn to respect those who have different needs. We shall need to use great skill and to persevere until solutions which go a long way to satisfying all interested parties are agreed. Without this there will be insufficient commitment for sound implementation.

This may sound utopian, but work has been done in many spheres for several years on creative ways to solve problems and resolve disputes. Successful applications are known to exist in business organisations, areas of social strife, environmental disputes and domestic situations. We need to promulgate this learning more widely and more quickly.

Emerging Trends

My own subjective view of the trends which appear to be emerging and are desirable for the creation of a sustainable society, are discussed below using the following broad themes:

- quality of life;
- more autonomous ways of working;
- democratic forms of government;
- benign technology;
- socially and environmentally responsible enterprise;
- creative ways in which to manage conflict;
- new economics;

Chart 16: Conflict Resolution

Conflict and communication are closely associated. When communication breaks down the result will often be disagreement. Simple but sound guidelines for effective communication are:

- Between people
- Within groups
- Between groups

Between People

Two people communicate effectively not only when their messages are clearly delivered but also when they receive messages and demonstrate that they have done so, accurately. This calls for:

- Attentive listening
- Accurate paraphrasing of the other person's message
- An ability to identify with how the other person feels.

In addition to these familiar listening skills it is very helpful to work together to identify common ground and the desired outcomes for both parties.

Within Groups

Effective working within groups requires skill and mutual respect between group members. The group itself needs to have jointly agreed clear goals, sound working procedures with a mutually agreed agenda for each meeting. The principles for sound communication described above apply equally within groups.

Conflict within groups can be greatly reduced if group members:

- Communicate effectively
- Understand each others' needs
- Search together for common ground
- Help the group to adopt effective working procedures and clear goals.

Between Groups

Communication between groups is infinitely more difficult. It requires great skill and awareness of how easy it is to upset those who belong to groups other than your own. Intergroup conflict is never easy to manage but can be reduced significantly if certain guidelines are followed:

- Identify a shared goal which both parties wish to achieve and which is hard for either to reach alone
- Develop mutual understanding and agreement of the ground rules for communication between the groups, for example when there is direct contact is the representative:

    * An observer with a restricted brief?
    * A delegate with a closely defined brief?
    * A plenipotentiary with full authority?

Both parties need to understand each others' roles. Without this it is easy for misunderstandings to give rise to suspicions which in turn results in conflict.

Strategies for resolving conflict

There are five main strategies for trying to resolve conflict each of which is used in different circumstances:

- Avoidance or denial that there is disagreement
- Compromise where splitting or sharing occurs
- Dominance where superior power prevails
- Smoothing through deflection or calming feelings
- Reconciliation through consensus.

Only the last really achieves results to which people are committed and therefore stands a good chance of being followed through to effective implementation of agreed outcomes.

Avoidance leaves feelings of frustration and disappointment that no one is facing up to the real issues.

Compromise is appropriate in some circumstances. If two people are arguing about a chicken and it is killed so the meat can be shared rather than one person getting it all the compromise is appropriate if both want meat. But if one party is interested in eggs, half the dead chicken is useless. It is important to recognise when and the sort of compromise that is appropriate.

Dominance which requires compliance from the other party is often used in hierarchical situations. It may work in the short term, and where this is an acceptable culture, but often leads to resentment later and perpetuates the feeling of dependence.

Smoothing ruffled feelings, deflecting from the issue, or using other diversionary tactics is seldom effective. It usually originates from a dislike of conflict and a desire to do almost anything rather than face up to the matter in hand.

Reconciliation through consensus is a demanding way of dealing with conflict. Both parties need to understand each other's perspective and desired outcomes and to have the skills to work for a solution, through negotiation, that meets these expressed needs in some acceptable way. It is time consuming but often saves time and money later because implementation of agreed outcomes is more thorough and more enthusiastic. In the chicken analogy both parties might agree to share the eggs.

The five strategies can be represented diagrammatically:

```
                        High concern
                        for Outcomes
                             |
        DOMINANCE            |         RECONCILIATION
                             |
                             |
                        COMPROMISE
Low concern  _____|_____  High concern
for People                   |                    for People
                             |
                             |
        AVOIDANCE            |           SMOOTHING
                             |
                        Low concern
                        for Outcomes
```

- holistic visions, pluralistic objectives and systems thinking; and
- managing through support and challenge to maintain quality.

In the industrialised countries there is an underlying trend away from sustenance driven-people towards those who are outer-directed and a second shift from outer- to inner-directed. I believe there is a gradual trend towards growing numbers of people placing more emphasis on quality of life rather than simply on higher material standards of living.

The trend towards a higher proportion of inner-directed people means that more people feel empowered to take responsibility for their lives. By their action they are demonstrating that if you give people the space and opportunity to behave responsibly most of them will do so. This has considerable implications for business and should be welcomed. As organisations reduce the layers of management – a widespread trend in Europe – and grant more autonomy to their staff, they need people who can produce effective results with less supervision. Small and medium sized organisations also need to realise that they should create jobs with scope for incumbents to exercise a high degree of autonomy, within guidelines.

Politically there are many countries struggling to move towards more democratic forms of government and to create various forms of modified free market economies. There is also pressure for information to be more freely available and for human rights to be enshrined in some sort of citizens' charter.

In the technological sphere there is increasing demand for benign technology, more recycling processes in manufacturing and farming, more efficient use of energy and the development of renewable forms of energy. All this will help to reverse the trends which are leading to further destruction of the ozone layer, global warming and acid rain. Big business needs to become more socially and environmentally responsible and:

- find ways in which to internalise environmental costs;
- manage waste responsibly and reduce toxic waste to a minimum;
- direct capital investment towards projects, products and processes which help communities and improve the environment;
- cooperate with developing countries in new forms of technology partnership;
- use energy and material resources efficiently; and
- educate employees to understand the new realities.

The pursuit of these objectives will inevitably give rise to internal conflicts which will need skilful managing. Once again it will be imperative to have a Mission Statement, aligned strategies and an organisation culture which adapts to changing circumstances. This will help to determine the appropriate choices in ways which ensure that profitability is

Chart 17: Support & Challenge Groups

The obvious questions are what are Support and Challenge Groups
(S & C Groups)? Why have them? How are they organized? What
are the benefits? The notes below provide some answers.

What are they?

Autonomous or semi-autonomous groups where the members have
agreed how they will work together, which include ground rules
for supporting and challenging each other on the content,
procedures and feelings which emerge in the course of the group's
work. A typical S & C group would have 4 to 8 members.

Why have them?

Performance within a group is at an optimum when the degree of
pressure exerted on members is about right. This will vary from
person to person and from one occasion to another. However, in
general if the pressure is insufficient performance will suffer.
A violin cannot perform well with a slack string! Likewise if
the pressure is too great performance suffers because of the
resultant stress. A violin string that is too tight not only
produces the wrong note but may snap! S & C Groups which work
well help to keep the pressure about right for everyone, use
effective procedures and have productive outcomes.

In hierarchical groups it is often assumed that the leader will
do what is required to challenge or support the members.
Responsibility for outcomes and choice of procedures is
frequently left to the person in charge. When autonomous or
semi-autonomous groups meet there is often concern that whilst
collaboration will be good, quality of output will suffer.
Explicitly agreed ground rules for 'support' and 'challenge'
strengthen the likelihood of effective outcomes without
undesirable side effects.

People who have experience of working in S & C groups often find
that giving appropriate and explicit support is just as demanding
as making an effective challenge.

How are they organised?

They are organised by the members. Some criteria for selecting
the members of your S & C group are described below. The aim is
to establish a climate of openness and trust so that feedback can
be given and received in ways that are helpful to each
individual, working procedures really do work and the results are
satisfying achievements of a high standard.

What are the benefits?

Those who wish to establish networks for various purposes will
find that it is very valuable to have a group of like minded
people with whom they can meet regularly in order to learn more
quickly and both give and receive support. Some important
considerations in forming groups are:

* People who live nearby.
* Complementary (probably different) interests and skills.
* Mutually convenient time(s) and place(s) to meet.
* Agreed understanding for frequency/duration of meetings.
* Willingness to respect different interests of members.
* Mutual interest in learning and feedback.
* Shared understanding of the desired group climate
* Broadly agreed aims and objectives.

The model below describes four different sorts of group climate
which are the result of a different mix of support and challenge.

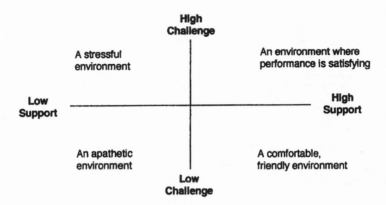

Some examples of different kinds of behaviour are:

Supporting Behaviours :

Listening and paraphrasing
Reflecting feelings
Asking open questions
Seeking common ground
Summarizing conclusions

Challenging Behaviours :

Being assertive
Saying what you want
Asking leading questions
Expressing contrary views
Applying pressure

It is important to recognize the difference between:

* Assertive behaviour which respects the other person and
  aggressive behaviour which does not.

* Supportive behaviour which draws others out and passive
  behaviour which is weak.

* Questions which are intended to be open/supportive but are
  experienced as probing/challenging. How the questions are
  experienced is more important than the intention.

not seriously undermined – but might even be enhanced.

Economics is the most difficult area in which to recognise a discernible trend. However, there is much creative work being done to explore the field of new economics and ways in which current practices could be changed or supplemented to take more account of the known, but not measured, impacts on people and the environment.

As organisations discover that they have a heart as well as a head, and when the recession eases sufficiently to allow more attention to be given to fundamental strategic considerations, much is likely to change. Holistic visions, pluralist objectives, systems thinking and reduced hierarchies will all contribute to the new world of business. Information technology will enable more decisions to be passed down to those closest to the action. As the number of specialised disciplines grows it will be increasingly difficult for senior executives to stay ahead of competition if they perpetuate the dominance/compliance culture. In order to maintain standards, especially if a higher proportion of staff are inner-directed, new ways will have to be found to maintain cohesion and performance standards. One way to do this is by introducing support and challenge groups.

Empowered people will seek more autonomous roles, with cohesion maintained through agreed visions, strategies and operating guidelines. Inevitably this will require enhanced skill in establishing mutual agreement, creative problem solving and conflict resolution. Those companies which are best able to spot emerging trends early, and which have the ability to align the human effort within their organisations, will gain market leadership.

New Beliefs and Values

We can now revisit the inappropriate beliefs set out at the beginning of this chapter, and describe a set of beliefs that would be more appropriate for the twenty-first century:

(1) Earth is a small planet and human activity is imperilling its life-support systems.
(2) Many of the Earth's resources are limited and need to be used wisely.
(3) The atmosphere and oceans on which all life depends can be permanently harmed by pollution and human activity.
(4) Population growth can and should be limited through sensitive education and action.
(5) People should be educated and empowered so that they will behave responsibly, with a limited amount of legislation.
(6) Poverty needs to be tackled directly by providing those in this

predicament with appropriate aid to enable them to help themselves.

(7) Justice depends primarily on fair dealing between individuals and groups.

(8) Our responsibilities span both the present and future generations.

If these beliefs were to become more widely accepted, then we would move towards closer harmony with the Earth and would create communities which are more compatible with human needs.

The values which we need at the centre of our being are not so much new, as requiring more widespread acceptance, and include:

- honesty within ourselves;
- honesty in our dealings with each other;
- justice for all;
- spiritual understanding;
- peace between peoples and nations;
- respect for all life on Earth;
- democratic principles of government;
- freedom of speech; and
- modified free market economies.

Summary

There is some evidence that values are changing, and little doubt that they need to do so if we are to move towards a sustainable society at some future date. New beliefs and values can be encouraged and everyone can contribute to this process.

There is an urgent need for new economic thinking, wise use and conservation of physical resources, and improved respect for ecology and biodiversity – three of the elements in chart 1: 'The Key Elements'. However, the moving force for these changes will come from the fourth element – human communities. This is why our beliefs are so important and why we should articulate them as we approach the twenty-first century. Our core values have been around for a long time but they need to be restated.

As Mikhail Gorbachev, the former Soviet leader, who has formed The International Green Cross which aims to bring together people with high credibility from around the world to lobby world leaders about environmental issues, has said:[9]

"We need an ecology of the soul. Without it all our efforts to save mankind would be pointless. When science and rationality cannot help us, there is only one thing that can save us: our conscience and our moral feelings...Without a change of values within myself, there would not have been perestroika or The International Green Cross."

Our values and beliefs, which are an integral part of our lives, need to be reviewed (see chart 52 for a suggested method). This is not a task confined to leading politicians, captains of industry and learned academics. It is a challenge facing us all. We can contribute by making it happen in our homes, where we work, and among the people with whom we make contact.

Notes

1　Toffler, 1980.
2　Clark, 1989.
3　Russell, 1992.
4　Higgins, 1978.
5　Clark, 1989, pp. 496–7.
6　See Sources of Help.
7　Kinsman, 1990.
8　Synergy Brand Values, 5th Floor Bilton House, 54–58 Uxbridge Road, London W5 2TL.
9　Observer, 25 April 1993.

CHAPTER 5

What Is Sustainable Development?

Sustainable development is development that meets the needs of the present without compromising the ability of future generations to meet their own needs.

Gro Harlem Brundtland[1]

Sustainable development is a business issue that needs to be made a reality in each line function in every company.

Dr Stephan Schmidheiny[2]

We saw in chapter 2 that many aspects of life on Earth are not sustainable, and if continued unchecked could deplete or destroy our life support systems. These include increasing emissions of CO_2, the depletion of fossil fuels, the escalation of wastes for disposal, increasing emissions of persistent pollutants which natural cycles do not break down, the depletion of forests and fish stocks, the erosion of topsoil by destructive agricultural practices the pollution of fresh water and the depletion of underground aquifers.

Most of these trends result from continuing with present forms of industrialisation. People everywhere strive for higher material standards of living, not least in the developing world where the inequity of current terms of trade compounds the problems. New methods have to be found to meet the legitimate needs of people in ways which do not degrade the Earth for our children and their children.

To meet this challenge the concept of sustainable development has evolved over a period of years. Business enterprise is the prime user of resources and, along with agriculture, is the main source of environmental pollution. The onus of achieving a form of industrial development which is sustainable rests squarely with businesses of every kind. This includes the service sector, which employs two-thirds of the workforce in developed countries and exerts considerable influence on how business is conducted.

Some of the significant landmarks in the evolution of the concept of sustainable development are described below.

How the Idea Evolved

The term 'sustainable development' gained credibility after the publication of the Brundtland Report with the definition quoted at the beginning of this chapter. The term is now widely used as a frame of reference.

The definition is followed by amplifying two important concepts. The first is that 'needs' relate in particular to the world's poor, and to give their 'needs' priority. The second explains that development must take account of the environment's limitations, bearing in mind available technology and prevailing social organisations.

The World Commission encouraged economic growth but also challenged the quality of growth, and we shall return to this shortly. The Commission was strongly motivated towards the relief of poverty in the world today, the inevitability of considerable further population growth in Africa, Asia and Latin America, and to our collective responsibility to future generations. It sought to describe ways in which these three responsibilities could be met without destroying the Earth as our home.

While Brundtland's definition aroused interest in the idea of sustainable development, it is salutary to note that it was not a new idea. The concept of 'carrying capacity' was given wide publicity among environmentalists after publication of Garret Hardin's article entitled *The Tragedy of the Commons*.[3] The point made in this article is that cattle farmers all seek to increase the size of their respective herds. This works well until the total number of cattle being grazed approaches the limits of a particular tract of land, or commons. At this point it is still profitable for each individual farmer to increase the size of his herd even though the 'carrying capacity' is exceeded and the total output of cattle declines.

If a common is capable of supporting 100 cows owned by twenty farmers, the farmer who adds one more cow gains the productivity of one cow (20 per cent of his previous herd) and loses 1 per cent of six cows. Similarly for the next farmer, and so on. The unregulated market ethic states that every farmer should increase his herd up to the point where the loss exceeds the gain – by which point the whole herd will be very scraggy.

Examples which provide parallels today include population growth, disposal of wastes, and depletion of limited resources. It is only recently that most people have begun to recognise the seriousness of the situation described so eloquently by Garret Hardin in 1968.

In 1966, the US National Academy of Sciences – National Research Council appointed a Committee on Resources and Man, which published its report in 1969.[4] Frederick Steitz, President of the National Academy of Sciences at the time, said in his foreword:

> The adequacy of resources stands with peace and population control among the crucial problems of our time and the future.

The report looked both at global issues and at those facing the USA. It considered the human ecosystem, how man interacts with resources, population, food, minerals and energy. It recommended twenty-six policies including:

- the need for early action to classify land use;
- policies to reduce population;
- investigation into the sources of food;
- assessment of mineral resources from land and sea;
- conservation of fossil fuel energy;
- an extensive research programme; and
- strengthened organisation to tackle the issues.

The report's conclusions included the following:

> To summarise ... the problem: since resources are finite, then as population increases, the ratio of resources to man must eventually fall to an unacceptable level ... The inescapable central conclusion is that both population control and better resource management are mandatory and should be effected with as little delay as possible.

In the following year, 1970, another significant report was published. This was the report of the Study of Critical Environmental Problems (SCEP), which was sponsored by the Massachusetts Institute of Technology.[5] The report considered the climatic and ecological effects of man's activities and went on to consider the implications of change, methods of monitoring, industrial products and pollutants, domestic and agricultural waste, and energy products. Its recommendations concentrated on:

- methods for gathering and disseminating information;
- the creation of international standards for measuring physical, chemical and ecological effects with prompt feedback mechanisms; and
- an immediate study of an integrated global monitoring programme.

The January 1972 edition of *The Ecologist* was devoted to the 'Blueprint for Survival'[6] which set out to describe what was wrong with society and to explain that the challenge was:

> To create a society which is sustainable and which will give the fullest possible satisfaction to its members.

The Blueprint was endorsed by thirty-three eminent people from a wide range of professional and academic backgrounds. The publication made a considerable impact but was criticised because it challenged the idea of continuous economic growth and recommended a decentralised society.

The idea of a sustainable society was mentioned in a policy statement prepared in 1973 by The Conservation Society for the Conservation Trust.[7] This statement discussed the important educational priorities which included:

- man's place in time;
- the significance of ecology;

- conservation which embraced population, resources and environment; and
- the necessity of social stability.

The key points were summarised as follows:

> ...the debate on the social conditions required to effect a smooth transition to a sustainable society and to maintain us in that state must be continuous and public...

It is interesting to note the emphasis on the social conditions required, and that there should be public debate on what a sustainable society would be like.

In 1974, I undertook a survey among the members of The Conservation Society in order to find out their views on the features of a sustainable society. The first phase involved some 500 people in about a hundred group discussions based on the following questions:

- What is wrong with life today?
- What are the features of a sustainable society?
- What obstacles have to be overcome?
- What are the benefits of a sustainable society to the individual?
- What are the best ways to accomplish change?
- What ideas, if widely understood, could lead towards a sustainable way of life?
- What features of our present society provide the basis on which to build?

The structure of the survey, and twenty-three statements describing a sustainable society, were derived from ideas which emerged from these group discussions: 182 replies to the detailed questionnaire were analysed and the findings published in a booklet.[8] Many of the findings are still valid today; but the emphasis has altered, giving greater importance to the link between environment and development. Relevant information from this study is incorporated into the section on sustainable society, which follows shortly, below.

In the period 1975 to 1987 many important books were published which developed our understanding of the environmental challenge, but the phrase 'sustainable development' does not seem to appear again until the *Brundtland Report*, mentioned earlier.

Refining the Definition of Sustainable Development

Some helpful ideas are contained in a book published jointly by three of the world's most respected environmental organisations.[9] They describe sustainable activities as those which can continue more or less indefinitely and make some useful distinctions. For example sustainable use applies only to renewable resources and means a level of consumption within the capacity for renewal. Examples are harvesting fish or trees at rates which do not reduce annual yields. It is very difficult to state specific quantities because other factors such as the weather, affect the likely level of the sustainable yield, but the principle is clear.

Another term which is widely used is 'sustainable development', defined as 'improving the quality of human life while living within the carrying capacity of supporting ecosystems'. It is equally applicable to industrialised and developing countries but each would have different priorities for action as they applied the principle.

Sustainable economy is described as the result of sustainable development and as one which 'maintains its natural resource base'. Development can continue by adaptation, widening the knowledge base, improving the efficiency of resource use, and enriching the quality of life. The difference between indiscriminate growth and sustainable development is very important.

A sustainable society follows the nine key principles defined in the book, namely:

(1) Respect and care for the community of life.
(2) Improve the quality of life.
(3) Conserve the Earth's vitality and diversity.
(4) Minimise the depletion of non-renewable resources.
(5) Keep within the Earth's carrying capacity.
(6) Change personal attitudes and practices.
(7) Enable communities to care for their own environments.
(8) Provide a national framework for integrating environment and conservation.
(9) Create a global alliance.

Some people use the expression 'sustainable growth' but this is dismissed as a contradiction in terms. No growth is sustainable indefinitely. All forms of life grow, reach maturity and then decline – or at least level off.

An obvious example of the contradiction is to relate 'sustainable' to any form of extraction industry such as the mining of minerals or the exploitation of fossil fuels. In these cases there are absolute limits, but the more important factor will be the practical limits where the concentration of the commodity becomes too dilute for extraction to be feasible and cost effective.

There are already many new terms being used, each starting with the word 'sustainable'. These include sustainable forestry, sustainable energy, sustainable fisheries, sustainable agriculture, and sustainable jobs. Many more are likely to emerge, but we must guard against the contradictory use of the word sustainable, as in sustainable mining. A useful distinction can be made between short term sustainability, which would see us through the transition from present unsustainable practices to ultimate long term sustainability. Each topic will require a lot of work to really understand what it means not only in theory but in practice. The most significant topic for industry and commerce will be the meaning of sustainable business, translated into the requirements for each industrial sector and for each specific business.

A concluding thought in this section is that a sustainable nation is only appropriate in a global context. No country can accomplish the transition to a sustainable society alone, because the Earth is a global commons. Those countries which perpetuate business as usual will destroy the life support systems on which we all depend. The only way to move forward is through some form of global alliance which leads to individual national action undertaken in cooperation with other nations, and guided by mutually agreed treaties and conventions.

The Natural Step[10]

An interesting example of an individual within one country making a real difference is provided by Karl-Henrik Robèrt, a leading cancer researcher in Sweden. He was very concerned about the condition of his patients and believes that our treatment of the environment is leading us towards sickness and poverty in a poisonous, global garbage dump. For a long time he dreamed of educating the whole nation with a new perspective on the environment. The educational material would be more influential if it was already agreed by the most respected scientists of the country. So he wrote a paper setting out basic knowledge about the environmental situation and sent it to leading scientists in Sweden asking them to point out the errors. They helped him very well, spotting numerous areas where the text could be improved to make it clearer and more informative. Karl-Henrik redrafted the paper twenty-one times before all the scientists could endorse the final version. By this time there were fifty scientists forming the first 'Natural Step' network. The statement had become more radical rather than diluted as a result of a consensus–building process which avoided peripheral details and focused on fundamental issues.

As the paper was nearing completion he approached some of Sweden's top entertainers and asked if they would help celebrate the launch of the Natural Step movement with a party on television. Annifrid, of former ABBA fame, took upon herself the initiative of building a network of 'Entertainers for the Environment'. Karl-Henrik Robèrt then approached, in succession, television executives, the government's education department, school boards and, finally, the King of Sweden with the same question:'If we succeed, would you like to take part?'. By the time he came to approach potential sponsors he had a complete package ready to go.

The message of the Natural Step was presented as a booklet and an audio tape and mailed to every Swedish household and school in April 1989. Since then, the movement's public education initiatives have been gaining strength and the networks of professionals 'for the environment' have widened. There are now sixteen networks of professionals involving some 10,000 people. Similar initiatives are being explored in several other countries, including the UK, and a consulting arm has been established in Sweden to work with businesses.

The Natural Step never gives advice, thus ensuring that the responsibility for action remains with those in the best positions to act. Instead, certain basic principles and non-negotiable conditions for sustainability are presented, based on the consensus of scientists.

The scientists agreed four basic principles, derived from natural laws:

(1) Everything disperses. All the human activities we consider productive always cause greater dispersal and disruption elsewhere.
(2) Nothing disappears. The biosphere is essentially closed for matter, so there is no magic to allow society's wastes to vanish.
(3) Material value corresponds to the order and structure of the biosphere's resources, so our economy depends on the quality of these resources.
(4) The only true production unit for material value is the green cell. Plants can create order without degrading matter elsewhere.

Over the past three-and-a-half billion years living cells have processed matter in natural cycles, transforming the original toxic stew into a clean, diverse biosphere. However, for the last hundred or so years human societies have been processing resources in a linear direction, into visible and molecular rubbish which accumulates and threatens our well-being. This is evolution in reverse. Adapting our societies to cyclic processes is a non-negotiable requirement if we want to keep our health and prosperity. Such a 'cyclic society' is the minimum requirement and lowest common denominator of all possible sustainable societies.

A neat way to summarise what we, especially in the industrialised countries, have been doing wrong and how we should change is provided in a paper on energy from the Natural Step:[11]

> We have been processing materials in a manner that is linear, wasteful and toxic, instead of cyclic, resource-conserving and healthy. Such a linear flow of materials cannot continue because, in accordance with natural laws, it is not sustainable.

In all areas of activity we need positive models showing practical steps towards a cyclic society. To provide an attractive role model these good examples should be economically and ecologically sound, and capable of being further developed.

There are four ecological system conditions for a good example:

(1) Stored deposits: less use of underground mineral deposits.
(2) Alien compounds: less use of persistent, non-natural substances.
(3) Eco-systems: allowing greater diversity and capacity.
(4) Metabolism: reduced rate of use of energy and materials.

An example of the results of the work of the Natural Step with business is the decision of Electrolux to replace their non-natural refrigerants with substances capable of being degraded by natural processes.

Endorsement from Business

Reference has already been made (*see* chapter 3) to the formation of the World Industry Council for the Environment, the work of the International Chamber of Commerce, and the Business Charter for Sustainable Development, all of which provide an endorsement by business of the underlying principles of sustainability. Another endorsement is provided by the Business Council for Sustainable Development (BCSD) – mentioned in chapter 3.

In their book, *Changing Course*, which was their contribution to the Earth Summit, the Council give their perspectives on development and the environment.[12] The declaration at the start of the book is signed by all members of BCSD and includes the following:

> A clear vision of a sustainable future mobilises human energies to make the necessary changes, breaking out of familiar and established patterns. As leaders from all parts of society join forces in translating the vision into action, inertia is overcome and cooperation replaces confrontation.

They went on to commit themselves to promoting this new partnership and examples of what some companies are doing are described in later chapters here.

In the UK, the Advisory Committee on Business and the Environment (ACBE), and Business in the Community, both involve many senior industrialists and leaders of service sector businesses who are frequently making statements which endorse the principles of sustainability. They go beyond endorsement, because growing numbers of companies are developing environmental policies and allocating substantial resources to environmental matters. Most of this activity is directed at reducing environmental impact, which is a vital first step, but there are now some companies which are making serious moves to address the question of sustainable development. In chapter 6 we consider ways in which companies have reacted to the environmental challenge and in chapter 7 we examine what is involved in a strategic approach.

Signs of Hope

Any move towards a sustainable society requires enlightened leadership. A powerful driving force for this to emerge comes from customers who are concerned about the environment, appreciate the need for change and buy products and services which are sustainable. They are making moves towards sustainable life styles and collectively applying pressure on business to meet their changing needs. Chart 18 shows the degree of concern that is felt throughout Europe on three of the major problems:

• the greenhouse effect;
• acid rain; and
• ozone depletion.

Chart 18: Perceptions of Problems

	% thinking problem is serious		
Country	Greenhouse Effect	Acid Rain	Ozone Depletion
Belgium	63	75	74
Denmark	67	68	72
France	64	74	77
Germany	78	75	83
Greece	89	85	91
Irish Republic	65	64	73
Italy	79	77	85
Luxembourg	85	84	88
Netherlands	55	70	66
Portugal	75	74	83
Spain	76	78	82
UK	65	72	73
European Community	72	74	80

Source: Social Trends 1993 p 126
Quoting Statistics Office of European Community

It is not enough to perceive the problems. People need to act by changing their behaviour. Chart 19 shows the percentage of people in the UK who have taken positive action to reduce their personal environmental impact. Figures for other countries will be similar and some will show even stronger commitment to changes in buying habits.

Chart 19: Actions in UK to Improve the Environment 1991/2

Action taken	Percent taking action
Use ozone friendly aerosols	67
Buy recycled paper	55
Take bottles to bottle bank	51
Buy biodegradable products	46
Use unleaded petrol	39
Take cans for recycling	32
Leave car and walk or cycle	28
Buy organic produce	22
Lobby MPs, Councillors	3

Source: Social Trends 1993
Approximate figures from bar chart

Changes in Energy Consumption

One of the crucial changes we need to make is to move away from our wasteful consumption of and very high dependency on fossil fuels. Two changes are required. We need to make much more efficient use of energy and we need to move towards more renewable sources of energy. Technological advances are helping in both these respects and in particular in bringing down the cost of wind, photovoltaic (electricity from solar power) and solar thermal energy, as is shown in chart 20.

An example of a problem which will require considerable understanding, cooperative effort and persistence, to bring about change is car emissions. In 1990 some 19 per cent of CO_2 was attributable to road transport and 50 per cent of this was caused by cars.[13] In order to bring this figure down there is a part to be played by five different initiatives:

(1) Government transport policy.
(2) Financial incentives and pressures.
(3) Company car policies.
(4) Motor manufacturers.
(5) The public.

The combined effect of all five could make a considerable difference but if any one initiative is weak or omitted then the speed with which we can reduce emissions will be reduced. This is illustrated in chart 21. Although the measurements would be extremely difficult the concept is indicated by the cumulative effect of each element.

Chart 20: Costs of Renewable Electricity 1980 - 2030

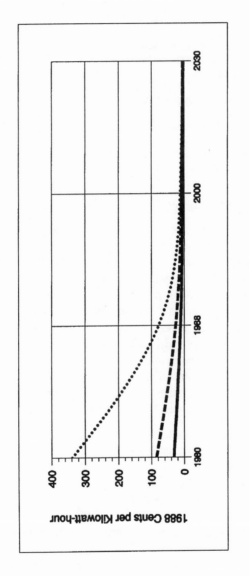

1988 Cents per Kilowatt-hour

——— WIND · · · · · PHOTOVOLTAIC – – – SOLAR THERMAL

Source: Brown, Lester et al, State of the World 1991

Chart 21: Reducing Car Emissions

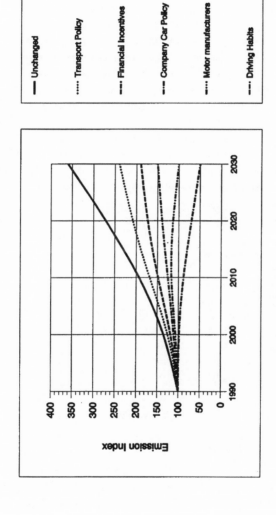

Author's figures to illustrate the value of a multiple approach.

Legend:
- — Unchanged
- ⋯ Transport Policy
- —·— Financial Incentives
- —·· Company Car Policy
- ⋯ Motor manufacturers
- --- Driving Habits

Emission Index

Overcoming Resistance to Change

There is some evidence that the main requirements for bringing about change towards a sustainable society are slowly coming into place. These include awareness that the current situation cannot continue, some perception of a more desirable future, and practical steps to make change happen. However, resistances are always present in any situation involving change. These resistances are always greater when the change is imposed, and can be reduced significantly when people are involved in changes which affect them. They can even seek out changes they want to make. So the crucial question is whether the forces for change are sufficient to overcome the resistances, and whether the resistances can be reduced. It is often easier to reduce hindering forces than to apply strength in the hope of overwhelming the resistance. This idea will be developed in chapter 11, and other useful processes and techniques will be described.

There are four elements which help to bring about change. These elements are distinct and do not necessarily appear in the sequence shown. However, when all are present the change is likely to happen. The four elements needed to make a real difference are:

(1) Dissatisfaction with the present state (D).
(2) A vision of a desirable future (V).
(3) A practical action plan (A).
(4) The will to make it happen (W).

The ability to reduce the resistance to change is always greater when there is involvement in the change process. The elements described here are a slightly adjusted version of the 'change equation'. This is a functional equation. It states that overcoming the resistance to change is a function of dissatisfaction with the present state (D), coupled with a vision of a desired state (V), where there is a sound action plan (A) and the will to make the change happen (W). The equation can be represented as follows:[14]

$$f(D, V, A, W) > R$$

One way to appreciate how this works is to imagine weighing scales with 'resistance' on one side. Now imagine adding dissatisfaction (D) to the other side – nothing changes. Add vision (V) and still there is no change. As you put the action plan (A) into the scales it lifts the resistance side off the ground and sometimes this is sufficient. However, if it settles again the final ingredient is needed. Now add the will to make it happen (W) and the scale swings over – a permanent change has been accomplished. Remove one of these and the situation reverts to where it was!

The ingredients need not necessarily be applied in the sequence described. Let us consider an example. A director believes that the company's environmental policy needs to be strengthened, and implemented more widely. Many others in the organisation agree that the existing policy is very weak; a few have expressed ideas which would make it clearer and more specific and some have even suggested how implementation could be improved. Despite this, nothing changes for several months. Clearly there is some dissatisfaction with the present situation. The vision of improvement is not widely shared, and because of this no one has done any serious work on how implementation might be achieved. The will to make things happen is insufficient. Using the change equation helps to identify which elements need strengthening. Every situation will be different, but in each case priorities will be more easily identified by using the equation to find out where the resistances are and how they might be overcome.

Vision of a Sustainable Society[15]

There is certainly a lot of dissatisfaction with many aspects of today's society, and especially with the damage we are inflicting on the environment. Plans for tackling the issues are slowly being formulated, as we have seen in chapter 3, and more people are declaring that they have the will to be involved. The vision described here may strike you as utopian, but bear in mind that it is a vision to be achieved at some indeterminate date. We need a vision and this attempt to describe it will surely be improved in the years to come. The key characteristics have been extracted from various books which are listed in the annotated bibliography, and articles referred to in the text.

The first requirement of a sustainable society on a finite planet is a stable population within the Earth's carrying capacity. With world population growing at a rate of 91m each year this is not achievable easily or quickly but should be the aim some time during the second half of the twenty-first century. The number of people the Earth can support will depend on their life styles and how these impact on the planet's life support systems and available resources.

Developed and developing countries will approach the vision of sustainability from different directions. The developed, industrialised countries need to change many of their established ways of doing things. This will require considerable revision of priorities and perceptions. In developing countries the first priority will usually be to achieve a viable economy, then to relieve poverty, both of which will often require cooperation and support from industrialised countries. It will also be important for developing countries to move directly towards sustainable societies rather than to copy the experience of unsustainable developed societies.

This will be difficult because so much attention is focused on emulating unsustainable characteristics of the industrialised world.

A major consumer of energy is transport. Reducing the energy used in transportation will be achieved by having fewer cars, with a higher proportion of them able to travel three or four times as far on each gallon of fuel. We need to rely more on public transport (which, to attract passengers, would need to be reliable, frequent, clean and efficient), encourage cycling or walking for short journeys, and use telecommunications to replace some travel. The transportation of goods should be by rail wherever possible and journeys should be reduced by locating manufacturing plants near to the markets they serve. Cities should be designed with more attention given to the way in which people need to get about.

It will be important for a sustainable society to differentiate between renewable and non-renewable resources and to strive to re-use and recycle the latter while keeping the former within their capacity to renew themselves. The current wasteful use of energy will need to change and the dependence on energy from coal, gas and oil will need to shift to renewable forms of energy. The type of renewable energy used will depend on what is available and appropriate locally. In warmer climates this is likely to be various forms of solar energy, while Northern Europe might make use of tidal and wind energy. A few places, such as Iceland and the Philippines, have the potential to develop geothermal energy. In all cases energy will need to be used much less wastefully than now through more efficient combustion and better insulation. These changes will also greatly reduce emissions and the damage they inflict on the environment.

Economic systems will change and measurement of progress will be more diverse and multi-faceted than is the case at present. The early signs of change are with us now in new economic thinking.

Lifestyles will have to change, with much greater emphasis placed on quality of life than on quantity of material consumption. Many countries will need to become more self-sufficient in food production to reduce the damage caused by transporting food over great distances – and there may be fewer places with surpluses to export. Food production will increasingly use organic principles, thereby enriching rather than impoverishing the soil. Cultural development, quality of life and personal growth will be the areas for dramatic and stimulating development. People will seek less stressful, more enjoyable, more creative and more stimulating lives and many will discover the deeper satisfaction to be gained from more purposeful life styles.

This in turn will place more emphasis on appropriate development of rural communities and the necessity for a fresh look at the whole concept of sustainable cities. Technology should be benign and aid the creation of cyclic process to replace the current linear processes. Technological efficiency should be focused on achieving more with less resource usage, on massive reduction in waste and emissions, and on the elimination of toxic substances being released into the environment. This will stimulate the demand for effective re-use and recycling of many products, thereby saving resources and reducing emissions.

The limitations of the biosphere will need to be widely appreciated and mutual commitment developed to respect its crucial importance to all communities. Respect for the different cultures and value systems which make up the global community will be necessary and this will happen only if there is much more equity and justice throughout the world.

Peace with the environment will only be achieved if there is also peace between the peoples of the Earth. It is not enough to think that this is an issue for governments. We all need to understand better the causes of conflict in our lives and to find creative ways in which to resolve our differences, whether they are between two people, within families, in work groups, among different departments and organisations, or are matters involving different cultural or ethnic origins. An approach to conflict resolution through consensus decision-making in which all parties gain something, is an important challenge for us all.

In a sustainable society our institutions will need to be both authoritative and legitimate, which will depend on sound democratic processes which are open and honest. The need for political leadership has never been greater, but we should not rely on that alone, there is scope for positive and effective leadership at every level.

As people everywhere feel that their basic material needs are satisfied and they are better able to meet their aspirations, peace between nations will be more attainable. If more emphasis is placed on quality of life, rather than the quantity of material consumption, people in the developed world may well be willing to see the gap between rich and poor narrowed and this will be a healthy step in the right direction.

Two major concerns are expressed to counter the case for sustainable societies: we cannot afford it, and it will increase the level of unemployment. In chapter 2 reference was made to the level of military expenditure which is close to $US1,000bn per annum. This expenditure is supported by a vast allocation of the best scientific talent available, and it absorbs an enormous amount of resources. When the weapons are used, especially weapons of mass destruction, the damage they wreak on human communities and the environment is colossal. One way to provide the capital requirements for work on a sustainable society is to reduce dramatically the amount of military spending. A further reference to this theme is picked up in chapter 7.

So far as unemployment is concerned there is increasing evidence that it is unfounded in an overall sense. It is true that there will be jobs lost as the change towards a sustainable future gathers pace. Old, wasteful, polluting industries which are not relevant to the future will need to decline, but the jobs lost here will be fewer than the new jobs available in cyclic, resource conserving and healthy businesses required for the sustainable society. This has been well researched and is described by Amory and Hunter Lovins in *Energy Unbound*, and in *Jobs in a Sustainable Economy* by Michael Renner – Worldwatch Paper No 104. Two examples illustrate the point.

The jobs required for generating electricity from large scale centralised utilities are far fewer than those required if the energy is derived from renewable sources and attention is given to conservation measures. Furthermore, the latter provides local jobs whereas the former provides only a limited amount of work, often some distance from the location where the energy is used.[16] A comparison of jobs required in New York City for landfills and incinerators, with those required for recycling facilities and mixed solid waste composting, shows that the latter requires 600 to 900 jobs whereas the former requires 150 to 350.[17] Certainly in the short term there would be no shortage of jobs in activities such as insulation, new forms of power generation, innovative benign products, engineering equipment for waste management and pollution control, etc.

Some ideas which will make a difference if widely understood are shown in chart 22.

Sustainable Business

Business enterprise is the most powerful, dynamic force in industrialised countries. The nature and scale of the response from business, influenced by communities and households, will be the determining factor in achieving a sustainable society. There is already a great deal of valuable experience in businesses of every kind and among managers at every level, which is going to be vitally important. This includes the development of new technology, the creative skills to devise and market appropriate products and services, the management of individual and organisational change and the ways in which cooperative relationships can be developed and strengthened in joint endeavour.

Sustainable business, and sustainable societies, need to achieve the goal of meeting the needs of today, in a global context, without jeopardising the ability of future generations to meet their needs. The elements of a sustainable society have already been described, and indicate many business opportunities. A general checklist for businesses striving towards a sustainable future is provided in Appendix 1.

In order to accomplish this kind of transformation, fundamental

Chart 22: Ideas Which Will Make a Difference

1 Our present way of life is not sustainable and unlimited growth in population and production is not possible.

2 Humans are part of nature - to upset natural laws is to court disaster; life - all life - is precious and dependent on the Planet's life support systems, which are now threatened.

3 Some resources such as fossil fuels and minerals are non-renewable; there is a theoretical limit to their availability and a much lower practical limit. We should value their scarcity.

4 Renewable resources such as fish, food and forests should be used at rates which are within their ability to renew themselves.

5 Energy from renewable sources such as sun, tides and wind should be developed rapidly - prices are coming down fast.

6 We should use public rather than private transport as much as possible, bicycles for short journeys, and seek long-life, durable goods which can be recycled.

7 Each one of us can contribute by moving towards more sustainable life styles - the more people that become involved the greater the chances of success.

8 Population should be stabilised at a level that is within the Earth's carrying capacity. This is best achieved by avoiding unwanted children and limiting family size to two children.

9 Food and forest products should be produced by organic methods and grown near their markets, wherever possible.

10 Quality of life, happiness, cultural development and personal growth depend more on emotions than money.

11 We have no right to endanger our children's future by leaving them an impoverished environment with diminished resources and large quantities of long lived toxic wastes.

12 The individual appreciates a human scale in communities and institutions; more decentralisation makes sense.

13 Time is running out - we must be convinced that there is a crisis and that action is needed now. Delay may make the problems insoluble.

14 The Earth is one world and international cooperation is essential; peace, sustainable development and environmental management must be tackled together - in all our interests.

15 Democratic government and institutions which are seen to be both legitimate and authoritative are a necessity.

16 The transition to a sustainable society will give rise to much dispute and conflict - we need to learn better ways to achieve outcomes where all parties gain something.

© Colin Hutchinson, *Vitality and Renewal*, Adamantine, 1994

rethinking of how things are done will be needed. Companies should be at the forefront of this challenge. Chief executives should provide leadership which includes opportunities for managers and staff to re-examine their values, become increasingly involved in refocusing the corporate mission, goals and strategies, to cope with managing change more smoothly and to do it in less time. This is the area in which companies can strengthen their reputation, attract and keep good people and compete effectively in a changing world.

All this will need to be achieved within the context of a peaceful world where human rights are respected, people gain satisfaction from what they do, the community is stable and people are involved in decisions which affect their lives. Through their organisation culture and management style, businesses can hasten these trends. A few of the more enlightened businesses are already contributing to the creation of a sustainable society.

For this to work well, the major institutions and organisations of society will need to be valued, authoritative and legitimate. At every level throughout the community, in the interaction between organisations, in the relationships within companies and in the way in which people deal with their issues, the challenge will be to find creative and positive ways to deal with and resolve conflict in all its forms. More training and development of this kind is an urgent priority for many businesses and will help them improve their own effectiveness.

Summary

We have seen that many aspects of our current way of life are unsustainable and we have explored the meaning of sustainable development. We clearly need a shared vision of a sustainable society so that we can apply the principles of sustainable development to help make it happen. We need to strive to switch away from the limitations of non-renewable resources, linear processes, our profligate ways, and the dispersal of toxic wastes towards sustainable use of renewable resources, using cyclic process which enable the environment to heal itself. Business organisations can play a major part in this transition because they make a significant impact on the model we have been using – see chart 23.

Moves towards sustainable business are going to be vitally important – probably the most powerful driving force for change that is available to us. This in turn will need to provide new insights into the management of global, national and corporate economies.

Finally, we recognise that results will only be achieved through enormous collaborative effort but there are signs of hope from every sector of the community. The challenge is daunting but the direction in which we need to move is becoming clearer, as can be seen in chart 24.

CHART 23: SUSTAINABLE SOCIETY: A VISION

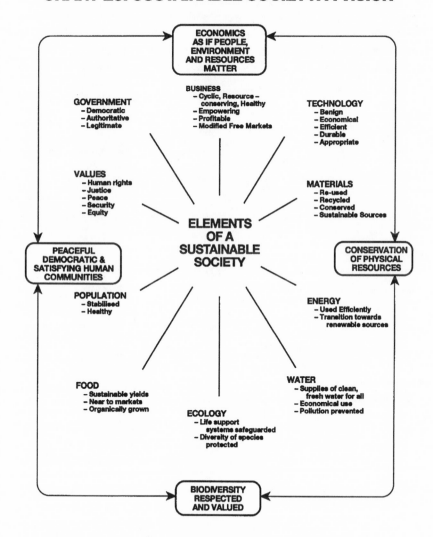

© Colin Hutchinson, *Vitality and Renewal*, Adamantine, 1994

Chart 24: A Daunting Transition

If we are to create a sustainable society it will need to be achieved
during the 21st century. The conditions required represent a daunting
challenge, as indicated below:

Topic	Past	Present	Future
Human Communities:			
Human Rights	Denied	Uneven	Universal
Justice	Unjust	Justice for some	Justice for all
Minorities	Prejudiced	More equal Opportunity	Mutual Respect
Peace	Frequent Wars	Potential for annihilation & internal wars	Peace
Population	Accelerating growth	Growth	Arrested growth
Empowerment	Many people disempowered	Awareness of empowerment	Widespread empowerment
Conflict	Aggression used to win	Trying out alternatives	Resolution through consensus
Physical Resources:			
Poverty	Widespread	More widespread	Relieved
Resources	Unconscious wastefulness	Conscious wastefulness	Conscious conservation
Aid	Limited	Help the disadvantaged	Help others to help themselves
Equity	Widespread inequity	Awareness of inequity	More equitable worldwide
Biodiversity:			
Environment	Ignorance	Awareness	Respect
Economics:			
Military Spending	Increased	Reduced	Disarmament
Economics	Capitalist/ Communist	Capitalist	New Economics
Industrialisation	Linear & toxic	Recycling emerging	Cyclic & healthy

© Colin Hutchinson, *Vitality and Renewal*, Adamantine, 1994

Notes

1   World Commission on Environment and Development, 1987, p. 43.
2   Schmidheiny, 1992 p. 183.
3   Hardin, Garrett, *The Tragedy of the Commons*, in Science vol. 162, 13 December 1968, pp. 1243–8. This and other landmark articles are summarised in Allaby, 1989.
4   Committee on Resources and Man appointed by the US National Academy of Sciences – National Research Council, *Resources and Man*, W.H. Freeman, 1969.
5   Report of the Study of Critical Environmental Problems, *Man's Impact on the Global Environment*: Assessment and Recommendations for Action, MIT, 1970.
6   Goldsmith, Edward; Allen, Robert; Davoll, John and Lawrence, Sam, *The Blueprint for Survival*, in The Ecologist, January 1972. Edward Goldsmith still publishes The Ecologist, Agriculture House, Bath Road, Sturminster Newton, Dorset DT10 1DU. John Davoll and Sam Lawrence were Director and Honorary Secretary respectively of The Conservation Society in 1972. A summary of the Blueprint is contained in Allaby, 1989.
7   The Conservation Society, *Education For Our Future*, published by The Conservation Trust, 1973. Since then The Conservation Society has closed down and The Conservation Trust has merged with The Environment Council, 21 Elizabeth Street, London SW1W 9RP.
8   Hutchinson, Colin, *The Crisis of Life Styles*, published by The Conservation Society, 1975. The booklet was intended to launch a campaign but this never materialised due to lack of funds.
9   IUCN, UNEP and WWF, 1991, *Caring for the Earth*.
10 The Natural Step, Sweden and UK, (see Sources of Help).
11 The Natural Step Science Advisory Council, Energy Policy from an Ecological Perspective, presented at IFAP Conference, Reykjavik 1991.
12 Schmidheiny, 1992.
13 Department of the Environment Discussion Document, Climate Change, Department of the Environment, PO Box 1150, London N4 1UB.
14 The change equation was devised by Kurt Lewin in the 1940s and has been widely quoted and variously presented since then. It is better known with three ingredients being necessary to overcome the resistance, namely dissatisfaction (D), vision (V) and practical steps (S). I have added 'the will to make it happen' as a result of experience in many situations.
15 This section draws on *A Sustainable Future* by Lester Brown, in Resurgence, no. 147, July/August 1991 and *A Sustainable Society* by Fritjof Capra and Ernest Callenbach in Resurgence no. 149, November/December 1991, as well as Crisis of Life Styles by Colin Hutchinson, booklet published by The Conservation Society, 1975.
16 Lovins and Lovins, 1986.
17 Renner, Michael, Worldwatch Paper no. 104, September 1991.

CHAPTER *6*

Tactical Approaches to the Challenge

Sustainable development is not one more burden on business, but is a way to re-invigorate their companies and to enable them to survive and prosper in a turbulent world.

Jan-Olaf Willums & Ulrich Goluke[1]

A group of environmentalists climbed over the perimeter fence of a chemical plant and took soil samples which they then had analysed. The results, indicating a high degree of soil toxicity, were released to the press. The firm was horrified and initially reacted with denials, and consternation over the break-in. Later they took their own soil samples and their analysis revealed similar results. They agreed to meet the environmentalists and in due course accepted responsibility and the need for action. Later the firm became environmentally active and increasingly open about their policies and practices. In due course environment was incorporated into their public relations strategy as a central theme. This story is based on real events and the response of a major company.

Accidents and spills of toxic substances, often the result of human error, occur periodically in oil and chemical companies. Sometimes they are dramatic and gain worldwide headlines such as Bhopal (Union Carbide) and the Exxon Valdez (Exxon). Companies such as these have had Safety and Health officers for many years, but in the past decade there has been an increasing tendency to add 'environment' to the responsibilities of their job.

Oil and chemicals companies are obvious candidates for environmental policies but they are not alone. IBM became concerned about the use of chlorofluorocarbons (CFCs) in the manufacture of their computers and have had an environmental policy since 1971. Ernst & Young, an accounting and financial services partnership, received requests from their staff that something should be done about the enormous quantities of waste paper generated in their offices. 3M have had pollution prevention schemes for some twenty years and claim that these have saved them millions of dollars.

The reasons why a particular firm decides to do something about the environment may develop gradually, or an incident may stimulate the need not only for swift action but for more fundamental change. In the first instance the focus will usually be on reducing environmental impact rather than on striving for a sustainable business. In this chapter we shall consider tactical responses; moving on to the strategic approach in chapter 7.

Chart 25 provides a diagram which shows how the realisation that action is needed often emerges. People in firms which are not involved with the environment usually start from never having thought about it, or from the belief that environment does not concern them. The reactive response is usually the starting point and is triggered by such considerations as the need to comply with the law, to improve health and safety, to save money, or to protect their reputation. Once the firm has an environment policy there is also the need to comply with that policy.

Any organisation which decides to take the environment seriously does so as a result of a strategic decision. That decision may in fact result in a low key, reactive response to environmental matters. The seriousness of the response will be evidenced by the seniority of the person with this responsibility, the job title of the incumbent and the way in which policies evolve and are implemented. A great many firms deal with environmental matters at a middle management level and position

Chart 25
REACTIVE ENVIRONMENT INVOLVEMENT

STRATEGIES TOWARDS
SUSTAINABLE BUSINESS

"Never thought about it"

STRATEGIC RESPONSE
Re-defined mission statement
Corporate values declared
Aligned business strategy
New products / markets
Changing corporate culture
Paradigm shift.

UNINVOLVED ——————————————— INVOLVED

"Environment does not affect us"

REACTIVE RESPONSE:
Compliance:
legislation
company policy
Reducing costs
Improving safety & health
Enhancing reputation

TACTICS TO
REDUCE
ENVIRONMENTAL
IMPACT

it to be reactive. Job titles of those attending environmental conferences and seminars are often a good indication of how a firm regards its environmental responsibilities. Some typical job titles in the early 1990s were:

- Health, Safety and Environment;
- Public Relations;
- Corporate Communications;
- Quality and Environment;
- Environmental Affairs; and
- Engineering and Technical Manager.

Many of the people doing this work find that it is extremely difficult. When pressed, they describe how hard it is to gain the attention and commitment of their colleagues. This is frequently more significant than the technical aspects of their responsibility, but it is hardly surprising when many line managers regard the environment as peripheral to their responsibilities and not affecting their appraisal or rewards. Some also believe that if it was really important their organisation would make a more senior appointment. The outcome is that many of those with environmental responsibilities struggle to make an impact – their job is rather like pushing a heavy boulder up a very steep hill. It need not be like this, as we shall see in the next chapter. But first let us look at some of the achievements, despite the difficulties, that have been registered by those who have pioneered the environmental role.

The Pressures on Business

As environmental, social, legislative and ethical issues gain more prominence the pressures on business increase. In chapter 11 we shall be discussing these pressures again in conjunction with chart 54. These pressures sooner or later have a direct impact on cash flow and economic performance. This might be the result of an expensive clean up operation after an accident, deployment of extra resources to avert a disaster, or legal fees to defend a court case. However, a simplistic focus on the cost factors is unlikely to be the best way to deal with the situation.

Recognising the importance of these pressures and the need to adopt a responsible attitude towards the environment is no more than enlightened self-interest. It is increasingly important to adopt a holistic approach and to recognise that the enterprise has to monitor performance in several areas. This is not new; in fact the areas where results matter were first defined by Peter Drucker in 1955.[3] A slight modification of his list might be as follows:

- market share and reputation;
- innovation and creativity;

- productivity;
- management of cash flow and physical resources;
- profitability;
- leadership and management – at every level;
- staff attitudes, development and performance; and
- ethical and environmental responsibility.

Environmental and social pressures have direct effects on every business but the larger companies inevitably get more publicity. Small and medium sized companies which supply goods and services to larger organisations or act as distributors on behalf of their principals are now often required to meet more stringent standards. Failure to comply can mean that they are deleted from the list of approved suppliers or distributors.

A growing trend in the 1990s is the way in which corporate performance is being monitored and made public. For example *New Consumer* publishes assessments of corporate policies and their implementation.[4] The criteria used are wide ranging and cover:

- disclosure of information;
- equal opportunities for women and ethnic minorities;
- community involvement;
- environmental impact and action;
- policies towards other countries (e.g. South Africa and developing countries);
- respect for life;
- political involvement;
- respect for people; and
- military sales.

Some 130 firms have been assessed against each of the above criteria, with supporting text describing the findings and the degree of cooperation received from each firm when the survey was carried out. The notes on each company conclude with a brief summary of the overall assessment and the degree of openness in responding to the questions asked.

Another form of assessment is carried out by Jupiter Tyndall Merlin Ltd for their Jupiter Merlin Ecology Fund, a unit trust launched in 1988. Their assessment focuses on environmental issues, with the aim of identifying those organisations which are taking positive action to improve environmental health. If companies also receive a positive rating in terms of their overall economic performance they will be considered as suitable for inclusion in the fund's portfolio. Investors receive copies of the Research Bulletin which provides information on the firms included in the portfolio.

Assessments like those of *New Consumer* and Merlin are likely to increase, with more firms coming under close scrutiny from different perspectives as the trend towards ethical investments grows. As this occurs the interest of shareholders in ethical considerations will also grow, and share prices and the ease with which capital can be obtained will be affected. During the 1990s this is becoming a significant pressure on many companies.

Financial pressure is also likely to become more intense from banks. The National Westminster Bank is already indicating a firm intention to take environmental factors more strongly into account when lending money to businesses. In part this is stimulated by ethical considerations but there are also practical reasons. For example contaminated land is becoming a significant issue and clean-up costs can be considerable. This might well affect cash flow or diminish the value of a plot held as collateral security against a loan. A firm which is in a potentially polluting industry might incur severe penalties should a spill occur, or it may find that it is unable to obtain insurance for certain kinds of risk. In either case it adds a new dimension for the bank to consider before agreeing terms for a loan.

Government action is increasing, with new legislation and fiscal measures designed to penalise those who ignore environmental considerations and to provide incentives to encourage desirable trends. In legislation, the penalties are becoming greater all the time, with firms being held responsible not only for their own actions but also for goods they receive from their suppliers. This liability is specifically directed towards individual directors, who can be brought to court and even imprisoned if their firm fails to comply with legislation.

Customer pressures are growing as eco-labelling becomes more prevalent and people can make more informed choices about the products they buy. Refusal to buy South African goods was a phenomenon for many years, but the practice ceased when the multi-racial government was elected. Many customers now avoid buying goods which impact adversely on people or the environment, select those which use resources more economically, choose products which are recycled, and decide not to buy goods with excessive packaging.

We have already seen in chapter 3 that many firms are taking action themselves by signing the Business Charter for Sustainable Development published by the International Chamber of Commerce. Many UK managers with environmental responsibility are joining the Business and Environment Programme of The Environment Council and similar trends are developing in other countries.

The wide range of the social, ethical and environmental pressures or potential threats means that every function of a business is involved.

(1) Boards of directors wonder if they are pursuing the right business strategy; if policies are still appropriate to the changing world; how to accommodate new thinking when preparing business plans; how

to allocate priorities; what monitoring procedures are effective, and whether the person in charge of environmental affairs is sufficiently senior, skilled and knowledgeable to establish a new function.

(2) Product development and marketing people wonder how fast customer buying habits are changing and whether they are able to pick up emerging trends early enough to maintain competitive advantage.

(3) Packaging decisions can be a significant element for some businesses and excessive packaging is expensive, as well as being rejected by environmentally aware customers. Purchasing, production, marketing and sales personnel are all likely to experience this pressure at different times.

(4) Advertising and sales people wonder if they have accurate information about products, resources used in manufacture, and performance in use, so that they can avoid making false claims and deal effectively with customer queries.

(5) Purchasing of materials, resources, services and supplies is an area where prices, availability and quality standards can change overnight and make a considerable impact on a business. Decisions invariably involve personnel engaged in other functions who do not want to be taken by surprise.[5]

(6) Public relations and internal communications personnel are finding that questions are becoming more difficult to answer and corporate reputations harder to protect. What do you tell the media, and how do you keep your own people well informed about increasingly complex issues?

(7) Personnel departments may find that they are closely questioned by new recruits about the company's ethical standards and environmental policies. This phenomenon is masked when unemployment is high but may emerge later when the company finds it has recruited people whose values are different from those of the company. When promotion is considered, are the old criteria still relevant or do candidates need to be sympathetic towards new corporate values? Does the reward system take account of good performance on environmental and social issues? If not, will the company be able to implement its newly declared policies on the environment? If company cars are provided as a job requirement, or as a perk might this policy need to be revised to reflect changing environmental policy?

(8) Managers of offices and other premises may wonder if their site makes efficient use of energy for heating and lighting, whether electrical equipment is being purchased with environmental criteria in mind. Do the cleaning contractors avoid ozone-damaging aerosols and deal effectively with the collection of waste for re-use or recycling? Who orders stationery and other office supplies and are they

changing their purchasing policies in line with any new environmental policy?

(9) The health and safety function has now often been extended to include environment, and this opens up whole new areas which have to be understood. Many people in this role face a daunting challenge in persuading people to exercise care in new areas of vital responsibility.

How Do Businesses Cope with These Pressures?

Henley Management College conducted a survey into management attitudes to environmental issues, with the help of their students in the UK, continental Europe and the Far East and published the results early in 1993.[6] Legislation and customer pressure were the two strongest overall influences on organisations. US businesses, however, experienced greater pressure from their parent companies and from employees than from other sources. General managers experienced most pressure from investors – which is not surprising in view of the key role of general managers in financial matters – whereas other respondents did not generally recognise this as a significant source of pressure. Firms involved with environmental activity were most preoccupied with waste management, recycling, monitoring systems and procedures, emission control, 'greener' raw materials and environmental impact assessment. Germany led the field in terms of the number of positive activities reported by respondents. Most respondents felt that it was important for them to be able to influence their company's environmental policy to some extent, and believed that they were able to bring their influence to bear to an appropriate degree.

The Advisory Committee on Business and the Environment (ACBE) conducted a survey among those companies known to be environmentally active, with the intention of finding out what they were doing in this respect and why they gave it such high priority.[7] The Committee wanted to learn from these companies in order to use this information to encourage others to do more. The response to the question: 'What are you doing?' revealed the following:

	%
Carrying out a review or audit	82
Recycling wastes	75
Establishing environmental policies	68
Improving energy management	61
Controlling emissions	58
Providing environmental training	54
Improving waste management	53
Improving Site management	22
Influencing the supply chain	19

The question about reasons for giving attention to environmental matters indicated that the primary factors were:

(1) Corporate image (65 per cent) – `if we let our guard slip we would lose business'.
(2) Bottom line results, either tangible or intangible (61 per cent) – 'our supermarkets have saved £10m on energy'.
(3) Better relations with neighbours, suppliers, local community and regulators, resulting in less hassle (40 per cent).
(4) Competitive advantage, especially for businesses in direct contact with the public (28 per cent).
(5) Survival (23 per cent) – `unless you conform we will not use you as a supplier'.

In this same survey respondents were asked to indicate where they went for sound advice and information on environmental matters. Their replies indicated:

	%
• trade associations	60
• Confederation of British Industry	19
• specialist groups	18
• suppliers/customers	18
• local government sources	16
• chambers of commerce	14
• corporate channels	14
• educational institutions	9

Thirty-five per cent of respondents, mostly international companies, felt that they did not have a 'level playing field' and believed that European regulations were applied unevenly. Although they believed that government action was necessary to resolve these discrepancies, they had taken action themselves.

The best way to promulgate the environmental message was believed to be through trade associations (60 per cent), followed by the CBI (19 per cent) and specialist groups and suppliers/customers (18 per cent). Other channels such as local/national government, the media, chambers of commerce, corporate channels and educational institutions registered 16 per cent or less.

The messages for companies which have not yet implemented an environmental programme were clear:

(1) Carry out an environmental review.
(2) Start recycling **now**.
(3) Start managing energy consumption **now**.
(4) Define a company environmental policy.

(5) Reduce emissions.
(6) Train your people.
(7) Listen to your Trade Association.
(8) These activities will improve the company's financial performance and its image.

Some Case Histories[8]

This section contains a small selection of examples which illustrate what some companies have achieved with their environmental policies. In many ways these examples demonstrate how the environmental challenge has stimulated sound business principles which are in fact long established. Identifying ways in which waste products can be used, changing extravagant practices and reducing the consumption of intermediates are traditional ways in which companies improve profitability.

Pollution Prevention

There is an important distinction between pollution control, which attempts to deal with effluents at the point of discharge, and pollution prevention, which seeks to reduce or eliminate the effluents. It is now widely acknowledged that prevention makes much more sense than control and that avoidance is less costly than cleaning up.

There are five areas which can be considered when addressing the question of pollution prevention:

- product design;
- efficient use of existing processes;
- substitution of materials;
- modification of manufacturing processes; and
- resource recovery.

3M and Dow Chemical are two companies with outstanding examples of pollution prevention. 3M have their famous 3P programme – Pollution Prevention Pays – which was introduced in the early 1970s. Their employees originated more than 3,000 projects between 1975 and 1992 which together stopped over one billion pounds weight of polluting emissions from entering the environment. 3M benefited by saving over $500m during this period.

Dow Chemical's programme originated in the late 1960s with a policy stating that the best solution was not to produce the pollutants in the first place. In 1986 this policy was strengthened, and their Waste Reduction Always Pays (WRAP) programme was introduced. The pay-offs include re-use of materials, increased yields, cuts in transport costs and reduced emissions. In the USA, Dow reduced its air emissions by half during the period 1985 to 1991. A reactant used in the production of agricultural products used to be incinerated after a single use. A project team using computer modelling techniques found ways in which the use of the reactant could be reduced by 80 percent through recovery and re-use. This eliminated 2.5m pounds weight of waste and saved the company $8m each year.

Monsanto have set themselves the target of reducing emissions to zero. They recognise that this is scientifically impossible but 'it is the only goal that will keep us stretching for ever greater improvement', according to Richard Mahoney, their Chief Executive. Monsanto's Fisher Controls International plant at Marshalltown, Iowa, reduced water consumption and non-hazardous waste by 50 percent and hazardous waste by 90 percent between 1988 and 1991. They expect to eliminate their hazardous waste emissions altogether.[9]

The potential for many companies to prevent pollution, recover resources and save themselves money is enormous. Anyone wishing to keep abreast of this work should get on the mailing list of an excellent free publication – the WARMER bulletin. The acronym stands for World Action for Recycling Materials and Energy from Rubbish and, as the name implies, examples are included from a wide cross-section of industries worldwide.[10]

Disasters

The ways in which companies deal with disasters provide a valuable indication of their attitude to the environment. There is little doubt that Union Carbide, after the Bhopal incident in December 1989, and Exxon, after the Exxon Valdez disaster in March 1989, initially dealt with their respective situations in ways which diminished their reputation, but later became very active in their efforts to regain what they had lost. Shell UK, on the other hand, dealt with a major oil spill near Liverpool in ways which some people believe resulted in a significant reduction in the fine that was ultimately imposed on them. Good results can only be achieved by sound contingency planning, honesty about the events which caused the disaster in question, swift action to reduce damage, a site visit by the chief executive as soon as a disaster has occurred, and appropriate follow-up action. This in turn requires an agreed strategy that is widely understood throughout the organisation.

Offices

Ernst & Young, an accounting partnership, came under pressure from their staff, who were concerned about the extent of paper consumption and wastage. Initially this focused on recycling paper and reducing wasteful use of energy. Later they sought help from Wastebusters, an environmental consultancy specialising in the office sector. The starting point was a 'green office' audit which identified the main environmental impacts and how they might be reduced. Board level commitment was given to a 'corporate environment policy' and a 'Green Committee' was formed. This committee works with Wastebusters and has established performance standards in purchasing, provided training for buyers and has sent a questionnaire to suppliers to assess their environmental standards. Monitoring results against the standards set takes place regularly.

The achievements include savings of £15,000 in the first year, development of longer term partnerships with suppliers and effective communication with staff.

Managing Office Paper

London Electricity undertook a survey of all paper used and purchased in their office and established a policy to reduce the amount of waste paper generated by their operations.[11] They identified each type of paper used and found their total spending amounted to £1,150,000 each year. They recognised that they needed to reduce overall paper consumption and generate demand for recycled paper, as well as collecting waste paper. An audit of paper usage, equipment and sources of supply was carried out. The company established a policy to purchase paper with a minimum of 75 per cent of recycled paper content, or which was chlorine free, and determined the practical steps necessary to achieve these aims. The steps included getting agreement from designers, printers and equipment suppliers to changes in the paper specifications for each classification of use. The outcome of the project was that London Electricity achieved its goals and saved money. However, recycled paper could not be introduced for the invoices sent to their customers because of objections from banks, who specify the standard required for processing on their equipment.

This project illustrates how thorough research and planning is essential and how important it is to work with others who are involved in the process. The solutions to many problems, such as London Electricity's invoices, require cooperation between different organisations.

Large amounts of paper can be saved by avoiding excessive revision of drafts, by photocopying on both sides of each sheet, and by using computers and electronic mail (e-mail) for internal communications. All these practices are becoming more common.

Environmental Improvement in a Service Business

Thorn EMI Rental (UK) Ltd employs 10,000 people and operates from over 1,000 sites in the UK. Its parent company, Thorn EMI plc, signed the Business Charter for Sustainable Development (reproduced in Appendix

3) in 1991, thus establishing its intention to tackle environmental issues.

The UK Rental company acknowledges that environmental protection is a significant business responsibility, that continuous improvement is the goal, and that this will be accomplished by working at the root causes of problems rather than by reducing environmental effects. The company states that implementation of its environmental policy requires a phased approach which includes raising awareness, setting clear targets, obeying the law, being well organised, and involving staff and suppliers.[12]

During the period from mid-1991 to mid-1993 the company progressed a long way towards achieving three important goals:

- eliminating ozone depleting substances, used to reduce temperature during electrical fault finding, as cleaning fluids and as solvents;
- recycling expanded polystyrene packaging wastes – which resulted in unexpected monetary savings; and
- establishing the basis for reducing energy consumption in operations which would in future be more closely monitored.

These examples show that much can be achieved when an organisation is determined to reduce its environmental impact. But goals need to be clear, research needs to be thorough, people need to be involved at every level, meticulous planning is essential and education and training needs to be provided right through the organisation. When all this is in place the organisation frequently finds that it not only reduces environmental damage but also improves quality standards and saves money which endorses the concept of enlightened self-interest.

The Penalties of Inaction

Firms which fail to respond to environmental pressures will find that their business is threatened and could be damaged in one or more of the following ways:

(1) Loss of business because of failure to meet changing customer requirements.

(2) Reputation harmed by false claims made in advertising and selling products.

(3) Deterioration of corporate image and public confidence as a result of an accident.

(4) Increasing difficulty in raising capital from banks and shareholders and loss of share value.

(5) Losing out to competitors who use resources more economically, recycle wastes, and therefore perform better than those who are slow to see the new trends.

(6) Heavy penalties for releasing pollutants to the environment, coupled with damage to reputation and possibly the health of staff and the public – jail sentences can now be imposed on directors who fail to comply with the law.

(7) Insurance premiums become more costly because the cost of cleaning up environmental damage is greater; some risks may become uninsurable.

(8) Recruitment and retention of good quality staff becomes more difficult as more people seek responsible employers who protect the environment, offer greater job security and provide opportunities for personal progress and development.

(9) Delay in re-focusing research and development priorities, resulting in loss of competitive edge; time lags prove very hard to make up.

(10) Lack of integration with the local community resulting in alienation, which in turn adversely affects business.

(11) Medium and long term future jeopardised because of failure to move with the times in a fast changing global situation.

The Potential Benefits

Organisations which are well managed and have a sound track record of devising and implementing new business strategies and corporate policies will be better able to tackle these new challenges competently. If they do, they are likely to derive several of the following benefits:

(1) Enhanced reputation and market standing.

(2) Ability to attract the green customer.

(3) Investment screening results in the company being included on ethical investment lists.

(4) Material costs come down as resources are used more efficiently.

(5) Pollution prevention contributes to resource economies.

(6) Pollution control results in effective re-use and recycling, as well as avoiding the risk of heavy fines or even imprisonment.

(7) It becomes possible to be an accredited supplier or distributor if the business so requires.

(8) Well positioned to be involved in partnership arrangements with others (where relevant).

(9) Insurance premiums rise less fast than for competitors and it is possible to get insurance cover for some risks denied to others who take less care.

(10) It becomes possible to attract and keep environmentally aware staff because they find the work rewarding and consistent with their own values.

(11) Relationships with the local community become positive and cooperative.

(12) Longer term prospects are good because it is possible to remain among the leading-edge companies.

A Checklist for environmental action is provided in Appendix 1.

Notes

1   Willums and Goluke, 1992, p. 10.
2   An earlier version of this diagram appeared in *Corporate Strategy and the Environment* by Colin Hutchinson, in Long Range Planning vol. 25, no 4.
3   Drucker, Peter, *The Practice of Management*, Heinemann, 1955, and recently reprinted.
4   Adams, Carruthers and Hamil, 1991 (see also Appendix 2).
5   Business in the Environment, *Buying into the Environment: guidelines for integrating the environment into purchasing and supply*, 1993.
6   Birchall, David; Stiles, Philip and Robinson, Helen, Management Attitudes to Environmental Issues – *A Survey of British, Continental European and far Eastern Companies*, Henley Management College, Greenlands Henley-on-Thames, Oxfordshire RG9 3AU, UK. The respondents were mostly middle managers who are registered students of Henley.
7   ACBE, Environmental Management Working Group, *The Case for the Environment*, Brian Whitaker, March 1993.
8   This section draws heavily on Schmidheiny, Stephan, *Changing Course*, MIT, 1992, and Willums Jan-Olaf, Goluke, Ulrich, From Ideas to Action, International Chamber of Commerce, 1992, as well as the much earlier publication of Royston, Michael G, Pollution Prevention Pays, Pergamon, 1979.
9   Schmidheiny, 1992, p. 116.
10 WARMER Bulletin, see Sources of Help.
11 Donna Clark, Company Environment Manager, London Electricity, gave a presentation to The Environment Council Workshop on 'The Environmental Implications of Using and Purchasing Office Papers', February 1993.
12 Ballard, David, *Agreeing Targets for Environmental Improvement*, in *The Environmental Management Handbook*, Taylor, Hutchinson, Pollack and Tapper, eds, Pitman, 1994.

CHAPTER 7

Strategic Approaches to the Challenge

I believe the 1990s will give birth to a broad-based technical revolution prompted by environmental needs, and will result in unprecedented new business development.

Richard M Carpenter, Chief Executive, SC Johnson[1]

Anyone wishing to consider a strategic approach to the environment wants to know the nature and scale of the business opportunity that exists. The first part of this chapter considers this opportunity from seven perspectives. We then look at a wider view of strategic thinking, how business is changing, three examples of a strategic approach to the challenge, and conclude the chapter by contrasting tactical and strategic approaches.

The seven perspectives are:

(1) Nature of the market: what issues need to be tackled and how big is the market?
(2) Industrial infrastructure: the need for change towards an infrastructure which is cyclic, resource-conserving and healthy.
(3) Capital requirements: can the necessary changes be funded?
(4) Technologies required: what technologies will be most useful?
(5) Market readiness: is the market ready?
(6) Underlying trends: what underlying trends might stimulate the market?
(7) Eco-labelling: will people be able to distinguish the less damaging products/services on the market?

Increasing evidence is emerging around the world to show that there is a very large potential market for goods and services which help solve environmental problems. The capital required for this can be made available on a scale which is relevant to the size of the task, but will require considerable re-allocation of priorities. Most of the technologies that are required are already available. The market is ready and the underlying trends indicate that market demand will grow stronger within the next few years as children, who have gained their environmental awareness at school, become increasingly significant customers. They will be able to pick out which products and services to buy because eco-labelling will then be commonplace. Relevant information to support this statement is discussed below.

Large companies and public sector organisations could accelerate the development of this market by appropriate purchasing policies. The buying power represented by purchasing departments is enormous, and yet in early 1994 there is little evidence that there have been any significant shifts in the criteria used by them when establishing sources of supply. On the contrary there is some indication that a few companies have been disappointed that there is not already a more pronounced trend for products and services which do less damage to the environment.[2] Companies taking action on their own initiative have a beneficial effect, but collective action is essential for some issues, and governments have a vital role to play in creating the conditions in which market forces can work effectively.

It is important to bear in mind that the underlying trend is for governments to strengthen legislative and fiscal measures to prevent environmental damage and encourage businesses to take positive action towards sustainable development. Many major companies expect environmental standards to tighten[3] and leading firms are anticipating these measures in their business strategy.

Nature of the Market

An overview of the strategic opportunity is provided by the Centre for Exploitation of Science and Technology (CEST).[4] Their report describes the key environmental problems, the technologies that will be required to deal with them, and also provides an estimate of the size of the potential market in the UK, Europe and the USA. Chart 26 provides a list of the threats to the environment and the estimated expenditure required during the current decade to deal with the problems. These estimates, acknowledged as rough and ready, cover capital requirements, new products which cause less environmental damage, and associated services. The greenhouse effect, water quality and waste management are the likely areas for greatest expenditure. The figures were calculated for the UK and extended to Europe and the USA to arrive at the full estimates.

Industrial Infrastructure

We saw in chapter 3 that the industrialised world has created an infrastructure that is linear, wasteful of resources and toxic. This kind of industrialisation reproduced in developing countries would destroy the planet. We cannot expect developing countries to invent a new form of

Chart 26: Key Environmental Problems

ISSUES	ESTIMATED EXPENDITURE £bn 1991 - 2000		
	UK	EC	USA
Greenhouse effect	48	237	443
Water Quality	25	75-100	71
Waste Management	19	180-200	120-170
Acid rain	11	51	25
Heavy metals	9	80	52
Ozone depletion	7	70	76
Air quality	7	34	17
Noise	6	32	33
Volatile Organic Compounds (VOCs) and smells	3	26	27
Persistent organics	2	23	15
Contaminated land	2	25	150
Major spills	1	7	7
TOTAL	140	860	1,060

Source: Good, Ben; *Industry and the Environment: A Strategic Overview*, Centre for Exploitation of Science & Technology, 1991.

industrial development alone, nor can the developed world continue with its form of industrialisation unchanged. The industrialised world needs to accelerate the rate of change towards an industrial infrastructure that is cyclic, resource-conserving and healthy. The world is crying out for industrial leadership that will boldly set an example, entrepreneurs who will invent the processes and innovative ways in which this form of development can be extended to other countries through creative partnership arrangements. This is now beginning to happen but needs to be developed rapidly.[5]

Capital Requirements

The overall figures estimated by CEST to deal with the issues listed can always be compared with others' estimates for restoring environmental health. Barry Commoner has estimated that the overall costs of effecting a transition to an ecologically sound system worldwide could amount to $500bn per annum for a period of 10 years.[6] The Worldwatch Institute have made an assessment which includes a lower figure for the reduction of Third World debt. Their estimate is for an expenditure of $46bn in 1990, rising to $150bn in 1999, which gives an average annual expenditure of $125bn over the 10 year period 1990 to 2000.[7] This figure, however, does not include the cost of supplying the world with clean water and halting the march of deserts. Elsewhere these are estimated at $30bn per annum and $4bn per annum.[8]

Chart 27:
Estimated Expenditure Required to Restore Environmental Security 1990 - 2000

	$ billions
Protecting topsoil on cropland	213
Reforesting the Earth	59
Slowing population growth	297
Raising energy efficiency	330
Developing renewable energy	172
Retiring Third World debt	300
TOTAL	1,371
Average annual expenditure	125

Notes:

1 Tree planting helps absorb carbon emissions and arrest erosion.
2 Investment in energy efficiency also helps to reduce carbon emissions, whilst investment in renewable energy meets much of the projected growth in energy demand.
3 Expenditure on conservation and population stabilisation are recurring costs, whereas investment in energy efficiency and renewable energy is mainly capital expenditure incurred once.
4 In these figures the cost of retiring Third World debt rises to a peak around $50 billion per annum in 1994, then declines to 0 by the year 2000, whilst other investments increase through the period.

Source:
Brown, Lester R & Wolf, Edward C *Reclaiming the Future* in Brown, Lester R et al **State of the World 1988**, New York, W.W. Norton & Co, 1988.

These figures are so large that reduction of other expenditure will be necessary to release capital for dealing with the environmental threat. Fortunately the end of the Cold War, and significant nuclear disarmament agreements greatly reduce the need to maintain expenditure on armaments at the levels that prevailed during the 1980s. Current military expenditure worldwide is estimated at $1tn ($1,000bn) per annum. The Worldwatch Institute estimates for environmental expenditure represent the equivalent of only two months military expenditure, and Barry Commoner's estimates are only six months at this rated expenditure. Obviously it is not easy to effect the transition, but the scale of expenditure is possible if we have the collective will to make radical changes. It would be possible for the environmental capital requirements to come from arms budgets, and this would represent a better investment in national security.[9]

There are signs that weapons manufacturers are seeking ways in which to deploy their skills and technology for civilian purposes – a prudent strategy to protect employment. This is reflected in increased R&D expenditure in new spheres and the application of the latest technologies in electronics, communications and energy efficiency.[10]

Technologies Required

CEST described the technologies which are most likely to prove helpful in dealing with the environmental threats. They were also described in an article published in April 1993 based on the work of the World Resources Institute (WRI).[11] CEST took a direct approach and described specific technologies which are available to deal with each of the threats they listed. These were classified into 'commercially proven' and 'not commercially proven' in relation to specific threats which need to be reduced or eliminated. WRI discussed the growing competitive market to provide leadership in the technologies that are required now to mitigate environmental problems.

Countries such as Canada, Germany, Italy, Japan and the Netherlands encourage collaboration between government and industry to develop technologies which help to solve environmental problems. The USA, on the other hand, while presidents Bush and Reagan were in the White House, saw measures to protect the environment as a threat to jobs and a drain on the economy. This attitude has changed since President Clinton took over and, hopefully, the situation will now change. Vice President Al Gore believes that industry has a major role to play in solving environmental problems and that this can be a source of productive development.[12]

A brief summary of the technologies that will be required, largely based on those identified by WRI, is:

(1) Energy: renewable sources such as sun, wind and tides, biological fuels, storage in batteries and fuel cells and increasing the efficiency of combustion.
(2) Agriculture: biotechnology and other improved techniques for food production without damaging the environment.
(3) Science and engineering applied to manufacturing processes, monitoring devices and mechanical equipment such as pumps, valves and robots.
(4) Alternative materials which come from abundant sources: e.g. ceramics in place of metals, and plastics from plants.
(5) Catalysts which can help prevent pollution by reducing the quantity and range of undesirable side effects produced by certain industrial and agricultural practices and products.
(6) Operations which dry, distil, evaporate and clean products and processes to reduce unwanted pollution.

(7) Increasing precision in fabrication, resulting in less waste of resources.
(8) Design revolution leading to new ways in which metals, polymers, ceramics and composites are made, thereby reducing waste of materials and energy.
(9) Information technology which can be applied to achieving better understanding of issues and improving communications.
(10) Contraceptive methods to assist with birth control.

Market Readiness

We have already seen in chart 18 that over two-thirds of the people in European countries perceive the greenhouse effect, acid rain and ozone depletion as problems. We now need to know if people are prepared to let this concern influence their buying behaviour. Two broad categories of consumer can be identified: those who are generally committed to the environmental cause, and the rest of the public. MORI have been conducting regular surveys of buying behaviour since 1990. The results for the years 1990, 1991, 1992 and 1993 are given in chart 28: Britain's Green Consumers. It is interesting to see how resilient this behaviour is, despite the recession, in response to most of the questions.

There is a strong underlying tendency towards green consumerism, which exerts a powerful influence on buying habits.

The moment of truth is when more and more people habitually make their buying decisions taking account of ethical and environmental considerations. Every individual can participate in the process of bringing about desired changes by exercising the power of choice when buying goods and services. By rejecting products and services which do not meet the new ethical and environmental standards and selecting only those which do, the transition will be accelerated. It is salutary to witness customers doing this – a few now, many more in the future.

Underlying Trends

Environmental subjects have been included, as a cross-curricular theme, in the UK school curriculum since 1990 and young people have been involved in studies and practical work during the course of their full-time education. There is a direct link from these subjects to the teaching of geography and science, but the link also extends to subjects such as technology, history, mathematics and languages. As many parents will know, this has led to various requests for time, information and materials on environmental subjects in schools. Parents with children who are in, or have passed through, the seven to thirteen age bracket will be aware of some of the penetrating, occasionally embarrassing, questions asked at the breakfast table about their parents' work activity and how it impacts

Chart 28: Britain's Green Consumers

*Q Which, if any, of these things do you do or have done in the last
12 months as a result of concern for the environment?*

| | GENERAL PUBLIC | | | | GREEN CONSUMERS | | | |
	1990	1991	1992	1993	1990	1991	1992	1993
Base %	100	100	100	100	50	49	40	44
	%	%	%	%	%	%	%	%
Buy 'ozone friendly' aerosols	73	71	65	71	92	91	88	90
Buy products which come in recycled packaging	41	55	52	50	58	74	77	71
Buy products made from recycled material	40	52	51	54	58	72	75	75
Buy household, domestic or toiletry products not tested on animals	43	51	47	51	59	70	70	72
Buy free-range eggs or chickens	44	46	44	45	55	58	58	56
Regularly use a bottle bank	39	39	43	46	53	58	55	57
Keep down the amount of electricity and fuel your household uses	44	44	42	51	49	55	52	58
Send your own waste paper to be recycled	31	36	36	38	51	43	47	47
Buy 'environmentally' friendly phosphate-free detergents or household cleaners	38	37	35	36	37	56	58	55
Avoid using chemical fertilisers or pesticides in your garden	41	38	31	40	55	49	45	53
Buy products which come in biodegradable packaging	26	34	29	36	52	53	43	57
Buy food products which are organically grown	25	28	24	27	43	41	36	41
Avoid using the services or products of a company you consider has a poor environmental record	23	19	16	22	33	31	30	38
Keep down the amount you use your car	19	19	13	16	23	25	21	21
Avoid buying chlorine bleached nappies	13	10	7	7	19	15	10	10
Have a catalytic converter fitted to your car	9	7	6	9	12	9	7	12
Loft insulation				9				36
TOTAL	549	586	541	626	727	791	782	849
AVERAGE	37	39	36	37	49	53	52	50

Source: MORI

on the environment. There is every indication that as teaching methods are refined this trend will continue and the pressures will increase.

Alison Clark has worked out a 'JIMM' theory – the initials stand for Jolly Interesting Moment for Management. It is predicted that around 1999 every manager will experience the JIMM theory in action, because that is when children who have received significant environmental education will enter the phase of their lives when they become significant consumers. Armed with their environmental awareness, which will have affected their personal values, they will begin to make a significant impact on the trend towards products and services which cause least damage to the environment. This is one way in which they can contribute to creating a sustainable society for themselves and their children.

Broadly speaking, children born between 1981 and 1986 will receive nine years environmental education incorporated into many different subjects, as we have seen above. Children born between 1976 and 1981 will have learned about the environment for four to nine years before leaving school. For those born before 1976 the proportion drops dramatically to about 20 per cent, and for them environmental education is more likely to have been received informally through television and radio programmes, magazine articles or books. Those who now have school age children are already being influenced by them. From 1999 onwards there will be a rapid increase in environmentally aware people entering the phase in their lives when they are major purchasers of goods and services – generally regarded as the group between the ages of twenty-five and forty-five.

The 'JIMM' will need to be taken into account in three ways:

- during recruitment and selection of staff;
- when managing or supervising younger people; and
- when trying to attract customers.

All three categories will involve new challenges for managers involved with providing goods and services to the community. More exacting requirements will be necessary from a rapidly changing market. See chart 29 which illustrates the JIMM theory graphically.

Eco-labelling

One of the consequences of increased environmental activity has been increased confusion about which products really are less damaging to the environment. This has, in part, been caused by much more detailed research becoming available as corporate research departments become more active in this area. They augment the information resources of the environmental organisations working in this field. Unfortunately some firms are also guilty of false claims, which contribute to the confusion.

Chart 29: The JIMM Theory

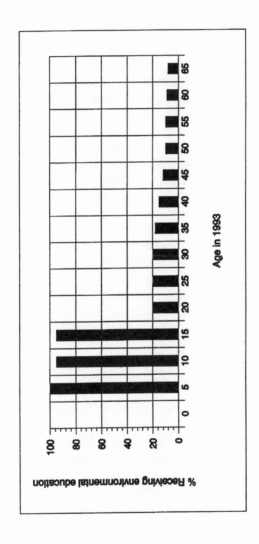

% Receiving environmental education

Age in 1993

Cross curricular environmental education introduced 1990. By 1995 school leavers will have 5 years exposure.
Managers should consider the implications for recruiting and managing people & market buying trends.
Source: Alison Clark, Shandwick Public Affairs. JIMM is the Jolly Interesting Moment for Management.

Many people now remain doubtful about what to buy: for example, the best paper products, petrol or diesel cars, choice of washing powders or detergents, and towelling or disposable nappies. In many cases such as these the least damaging product is not obvious. The choice of paper products will be influenced by the intended use. The choice of car by the type and amount of motoring, as well as by how the car is built and the degree to which it can be recycled when it becomes scrap. All of this makes eco-labelling a complex issue. Up-to-date information on labelling is available from the Confederation of British Industry and the UK Eco-labelling Board.[13]

Eco-labelling became an official European scheme for consumer products from 1993. The scheme is based on independent assessment, taking account of all phases of manufacture, use and disposal of products. Manufacturers can apply for a label and will be charged a fee as well as an annual licence payment if an eco-label is awarded. The scheme will be monitored under the Trade Descriptions Act by Trading Standards Officers. Because the scheme is voluntary firms may also devise their own labels and product descriptions as they do now. The discerning customer will be armed with more information as the years go by and will be able to make more informed purchasing decisions. This trend is set to grow stronger, aided by eco-labelling, stricter legislation and more use of voluntary schemes. It is spreading beyond the industrial countries to affect the whole world.

Organisations can help themselves by being more explicit about performance characteristics of their products – which can be important selling points – and by recognising the desirability of designing products which meet environmental standards as well as customer preferences.

Rethinking the Business

A firm which deals with its environmental responsibility only in a reactive or tactical way will fail to see the business opportunities and will lose out to more enlightened competitors. These firms are likely to find that several departments identify environmental issues in the course of their normal work, but find it increasingly difficult to make an effective response. For example, purchasing departments will identify changes in their sources of supply, marketing departments will discover that competitors' product descriptions contain environmental information, personnel departments will be questioned more closely about environmental policies during recruitment, and financial departments may find that the business is being unfavourably screened for investment purposes. The absence of a cohesive strategy will mean that each department tries to develop an appropriate response, but the separate and independent solutions remain inconsistent. Consistency can only be achieved by a strategic approach for the whole business, preferably developed through the involvement of all major functions.

Several businesses have discovered this for themselves, made a more senior appointment in relation to environmental issues and involved key people from major departments in the process of rethinking the business. Most firms will meet resistance to change – in one form or another. However, it is helpful to remember that the changes which are most strongly resisted are those that are imposed. When people participate in effective joint problem solving the disagreements which occur can be used creatively to develop robust solutions.

Every business faces a triple challenge, which in today's world needs to include the environmental dimension. First, every business needs to be effective today and to make its environmental impact acceptable. Secondly it needs to identify and realise its potential to become a sustainable business. Thirdly, it needs to change to a sustainable business for a future that will inevitably be different.[14] These three challenges need to be tackled together. An attempt to deal with them sequentially will almost certainly fail because the first two can each become a never-ending task. The more that this happens the longer the need for change is deferred. A fragmented, as opposed to a holistic, approach will not work either, because too many elements are inter-connected.

To establish a holistic, integrated approach requires a clear corporate strategy. In order to start the process of a dialogue, some companies, such as IBM and Rank Xerox, have created cross-functional teams on environmental matters. They have not necessarily altered their focus from reducing environmental impact to creating a sustainable business, but have taken an initial step which could move in that direction. We now need to revisit an earlier chart in an amended form. Chart 30 identifies what is involved in making a strategic response towards creating a sustainable business. This emphasises the fourth segment rather than the tactical response which was stressed in chart 25.[15]

A dramatic change to this strategic approach will be a daunting prospect, with a high risk that the business will suffer because it attempts to make a change that is too radical, too quickly. However, there is also the risk of sticking too long with the proven products of yesterday's world and being outstripped by more alert competitors. Ways need to be found to address the fundamental question of new strategies while continuing to market successful products and services which are reasonably acceptable in a fast changing world.

For any business, serious involvement with environmental and ethical issues means commitment from the top. An effective strategic approach is dependent on board agreement – and preferably a statement from the chief executive demonstrating personal commitment. This alone is never enough, because what is done is always more important than what is said. However, without a clearly expressed intention from the board the

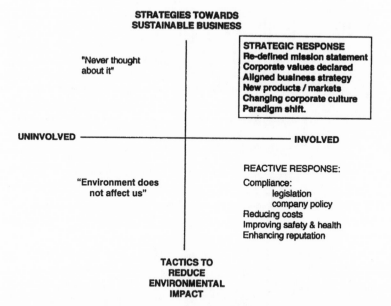

Chart 30
STRATEGIC ENVIRONMENT INVOLVEMENT

STRATEGIES TOWARDS
SUSTAINABLE BUSINESS

"Never thought
about it"

STRATEGIC RESPONSE
Re-defined mission statement
Corporate values declared
Aligned business strategy
New products / markets
Changing corporate culture
Paradigm shift.

UNINVOLVED ——————————————————— INVOLVED

REACTIVE RESPONSE:

"Environment does
not affect us"

Compliance:
   legislation
   company policy
Reducing costs
Improving safety & health
Enhancing reputation

TACTICS TO
REDUCE
ENVIRONMENTAL
IMPACT

rest of the organisation has no coherent guidance. It is also necessary to locate the coordinating executive responsibility with a named director, which is now done in several major companies.

Widening the Debate

Some companies are already having meetings with environmentalists. They want their senior managers to be exposed to people with different perspectives, different values, different motivations, in order to understand better how the world is changing. For example Procter and Gamble and British Telecom work with John Elkington and Julia Hailes, the authors of several best selling books on environmental matters as they affect industry.[16] Sainsbury's have appointed Jonathon Porritt as an adviser. Shell UK have involved various people, including Chris Baines and John Button to provide information and perspectives not readily available within the firm.

The use of cross-functional teams is a good way to collect the facts about pressures, opportunities and options. A rich problem-solving process can be developed, leading to creative solutions which are unlikely to be achieved without this sort of cross fertilisation.

A useful framework for carrying out this process is provided in chart 31 which outlines the stages of a strategic approach.

CHART 31: A STRATEGIC FRAMEWORK FOR ENVIRONMENTAL MANAGEMENT

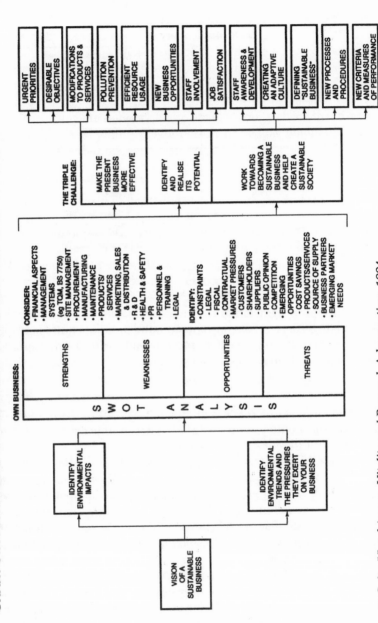

© Colin Hutchinson, *Vitality and Renewal*, Adamantine, 1994

Assessing Existing Products

A simple but powerful technique for analysing existing products in terms of their acceptability for a sustainable business scenario is to use a product strategy matrix such as chart 32. The company's products can be categorised on this matrix by identifying which segment best describes each product in terms of market potential and potential for sustainability. Those that fall into the bottom left segment because they have low potential both for the market and for sustainability should be abandoned. Those which have high market potential but low sustainability should be modified in ways which increase their sustainability, or substituted. For example peat is ideal for gardens but because its extraction is not sustainable and it cannot be modified the search for substitutes is already happening.

For those products which have high sustainability but low market potential, every effort should be made to increase market acceptance. This may involve the search for new materials rather than a simplistic attempt to persuade people to buy an inferior product – such as reverting to wooden spoons. Finally those products which have high potential for sustainability and high market acceptance are clear priorities for development. They are most likely to prove to be useful revenue earners for the future.

Chart 32
A PRODUCT STRATEGY MIX

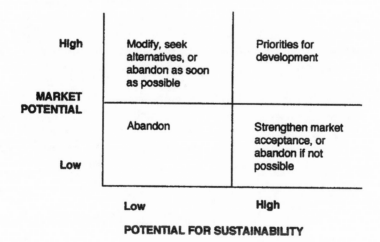

Life Cycle Analysis

So far as existing products are concerned, many companies are now using life cycle analysis to find out about all the impacts on the environment of a particular product 'from the cradle to the grave'. This is a demanding process and requires careful analysis and documentation of findings. It can then provide the base line from which to consider every aspect of the product, from the procurement of raw materials, through all the manufacturing processes, to the product in use, and to its final disposal after use. Changes can be planned and implemented at every stage of the process, in order to reduce adverse environmental impact, conserve resources, eliminate pollution, and often save money.

Identifying and Specifying Business Opportunities

As a result of the various considerations in this chapter, and after using the frameworks described in Charts 31 to 33, some ideas for new products will have emerged. It is now time to consider the new opportunities. An initial brainstorming session will help to identify a list of possibilities, which at this stage will contain many wild ideas. These should not be prematurely rejected, because they might be useful stepping stones to a really good innovation. A quick method for developing a short list is to ask those involved to select their top two or three priorities. Ideas which appear in several lists are likely to be the best possibilities for further development, feasibility studies and costings. The final identification of one or two new products can then go forward in the normal way, for market testing.

A useful notion for these products is to separate them into 'lifeboats' – those acknowledged as radical and different – and those which are in the mainline business. Mainline business ideas can be developed in the usual way. Those which are 'lifeboats' should be recognised as rescue vehicles and given appropriate treatment. Shell introduced a small heating services section within their oil marketing operation, recognising it as different and small scale. They probably did not expect it to grow into a major company, but after a few years it was launched as a wholly owned subsidiary called Emstar, which now, having merged with AHS, is a separately quoted company on the London stock exchange, trading under the name of AHS Emstar. The new company offers comprehensive energy management services and has had considerable success as a business, as well as helping its clients to reduce emissions and save money.[17]

Business is Changing

Several companies have in recent years revised their Mission Statements. For example the BBC states that it is in the business of making and

Chart 33
A FRAMEWORK FOR PRODUCT LIFE CYCLE ASSESSMENT

PRODUCTS	DESIGN CONSIDERATIONS	PROCURING MATERIALS	PRODUCTION PROCESSES	PRODUCT DISTRIBUTION	PRODUCT IN USE	DISPOSAL AFTER USE	NOTES ON OTHER LINKS
A							
B							
C							
D							
E							

Notes:

1. Consider: resource depletion, wastes, pollution of air, water and soil, recovery procedures, impact on the community and damage to the environment at each stage of the life cycle.

2. Quick ratings: give scores ranging from 1 (low impact) to 5 (high impact) for each product and each stage of the process. Develop strategies for dealing with all scores of 3 and above for any individual rating and all products which achieve a total score of 14 or more.

3. In depth analysis: develop descriptive information for each stage of one product, using a larger version of this chart. Review the method and the criteria being used. Refine as necessary to suit your business, complete the analysis, and then prioritise the product development plan.

4. Notes on other links: use this space when a product is closely linked to another product or requirement of another organisation. For example packaging may be influenced by criteria specified by hygiene or safety considerations, billing forms may need to meet processing requirement of banks.

broadcasting radio and television programmes. It is not a specialist in all the other 'businesses' that have grown up around its main function. The Corporation decided to let others supply the support services it needed, such as building maintenance, engineering, catering, security, and cleaning.

Both BP and Shell have had ventures into other spheres which were nothing to do with oil or chemicals; but in recent years they have shed most of these interests and now concentrate on their mainstream business.

Several organisations have discovered that they had too many layers – especially of management. In the seventies this applied in particular to oil and chemical companies, but in the eighties it spread to banks, insurance companies and public sector organisations. This is not just a question of overhead costs being too high but is also influenced by the development of information technology. As information systems become more sophisticated it is possible to make relevant information available to people close to where they work. For example, sales representatives and area managers are now supplied with information which enables them to make pricing decisions and to measure their performance in terms of contribution to profits rather than sales volume.

Many companies have declared specific goals to reduce staff numbers, to strengthen teamwork, to rely less on the hierarchy for decisions which could be taken at lower levels in the organisation, and to grant more autonomy at every level. This means that those now responsible for taking decisions need the relevant information to take sound decisions. Initially, junior managers are not used to this level of authority and a lot of learning takes place in a short time. Many of these managers comment that after such changes have been implemented 'there is nowhere to hide any more', but many also say: 'I have not enjoyed any period in my career as much as I do now.' This was one of the striking experiences when changes were made in the Commercial Division of Shell UK Oil in the mid 1980s. Once people feel the freedom and have the autonomy there is no going back. Work becomes exciting, challenging and infinitely more rewarding. The case history of Shell UK is dealt with in more detail in chapter 9 and approaches to personal growth and development are dealt with in chapter 10.

Improved information technology has also meant that many jobs can be done by people working from home. This requires considerable adjustment, but it suits many of those who now work in this way. It benefits the company because premises can be smaller and overheads can be greatly reduced. For the individual, sometimes this form of working is a stepping stone to becoming self-employed, through a gradual transition which is agreed by both parties.

Change can be brought about in surprising ways. For example, the market for facsimile machines increased as a result of a postal strike. It is also possible that the IRA bombings in London and other major cities might boost the demand for teleworking and contribute to a decline in demand for large office blocks in major urban areas.

These changes in business practice have been brought about by economic pressures, developments in technology, and government policy. Most organisations have become used to change, but it is likely that the scale and nature of the future changes stimulated by the environmental challenge will be even greater. Those organisations which come to terms with this challenge and learn to manage the changes will be well placed to succeed in the future.

Learning Organisations

In order to cope with the fast changing world, executives need to understand better how organisations function. When there is steady growth year after year, doing much the same things as before, this need is far less. But when organisations have to be formed or changed quickly to tackle new opportunities, or when there is a need to slim down as market demand declines, such understanding is essential. Several companies provide training to their senior managers in open systems theory, and including models which illuminate the functioning of organisations. These models have proved extremely beneficial for those responsible for planning and implementing organisational change.

Chart 34 is one example of such an organisation model.[18] It is based on open systems thinking which recognises that all organisations operate as 'open systems', interacting with many other organisations in the community. They receive inputs in the form of energy, materials, information and money, which are processed within the organisation to produce outputs for the community in the form of goods or services, information and wastes. Feedback loops provide information which enables performance to be measured and materials re-used or recycled. Within the organisation it is helpful to separate the direction-setting activities from the operational. Direction is set through establishing a Mission Statement, identifying values, agreeing policies, deciding which markets will be addressed and setting specific objectives, typically annually. When new directions are set, the implications for the operational organisation are considerable. Without an appropriate organisational model, widely agreed among senior managers, it is very difficult to manage change effectively. The implications of change have to be carefully considered right through the whole organisation.

Once the direction is set, attention shifts to operational issues. The objectives determine the work to be done, the people required to do the

work, how they will be rewarded (formally and informally), the organisation structure to have, what information flow is needed and the problem-solving and decision-making procedures required. The effectiveness
of the organisation will depend on the organisation culture that prevails,
how adaptable it is to changing circumstances and the degree of 'fit'
there is between the six operational elements. In a turbulent, changing
world the ability to adapt to new situations is crucial. Every time an
operational element is changed it will affect every other element, hence
the connecting lines in the lower half of chart 34.

As organisations develop strategies for tackling the environmental
challenge and move towards becoming sustainable, they face a very considerable challenge of change management. This has contributed to the
ideas behind the learning organisation, as one which promotes the idea
that it is not only individuals who learn, but that effective learning in fast
changing situations needs to be taken on board by the whole organisation. Learning needs to be a collective process so that groups and departments can work together smoothly to bring about change.
Organisational learning involves:[19]

- systems thinking;
- personal mastery;
- mental models;
- building shared vision; and
- team learning.

There is an obvious link between this approach and the research findings of Kotter and Heskett about the value of adaptive organisation cultures, which we shall discuss in the next section.

Corporate Culture

The culture of an organisation is made up of its traditions, its underlying
values, the procedures used for getting things done, how information
flows through the organisation, how decisions are made, and the way in
which people, especially those in positions of power, behave.
Organisation cultures exert considerable influence on people at all levels.
Everyone, consciously or sub-consciously, decides what they need to do
to fit in, get rewards, make progress and achieve results. In this way they
are all making assumptions about the organisation's culture, and usually
reinforcing it in subtle ways.

Some people believe that successful organisations need strong cultures
if they are to succeed. Others have said that it is more important to have
a culture that fits the organisation's Mission. Some interesting research
has revealed that the most successful companies have neither strong cultures nor cultures that are appropriate to their Mission. The most suc-

CHART 34: AN ORGANISATIONAL MODEL

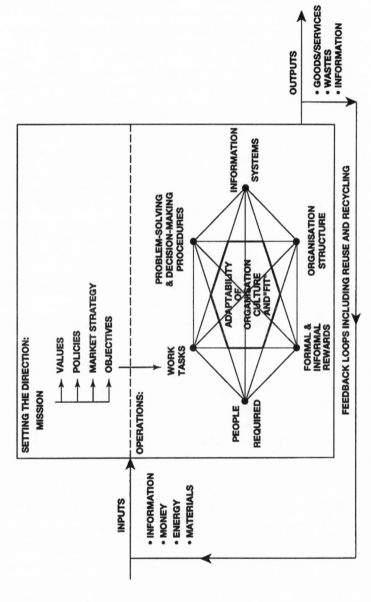

Adapted from Jay Galbraith & Sheppard Moscow

© Colin Hutchinson, *Vitality and Renewal*, Adamantine, 1994

cessful companies have adaptive cultures. Strong cultures are very hard to change, and when the organisation needs to alter its Mission, strategies, policies or objectives, the culture prevails and changes are often not brought about in time. Similarly those companies with an organisation culture ideally suited to the current Mission are effective only as long as the Mission, strategies and policies remain appropriate.

The outcome of the research was that:

> ...in the firms with more adaptive cultures, the cultural ideal is that managers throughout the hierarchy should provide leadership to initiate change in strategies and tactics whenever necessary to satisfy the legitimate interests of not just stockholders, or customers, or employees but all three.[20]

It is interesting to note that these findings used the idea of stakeholders, and emphasised the importance of leadership being exercised at every level. We shall return to the idea of leadership in chapters 8 and 9.

If your organisation does not have an adaptive culture and you want to stimulate action to change it, it is important to recognise that this is never easy, but it can be done. It requires great skill, competent leadership and relevant opportunities to help people at every level to make their own adjustments in behaviour – and it calls for perseverance over several years. How this can be done will be addressed in chapter 9.

In his address to a joint CBI/ICC conference in October 1992 Robert Kennedy, Chairman and Chief Executive of Union Carbide, stated that the greatest barrier to environmental excellence is requiring change in organisation culture and the behaviour of staff. He is not alone. Edgar Woolard Jr, Chairman of E.I. du Pont de Nemours, says: 'I'm calling for corporate environmentalism – which I define as an attitude and performance commitment that place corporate environmental stewardship fully in line with public desires and expectations.' ICI place much emphasis on the need for training which begins with an exploration of values – an approach being extended to 130,000 staff throughout the world.[21]

Examples of a Strategic Response

The examples given here are illustrative of companies adopting a strategic approach. The inclusion of these examples does not suggest that the companies have done all they need to do, nor that they are the only ones that are doing so. The companies mentioned would be the first to admit that there is a great deal still to do. However, they have won awards for the leadership they have given and are useful illustrations of what can be done if the will is there.

Procter and Gamble

Procter and Gamble is one of the world's leaders in environmental management and contribute to the state of the art by making it's work known.[22] The company states that it 'has a deep sense of commitment to help protect, preserve and enhance the quality of the environment in which we all live...something we have pursued for decades'.

The company's environmental quality policy is:

To provide products of superior quality and value that best fill the needs of the world's consumers. As a part of this, Procter and Gamble continually strives to improve the environmental quality of its products, packaging and operations around the world. To carry out this commitment it is P&G's policy to:

- Ensure our products, packaging and operations are safe for our employees, consumers and the environment.
- Reduce or prevent the environmental impact of our products and packaging in their design, manufacture, distribution, use and disposal whenever possible... We support the sustainable use of resources and actively encourage reuse, recycling and composting.
- Meet or exceed the requirements of all environmental laws and regulations.
- Continually assess our environmental technology and programs and monitor progress toward environmental goals.
- Provide our consumers, customers, employees, communities, public interest groups and others with relevant and appropriate information about the environmental quality of P&G products, packaging and operations....We...nurture open, honest and timely communications and strive to be responsive to concerns.
- Ensure every employee understands and is responsible and accountable for incorporating environmental quality considerations in daily business activities. We encourage, recognise and reward individual and team leadership efforts to improve environmental quality.
- Have operating policies, programs and resources in place to implement our environmental quality policy.

Scientific understanding and wise use of resources are central to Procter and Gamble's environmental work and the company undertakes projects in partnership with others where this is appropriate. They make sure that innovation and leadership is rewarded. This is vitally important to ensure that environmental management is kept within the main stream of business activity and is taken into account when appraisals, career progression and promotion are being considered.

Because Procter and Gamble adopt a strategic approach they have modified their washing powders, such as Ariel and Ultra, made them more compact or concentrated and thereby saved 200,000 tonnes of detergent in the UK alone during the period 1988 to 1992. They have been pioneers of refillable bags for washing powders, which use 90 per cent less packaging than the equivalent size carton and 50 per cent less packaging throughout the total packaging system. The Ariel liquid refill pouch alone saved over 700 tonnes of packaging over the eighteen-month period mid-1991 to the end of 1992. They have been at the leading edge of Life Cycle Assessment (LCA) and developed a spreadsheet which helps to predict the inputs and outputs of all processes in the life cycle of a packaging system.[23] They play a leading part in the work of the Society of Environmental Toxicology and Chemistry (SETAC).[24]

Procter and Gamble take part in the European Recovery and Recycling Association's (ERRA) kerbside collection scheme in Adur, West Sussex, England. They became involved in this project when they realised that the next phase of their work on reducing waste had to concentrate on what happens to packaging after the products have been used. This was a more productive area to tackle rather than to continue focusing within their own premises. Procter and Gamble's European manufacturing plants have reduced their waste per tonne of finished product by 44 per cent over the two year period 1991–1992. This is against a target of 15 per cent each year, as part of a long term objective to strive for zero waste.

Sometimes controversial issues arise, as has happened with Procter and Gamble's claims for disposable nappies versus the washable variety. The controversy has been debated in the *WARMER bulletin* and remains unresolved.[25] In summary, washable nappies consume less raw materials, create less waste, are less absorbent, consume more energy in washing and drying, consume detergents and are a cheaper option. Disposable nappies consume more raw materials, create more waste for disposal, are more absorbent, consume no energy or detergents in use and are a more expensive option. The decisive factor is often determined by the locality in which the parents live, the sort of waste disposal services available and whether or not a nappy washing service (which involves transportation costs) is used.

British Telecommunications

BT has declared its commitment to the environment and stated its policy which is that:[26]

> BT is committed to minimising the impact of its operations on the environment by means of a programme of continuous improvement.

In particular BT will:

- meet and, where appropriate, exceed the requirements of all legislation;
- where no regulations exist BT shall set its own exacting standards;
- promote recycling and the use of recycled materials, while reducing consumption of materials wherever possible;
- design energy efficiency into new services, buildings and products and manage energy wisely in all operations;
- reduce wherever practicable the level of harmful emissions;
- minimise waste in all operations and product development;
- work with its suppliers to minimise the impact of their operations on the environment through quality purchasing policy;
- protect visual amenity by the careful siting of buildings, structures and deployment of operational plant in the local environment and respect wild life habitats;
- support through its community programme the promotion of environmental protection by relevant external groups and organisations;
- include environmental issues in BT training programmes and encourage the implementation by all BT people of sound environmental practices; and
- monitor progress and publish an environmental performance report on an annual basis.

BT published its first Environmental Performance Report in 1992 together, with brochures on telephone recycling, environmental achievements, and energy, telecommunications and the environment. All these are very impressive and earned the company an award in 1993. The report gives quantified data on specific amounts of metals and minerals recovered through recycling cables and equipment. Specific targets are quoted for waste reduction and reduction in use of products which give rise to harmful emissions. BT gives details of its own purchasing commitment and how it intends to influence its suppliers. The community programme and training provided to BT staff are described. Finally the company explains its monitoring procedure and how it has set up its environmental liaison panel.

BT also published its Business Catalogue, in spring 1993,[27] which demonstrates that the company is in the fortunate position of being able to encourage people to make more use of the telephone and teleconferencing facilities to cut down on travelling long distances to meetings. The company acknowledges that remote contact cannot replace all face-to-face meetings, but it can reduce the need for meetings as people become skilled in the use of technology. BT emphasises that reduced travel cuts down energy costs and helps the environment. The figures they quote are impressive and are given in chart 35, which shows how the energy consumption of travel compares with the use of the telephone.

Chart 35: Comparative Energy Consumption - Telecommunications

Type of call	Mode of transport	Distance	Length of continuous time on phone to use equivalent amount of energy
Local	Car	10km	21 hours
Trunk	Rail	320 km	33 hours
Trunk	Car	320 km	7 days
International	Air	5,000 km	5 weeks

Source: British Telecommunications plc 1991

There is no doubt that BT has developed powerful arguments in favour of its business and has adopted a responsible attitude towards the environment. However, the company has not yet made all the strategic connections. For example there is no cross-referencing of BT's impressive environmental impact statement to its products. This means that a buyer of BT equipment is unable to select those items which do least damage to the environment. BT's work is still developing and no doubt this aspect will be covered in due course.

Xerox Corporation

Xerox is an organisation which recognises that 'the reactive approach is yielding to proactive compliance as companies anticipate the changes in regulation.' Xerox formally declared environmental leadership to be a strategic priority in 1990, and formed an Environmental Leadership Steering Committee. The company identified 300 people in the organisation who were committed to working on this project and provided each of them with a data base giving details of all the other people involved.

Xerox Corporation's approach is to take account of all environmental quality issues, adopting a total life strategy, at the design stage, while acknowledging that this is not easy. The company uses its quality programme which recognises the need to:

- understand customers' existing and latent requirements;
- provide all external and internal customers with products and services that fully satisfy their requirements;
- develop employee involvement and teamwork, through participative problem solving, as essential to improving quality; and
- recognise that error-free work is the most cost-effective way to improve quality.

The Corporation recognises that a key aspect of the quality process is reward and recognition for individual and team excellence and that this is essential if the goal of internalising environmental values within Xerox as a normal part of the management process is to be achieved.[28]

Abhay Bhushan, who is Manager of Xerox Corporation's Environmental Leadership Programs, believes that it is important to help people doing this type of leading edge work to deepen their understanding of environmental issues. He and the team took part in Terma's Box training and found it to be 'invaluable in creating a stronger connection between team members and the environment'.[29]

Contrast Between Tactical and Strategic Approaches

A tactical response to the environment is reactive, often defensive, and tends to deal with issues which are a nuisance because they seem to distract attention from the real, important business. The focus is invariably short term and the effort exerted frequently seems to be excessive for the results achieved.

A strategic approach, on the other hand, requires more thought at the top executive level, is highly active in implementation, tackles mainstream issues such as products or services offered to the market, involves every department in a creative endeavour, and seeks business opportunities which are congruent with responsible, ethical business practices. The focus is on the medium or long term and requires sound vision and leadership. Very soon companies realise that their environmental responsibilities are fulfilled better when environment becomes an integral part of the business in all its spheres of operation. We saw in the previous chapter that environmental managers often have great difficulty in enthusing their colleagues on these issues, when they are tackled piecemeal, because involvement in these issues has little or no effect on their colleagues' main line responsibilities, departmental performance and rewards. However, the situation changes if the organisational approach is strategic, because environmental impact is then a mainstream activity. As Edward Woolard of Du Pont has said:

> 'I have never seen a stronger force for coalescing the organisation about a common purpose than the environment. Our people were waiting to be empowered to do the right things.'[30]

As the strategic approach spreads throughout the organisation another perspective emerges. Every individual discovers that full involvement with environmental and ethical issues reaches the inner world and personal values. As Mikhail Gorbachev has said (and we noted in chapter 4), Perestroika could not have been undertaken, nor the Cold War ended, without a change in values; and this learning process continues. The realisation is now dawning on a few senior executives that a sustainable future can only be achieved if values change and this means entering the world of our inner beliefs.

The strategic approach will vary for different industries. For example, engineering companies will find many ways in which they can contribute by altering their products and services. For some industries, as we have seen in the case of BT, it will be possible both to promote their business and in doing so help others to reduce their environmental impact. Many businesses in the service sector will be able to find creative ways in which they can make a significant contribution. Many new businesses will grow up to provide products and services which it is difficult for large, established organisations to provide. When a company is making annual profits in excess of £100m any new venture which does not look likely to achieve a profit of £5m within three to five years appears too small to consider; but for many independent businesses this might well be a healthy, ambitious achievement.

Those industries which extract minerals from the earth will have a tough time because they make an enormous impact on the environment, and the concept of sustainability will be difficult if not impossible to achieve in practice. For these businesses the long term focus will need to be on alternatives to the product, while in the short term they should concentrate on minimising the harm done by the extraction process, making provision for cleaning up the residual mess, using energy as economically as possible, and trying to ensure that reserves last as long as possible.

Many companies may find that their approach to the environmental challenge goes through four phases:

(1) Reducing environmental impact using a tactical approach.
(2) Developing an holistic strategic approach, which may mean redefining the nature of the business.
(3) Exploring partnership arrangements to find creative ways to tackle projects where solutions depend on cooperation between different organisations.
(4) Realising that the search for a sustainable future depends on changes that reach the inner world and values of senior executives and in due course all staff.

A checklist covering both tactical and strategic approaches is provided in Appendix 1.

We saw in chapter 6 how the environmental challenge can be tackled tactically. In this chapter we have considered the strategic approach, which is likely to lead companies to explore ways in which they can contribute to the creation of a sustainable society such as the vision encapsulated in chart 23 and the daunting challenge described in chart 24. In terms of real contributions towards a viable future, this is where the effort needs to be developed.

A study carried out on behalf of the Royal Institute of International

Chart 36: Technology Sourcing

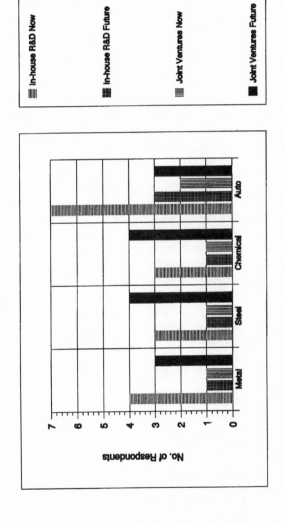

In-house R&D Now

In-house R&D Future

Joint Ventures Now

Joint Ventures Future

No. of Respondents

Metal   Steel   Chemical   Auto

Source: Environmental Profiles of European Business, Earthscan, 1993

Affairs jointly by the Centre for Exploitation of Science and Technology and the Association for Conservation of Energy examined the profiles of European Business. The study concentrated on six sectors – automotive, chemical and petrochemical, steel, metal processing, and electricity – and examined each sector in terms of the importance attributed to different environmental issues, the sources of pressure on the sector, and the level of government (local, national, European or global) the sector regarded as most significant. As might be expected the picture varied for each sector. For example, in terms of environmental issues, the greenhouse effect is very significant for the automotive and chemical industries, air quality for steel and acid rain for electricity. Pressure from the public is very significant for electricity and steel, pressure from the media for automotive and chemicals, and from customers for chemicals and metal processing. One of the most interesting findings of the study in terms of business strategy is that all sectors intend to move away from in-house R&D on environmental matters towards 'the formation of new joint venture companies to develop and produce technologies and processes for addressing environmental pressures.' Chart 36 gives the figures from the study.[31]

Moving from the Context to the Methods

So far in this book we have concentrated on the substantive issues (chapter 2), how people are responding (chapter 3), beliefs and values (chapter 4), sustainable development (chapter 5) and the tactical (chapter 6) and strategic (chapter 7) responses from business. These substantive issues need to be understood, but we also need to grasp what it will take to bring about change, in terms of both the learning that is required and the processes and techniques which will be helpful. We are now at the half way stage before we move from the context which stimulates the need for change to the methods that will achieve it.

Notes

1 Schmidheiny, 1992, p. 218.
2 Jones, Robert J, *Developing Business Opportunities in Energy Conservation*, in Taylor, Hutchinson, Tapper and Pollack (eds), 1994.
3 Vaughan and Mickle, 1993.
4 Good, 1991.
5 Schmidheiny, 1992, chapter 8.
6 Commoner, 1990, pp. 172–3.
7 Brown, Lester R. and Wolf, Edward C., *Reclaiming the Future* in Brown, Lester et al, *State of the World 1988*, W.W. Norton & Co, New York, 1988.
8 Myers, 1990, p. 162.
9 Lovins and Lovins, 1986, chapters 19 and 20.
10 Kenward, Michael, 'Learning to Live with Peace', in International Management, May, 1993.

11 Banks, Darryl R, *The Heat is On*, in Tomorrow no. 2, April 1993.
12 Gore, 1992.
13 See Sources of Help.
14 Drucker, Peter, *The Practice of Management*, Heinemann, 1955. The formulation in the text is an adaptation of what Peter Drucker wrote.
15 Earlier versions of Charts 30, 31, 32, 33 and 34 appeared in Hutchinson, Colin, *Corporate Strategy and the Environment*, in Long Range Planning vol. 25, no 4.
16 Elkington and Burke, 1987; Elkington and Hailes, 1988 and 1989: examples to illustrate why it is so important to develop an integrated, holistic approach.
17 Ashcroft, John, *The Need for Energy Management*, in CBI Environment Newsletter, no. 11, April 1993.
18 This model is based on work done by Jay Galbraith which was adapted by Sheppard Moscow Ltd for their consulting work on organisational change, and in the form used here has been further adapted by the author.
19 Senge, 1990.
20 Kotter and Heskett, 1992, p. 50.
21 ICI have produced four booklets covering environmental values, waste and pollution, chemical industry trends and environmental actions. These are being used worldwide.
22 Procter and Gamble, *In Partnership with Our Environment* and *Real Progress*, in Procter and Gamble's Environmental Review 1992.
23 This spreadsheet is available from the Environmental Affairs Department, Procter and Gamble Limited, PO Box 1EE, Newcastle upon Tyne NE99 1EE, Tel: 091 279 2000.
24 SETAC (see Sources of Help).
25 WARMER Bulletin nos. 36 and 37.
26 British Telecommunications, BT and the Environment: Environmental Performance Report 1992. This report and up-to-date brochures are available from BT's London Headquarters.
27 The BT Business Catalogue, Spring 1993.
28 Bhushan, Abhay and MacKenzie, James C., *Environmental Leadership Plus Total Quality Management Equals Continuous Improvement*, in Total Quality Environmental Management, Spring 1992.
29 Letter, May 1993 (see Sources of Help, for Terma Box Training).
30 Schmidheiny, 1992, p. 195.
31 Royal Institute for International Affairs, 1993.

CHAPTER **8**

Who Is in Charge?

Never doubt that a small group of thoughtful, committed citizens can change the world. Indeed it is the only thing that ever has.

Margaret Mead

> *A leader is best*
> *when people barely know that he exists,*
> *not so good when people obey and acclaim him,*
> *worst when they despise him.*
> *Fail to honour people,*
> *they will fail to honour you;*
> *but of a good leader, who talks little,*
> *when his work is done, his aim fulfilled,*
> *they will all say, 'we did this ourselves.'*
>
> Lao Tzu 600 BC

This chapter marks a change of emphasis. We now move from the substantive issues which represent the global challenge to the processes which we need to develop in order to understand better how to make an effective response. One of the most crucial issues in this context is the relationship between boss and subordinate. Is this characterised by dominance and compliance, or a feeling of shared responsibility and interdependence? The established organisation culture and the choices made for the future play a large part in determining who is in charge.

We look first at the boss/subordinate relationship from both perspectives, then at working in groups. We consider ways in which groups mature and become effective, as well as some of the ways in which they are blocked from doing so. We explore the relevance of group work in today's world and how important it is for tackling social and environmental problems. Finally you, the reader, are invited to consider the question: who is in charge of your life?.

The Subordinate's Perspective

'I disagree with what we are doing but I go along with it.' This was the comment, in a confidential interview, from a very senior executive in a large financial organisation. In response to the question: 'Have you told your boss?' the reply was: 'That would not be appropriate; it's not how we work here.'

Deferring to senior people is widespread in large UK organisations. Many would say: 'That's quite right and appropriate.' It is not the intention in this book to advocate anarchy, but to explore the consequence of undue deference and describe how shared responsibility can emerge in practical ways.

The deputy who does not speak up and passively accepts direction from the boss is in effect saying: 'I am not in charge, they are.' Subordinates often feel constrained, or fear that they run the risk of putting their career in jeopardy if they speak up. In a few organisations – probably very few – the fear may be justified, but in many more it is a constraint emanating from the organisation's culture. In these situations the assumption is that it is too dangerous to speak up – it may be taken as a challenge to authority and is therefore inappropriate. The tragedy is that the assumption usually remains implicit and untested. The result is that many subordinates are frustrated, and they contribute few of their ideas and little of their talent. They and their organisation are both losers.

Influencing skills courses and workshops usually include opportunities to explore and try out new ways of being more effective in real life situations. An overwhelming majority of participants, given a free choice, select their boss as the person whom they would like to influence more. The training event provides an opportunity to rehearse how a particular meeting might be conducted, and to repeat the rehearsal in a variety of ways until confidence is established that an initiative can be taken with a good likelihood of a positive outcome. An example helps to clarify what is involved.

Bill felt frustrated that Alan, his boss never really listened to him. Bill was working on a marketing proposal which had considerable significance for his department. He would be presenting his proposal within a few days and did not want a repetition of his last presentation when Alan rejected his proposal after limited understanding of the ideas. The new project required the cooperation of people in other departments and Alan's support was crucial for its successful implementation. Bill tended to undersell his ideas, with a hesitant delivery, and he now realised that this probably contributed to Alan's impatience and inattention. Bill wanted to practise giving a more confident presentation which would command attention. He tried out various ways of conducting the meeting, with one of his course colleagues taking the part of Alan so that it could be as realistic as possible. After four attempts and some coaching Bill was making the sort of impact he wanted. Some weeks later Bill was able to describe how his proposal had been accepted and how Alan had commented favourably on his new found confidence.

The Boss's Perspective

Discussions with senior people often reveal a very different perspective. Top level executives in many large companies periodically fear that they have insufficient competence beneath them to ensure an effective succession to the top jobs. They do not see the level of management below them taking sufficient initiatives or accepting adequate responsibility to demonstrate the sort of competence required to be effective at the top level. Some of these senior people say to their subordinates 'Bring me your solutions, not your problems.' They would like their subordinates to be more autonomous, and they feel frustrated when they are not. At times the way this is expressed by the boss is brusque and discouraging. If it is done sincerely and backed up by active listening, many subordinates will be encouraged and a more robust, effective relationship will develop.

In several companies the situation has been changing. A combination of factors has produced a powerful stimulus for this change. These factors include the need to reduce costs, recognition that there are too many levels of management, adoption of total quality programmes, and the development of improved information systems. The result is that organisations have slimmed down their middle management, granted more authority to people at lower levels and established clearer objectives with better information to enable managers to make informed decisions. Jobs have become more challenging, stimulating, satisfying and rewarding. Although this is sometimes quite threatening initially, in due course most people welcome the increased challenge and find new interest in the job.

Sometimes this trend is taken further with more autonomy granted to sales people and operators. Increasingly the trend is to encourage people to be more in charge of their own workplace.

This is consistent with the trend towards more inner-directed people, which we discussed in chapter 4. It is also consistent with the growing numbers of people from large organisations who work from home. Some of these have moved to a part time involvement and later become self employed. Overall there is a trend towards growing numbers of people feeling in charge of their work, their contribution, their own personal success and indeed their destiny.

Large Organisations

But this is not how it is for large numbers of people. A great many work for large organisations and will continue to do so. For them the message is that you can probably do more than you think you can. In many situations if you show initiative, take responsibility and act on your best judgement you are likely to enhance your reputation and progress your career. The number of organisations where you will be criticised or penalised for showing initiative is reducing. The responsibility remains with you to show initiative skilfully, in context and on issues where you have confidence in your own expertise. It will be necessary to plan a careful strategy to bring your influence to bear, and to use various change-management processes and techniques such as those described in chapter 11.

There is a demand for more effective leadership, not just at the top but at every level. More imaginative management contributions, clearer focus on customers, higher regard for the contribution that can be provided by staff, more satisfying jobs right through the organisation, and better methods for targeting results and reviewing performance are also required. The key elements of this trend are summarised in chart 37.

Chart 37: The Trend Towards Increased Autonomy

Leading edge organisations are setting the trend and encouraging their people to shed past or even current practices and move towards the desirable future. Those who do this best set the example from the top, recognise when their subordinates are responding appropriately and give positive feedback and encouragement.

Current/Past	Future
Seeking answers	Proposing solutions
Link in the hierarchy	Leader of a team
Passive	Active
Low creativity	Innovative & imaginative
Self contained	Networking
Focused on objectives	Focused on customers
Treat staff as workers	Regard staff as resources
Limited training	Development as part of the job
Avoiding responsibility	Seeking responsibility
Limited authority	Considerable authority
Not responsible	Feeling in charge
Dull, boring job	Exciting challenge in the job
Tell people if essential	Keep people informed
Poor level of listening	Listening to others is crucial
Low levels of trust	High levels of trust
Resists change	Encourages change
Accepting routines	Targeting & monitoring results
Poor staff appraisal reviews	Effective face-to-face reviews

Lasting solutions to the dilemmas considered in the first part of this book will, to a significant degree, depend on cultivating responsibility among large sections of the community. The willingness to accept responsibility grows out of the opportunity to behave responsibly. Children learn how to take on increasing responsibility as they grow older and more independent, but often rebel if the opportunity to take charge is delayed or denied. Premature withdrawal of parental responsibility can be disastrous, so balance is important. There are so many aspects of the environmental challenge where we need to rely on citizens behaving responsibly, through their own motivation, that it is important to understand some of the dynamics which affect how people behave.

Effectiveness in Small Groups

One of the consequences of the turbulence of recent years is that most organisations have faced enormous upheavals. This has meant that many people have had to learn how to work with strangers in new groups. Sometimes the rate of change has meant that these new groupings have broken up before they have settled down to work together. Even if the whole group has not dispersed, in many situations it is necessary to adjust to changes in group membership, almost as a matter of routine. It is never easy to make these adjustments, but it is helpful if there is a better understanding of how groups can learn to be effective. This is important when new groups form and when membership changes. The tendency in groups is to get on with the task but if this is all that is done the integration of members – reaching agreement on objectives and establishing sound working procedures – is neglected, and group effectiveness suffers.

The emphasis is placed on groups because this seems to be important for a great many organisations, even some that are quite small. It is not surprising that group work is favoured, because the information and knowledge explosion produces a situation where most projects and assignments require people with different skills to work together to produce worthwhile results.

When people come together in a group for the first time they are unsure how they will get on. As trust and confidence grows, communication becomes easier and it becomes possible to make decisions about the work to be done and the goals to be pursued. Successful progress then tends to focus on how control is exercised. This is usually a reflection of management style. If dominance of one or more members prevails, this behaviour will be acceptable to some, cause others to become passive, and may stimulate one or two to challenge the leadership, occasionally in an aggressive way.

If members' control needs are satisfied a group culture of shared influence emerges. This is characterised by members feeling interdependent, being willing to accept different roles, and exercising self-control in the pursuit of consensus decisions. In this context consensus means the meeting of minds and not a majority decision. In general this pattern is followed by most small groups which succeed in becoming mature and effective. Groups will, however, differ in the degree of trust that exists between members, the nature of the feedback system, the extent to which the goals are clear, and how control is exercised. Mature groups usually feel comfortable with the principles of support and challenge described in chapter 4 and summarised in chart 17, which they use quite naturally.

Some groups never get beyond the first stage of development, because some members continue to feel inadequate or not accepted. They never gain the self-confidence to express their views openly, they accept the goals defined by others without real commitment, and they remain submissive towards the leader. These groups fail to make effective use of the resources available to them and produce poor results. It is sometimes possible for groups to survive for years in this mode of operation although many will have been disbanded as a result of the shake out stimulated by the recession, because they were making an insufficient contribution.

It is also possible for groups to regress. If a group reaches an impasse and an authority figure decides to exert control this can lead to submissive behaviour or a counter attack. Either way it may result in apathy towards group goals, a return to cautious communication and a feeling among some members that they are no longer accepted. If this happens in a group which needs to work together, the whole process of rebuilding towards maturity has to start again. Trust has to be re-established, sound communication has to re-emerge, goals which were agreed have to be redefined and the form of leadership which is appropriate has to be agreed. The second time this is attempted, and every successive occasion, will be more difficult and require even greater patience and perseverance than the first.

A summary of the phases of group development is given in chart 38.

Chart 38: Effectiveness in Small Groups

Personal Concerns	Indications of Unresolved Concern	Indications of Resolved Concern	Group Capability
Acceptance	Feeling inadequate Suspicion of others Lacking confidence Lack of trust Reluctant cooperation	Accepting self Accepting others Confidence Mutual trust Willing cooperation	Belonging
Communication	Tentative Superficial Poor listening Unduly polite Keep ideas to self	Views expressed Openness Good listening Willing to challenge Offer ideas	Problem solving and decision making
Goals	Apathy Competition Own goals focus	Commitment Cooperation Goal integration	Productive work
Control	Dependence on leaders Attacks on leaders	Interdependence Role differentiation Self regulation	Organisation

Source: Based on the work of Jack Gibb in Bradford, 1978.

It is interesting to apply the model described here to family or household situations and the way in which domestic affairs are conducted. consider, for instance, how decisions about holidays, entertainment, domestic chores and meal arrangements are settled. Is your family or household trapped in an early phase of group development, or has it matured and become a satisfying community for all members? Consider in particular the indications of unresolved concern described in chart 38.

Working in a small, mature group can be very rewarding to all concerned because high quality results are produced and the experience is satisfying. The key to achieving this outcome and maintaining this way of working often depends on four factors:

- how conflict is managed;
- the management style of the boss or group leader;
- the willingness of group members to feel in charge; and
- the awareness of group processes and how they are managed.

Conflict has been discussed in chapter 4 and an approach to conflict resolution was described in chart 16.

The group leader's management style is a crucial element. The boss who always has to dominate and keep strict control will hold the group in a state of dependency. Group members will feel that to be accepted requires them to conform, remain submissive and contribute only when asked. Groups with this kind of leader fail to become mature. Passive leaders, on the other hand, who appear unconcerned about whatever happens, are also ineffective leaders, and these groups also fail to reach maturity.

The most successful leader is the one who is enthusiastic, wishes to understand and value each group member, listens well, contributes effectively, and is willing to give and receive both support and challenge. Groups with this kind of leadership have the best chance of reaching maturity.

When conflict is well managed and there is a participative leader the chances of the group becoming effective are greatly enhanced, but there is another ingredient. Each group member needs to be willing to contribute and to feel in charge. This does not mean that they dominate the group but rather that they are willing to work effectively with others. They feel that they share responsibility for how the group works and for the results it produces.

How Groups Develop

A variation on the description of effective groups is provided by Bennis and Shepard.[2] They identify two major areas of uncertainty for people working in groups, namely, relations with authority, and personal relationships with their colleagues. Those who are concerned primarily with authority tend to be dependent or counter dependent. They are likely to focus on the leadership issue more than on other matters, and either become over compliant or criticise the leader whenever the opportunity occurs. Those who are concerned mainly with relationships with other group members tend to be personal or counterpersonal. They are primarily preoccupied with the ways in which each person is fitting into the group and establishing sound working relationships. A third category are those who are not over concerned about either authority or relationships with other group members – these are the independents. They maintain a balance in their interest in outcomes, effective leadership and sound relationships.

The first phase of group development results in dependency and compliance, which moves on in the second phase to counter dependence, sometimes even to aggressive behaviour towards the leader. The third phase represents some degree of resolution which is often temporary. In phase four enchantment emerges, only to be followed in phase five with disenchantment. Finally, in phase six, the true consensus emerges and the group reaches maturity with interdependence and achievement as prime characteristics.

An interesting feature in studying group relationships is to consider the sort of people who prove most significant during the various phases of development. The early phases of group development tend to be dominated by the dependent and counter dependent people, whereas the personal and counter personal come to the fore in phases four and five. However, it is the independents who prove to be the most helpful catalysts for helping the group to progress through its various crises towards maturity. In effect this means that those people who are able to maintain a degree of detachment from leadership and relationship issues are best able to help the group to establish an effective working procedure and move towards maturity so that effective, satisfying performance is achieved.

A considerable body of knowledge, founded on extensive research both in the field and in training workshops, suggests the following propositions:

- when groups first form people are cautious;
- how groups move towards maturity is well understood;
- mature groups produce effective results;
- mature groups are characterised by interdependence;
- interdependence requires people to feel in charge;
- being in charge means sharing responsibility;
- shared responsibility requires participative leadership; and
- when we share responsibility life is satisfying and productive.

The way in which any meeting is conducted has a direct bearing on its outcomes, and it is worth summarising the things to do to ensure that meetings are productive. Chart 39 provides a brief description of how to manage three elements: task and content, arrangements and procedures, and feelings and emotions.

An Example of Group Development

A group of seven people faced an opportunity to buy the business in which they were employed, because the owners wished to retire. They met one evening to consider the proposition and whether they wished to go ahead. Obviously, if they intended to go ahead, the first meeting could only be a beginning, but they had to start somewhere. At that initial meeting everyone had an opportunity to say what they felt about:

• the proposition;
• their own needs;
• their confidence in the others as business partners; and
• their ability to raise funds for the buy out.

By the end of the first meeting it was clear that there was a general wish to go ahead. Other meetings were arranged, but had to be in the evening or at weekends because it was in everybody's interest to keep the current business in good health and normal work remained a priority.

At the second meeting the leadership issue was addressed in order to find out who would be an acceptable leader of the group and to consider the claims of different people to become the leader. This involved considerable debate because delicate issues and strong feelings emerged. An amicable way forward was found after much discussion and negotiation, which required clear communication and good listening about individual preferences. This was a necessary foundation for sound decisions. The group was then in a position to start negotiating the terms of the buy-out with the owners.

Matters progressed slowly and during this time the buy-out team had to establish how they would work together, assuming that the outcome of the negotiations was successful. In effect they had to develop a business plan for the company that they expected to own. One of the central elements was to describe the underlying values which would be at the core of all operations. Another was to agree performance standards for each individual and how performance would be reviewed.

The original evaluation of each individual was nearly undermined when one member felt that he was being excluded from the executive management group. Careful rebuilding and re-integration was undertaken and the threatened resignation forestalled. If this situation had not been retrieved it is quite possible that the whole deal would have collapsed.

Chart 39: Managing Meetings at Three Levels

Every meeting needs to be managed at three levels:

- The task or content
- The arrangements and procedures
- The feelings and emotions of participants

In order to move smoothly and productively from the start of a meeting to a productive conclusion all three levels need to be managed:

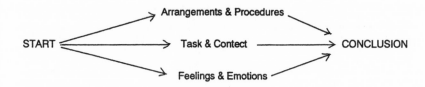

Arrangements & Procedures

Most effective meetings start with the arrangements and procedures for conducting the meeting. This includes such things as:

* Who should take part
* The task to be accomplished, remit or terms of reference
* Where it will take place
* Start and finish times
* The frequency of meetings
* The agenda and how it will be drawn up
* The information that needs to be prepared in advance
* Who will take notes/minutes

When the meeting begins, especially if people are meeting for the first time, the start should cover such things as:

* An opportunity for people to introduce themselves and cover such points as:
    - personal introduction
    - function, job title, special knowledge/skills
    - personal needs and desired outcomes
* Confirmation of the task, remit or terms of reference
* Review of the arrangements and procedures
* Confirmation of the agenda, sequence and timing for each item - which are important, which urgent?
* How the meeting(s) will be conducted

Task & Content

Because meetings assemble to tackle a task there is a temptation to start work on the task immediately. If this happens, with no prior discussion of arrangements and procedures, those taking part make assumptions which are not checked out with others and often differ. This results in confusion, frustration and at times arouses strong feelings later in the meeting. Undue attention to every detail of the procedures also causes frustration and a fear that the task will never be tackled.

The discussion about arrangements and procedures starts the process whereby people test whether they are accepted by the group, how easy or difficult it is to communicate with others, the objectives for the meeting and how control is being exercised.

Once there is broad agreement about the arrangements and procedures the task can be addressed. How this is done will strengthen or weaken each individual's feelings of acceptance. This influences the willingness to listen to others, the way in which contributions are made and the ability of the meeting to stay focused on the overall objective as well as the specific agenda item.

If the meeting strays from the agreed objective or agenda, someone (not necessarily the chairperson) needs to draw attention to the departure from the agreed procedures. A temporary switch to the 'arrangements & procedures' level should correct the situation and the task can then be re-addressed.

Feelings & Emotions

If the task is being tackled ineffectually, or if the procedures are unsatisfactory, one or more of the participants will begin to feel frustrated, disappointed or angry. It is easy to trigger emotions which are often associated with past experiences of meetings which never succeeded in working effectively. At some stage of every meeting feelings will be aroused. If they are ignored they usually get stronger and are harder to manage. Early identification of feelings (facial expressions, body language etc) followed by sensitive, open questions help to ensure that the emotions and feelings of all members are respected and managed appropriately. Likewise each individual should be encouraged to express his or her feelings. When this is done early it is surprising how helpful it can be to the conduct of the meeting because it relieves tension before it becomes excessive.

The strongest feelings are usually associated with the way in which the meeting is controlled by the chairperson. Both too much and too little control can be hamper progress or, when severe, result in a disruptive meeting.

Balance

The important point is that there should be balance between the three levels. Inexperienced people often give undue attention to the task and content and these meetings fail to be effective because too little attention is given to the procedures and the management of emotions. Meetings which concentrate on getting all arrangements and procedures right prove frustrating because they seem to accomplish little and this arouses negative feelings. Too much attention to emotions and feelings may result in pleasurable experiences but some people will be disappointed or even angry that time has been wasted and little or nothing has been achieved.

At effective meetings participants recognise the importance of all three levels and give appropriate attention to each. They maintain balance and move between the levels easily and naturally as they work towards agreed goals.

Eventually the group bought the company, and three years later could look back on excellent results and business expansion which were directly attributable to the painstaking process of group development that took place while the negotiations were being completed.

When Group Members Represent Different Interests

All that has been said about the way in which groups develop remains valid when the group is made up of people who represent different interests, but a significant added complication needs to be taken into account. Within a company people often come from different departments to work together in a cross-functional group. In these situations they bring with them an additional set of needs, constraints and challenges which can have a dramatic impact on how the group develops.

It is helpful to break this situation down into three phases:

- how people get briefed by their own department;
- the dynamics that arise when working with others; and
- the return to the 'home group' after a cross-functional meeting.

The briefings people receive when they are to go to a cross-functional meeting vary greatly from no briefing at all to very detailed and specific instructions. When no briefing is given, the individual often finds that problems arise during meetings, and we shall consider this later. The role of the representative can take many forms but three are typical:

(1) As observer: attend, but say little or nothing and report back.
(2) As delegate: deal with stated issues along the lines of your specific brief.
(3) As plenipotentiary: deal with any issue that crops up using your own judgement.

Most managers can recall occasions when they were briefed in accordance with these principles, or have come across people at meetings who clearly had one or other of these briefings.

When a cross-functional meeting starts, these roles are often not revealed; no one declares their remit or asks others to declare theirs. This can be a great source of confusion and frustration as the meeting progresses. For example, those with no remit may suddenly find that an issue has cropped up and they have to decide what role to adopt. It is too embarrassing to be open about the dilemma so the sudden realisation remains undeclared and tentative moves are made to create thinking time.

Problem solving and decision-making are therefore much more difficult in these cross-functional groups. It takes longer for people to feel accepted, to be able to communicate freely, to agree objectives and to decide how control will be exercised. It is also necessary to be sensitive to the needs of each person to check things out with their 'home group' before making final commitments in the cross-functional group. A series of meetings often becomes essential.

After the cross-functional meeting participants return to their 'home groups'. Those with a clear remit report back, to debrief on progress made, and to review the role and remit for the next meeting. Those who went to the cross-functional meeting with no clear brief may or may not find that there is any interest in a debrief. Whether or not there was a brief, each representative is exposed to some degree of scrutiny on how well their role was carried out. In the more extreme cases a representative can be seen by the 'home group' as a 'hero', if a difficult issue was handled in a way that is advantageous to the 'home group'. Conversely the representative may be seen as a 'traitor' if the 'home group's' interests are seen to have been compromised. This 'hero'/'traitor' dynamic can play a significant part in the functioning of a cross-functional group.

This explanation has focused on representatives of different departments from within one company but the same principles apply when a mixed group assembles and the participants are from different organisations. The dynamics are often more extreme, especially when the mixed group includes people who work in organisations as diverse as a company, an environmental organisation and local authority. This sort of mixed group is now coming together to tackle major issues, and great skill and awareness is needed in handling such meetings.

Sometimes a situation exists where two groups or organisations which need to cooperate fail to do so, or are in active opposition to each other. Such situations can be tackled, and cooperation can sometimes be achieved but this requires great skill and patience. If the situation has prevailed for some time then help from a professional mediator is usually required.

One powerful cohesive force is the growing realisation that the issues we face as a community are so enormous that the only way in which effective progress can be made is by mutual cooperation to find solutions which are generally acceptable.

Group Development to Tackle Environmental Issues

There is no doubt that there are many opportunities for group problem solving to resolve environmental issues. Within companies environmental directors are finding that it is very helpful to form cross-functional teams because so many issues cannot be resolved by departments working in isolation. A dialogue is being opened up by some companies with people from environmental groups and various organisations are forming partnership arrangements with others to tackle difficult issues. Sometimes these gatherings involve people representing many different interests. For example farmers, food manufacturers, supermarkets, packaging companies, product designers and local authorities might come together to look at the issue of waste management. All the issues that face people when they try to work together are present on these occasions. If successful outcomes are sought then considerable attention needs to be given to the way in which the group will work. It is not sufficient to consider only the substantive issue that brings people together.

The question of group work is not confined to business organisations. Within well established environmental organisations the changing environmental scene is creating new challenges and some realignment of strategies as new priorities emerge. This can result in major restructuring and it is never easy to make changes. At the very least, groups of people are re-aligned and new working relationships have to be developed.

New consultancies are forming and, within large organisations, new departments are being established. Government departments and non-governmental organisations (NGOs) continue to form and reform to tackle new issues or approach old issues in new ways.

In all these situations there is scope to apply the principles of group development and strive to develop mature groups which are capable of producing high quality results in ways that prove satisfying to those involved.

Who Is in Charge of Your Life?

The provocative title of this chapter is deliberate. The intention is to invite you to consider your own life. Where do you work and are you passively accepting a situation that is frustrating and demoralising? What assumptions guide your behaviour and have these been tested? Are they valid? Do you wish to join those who have found that it is rewarding to work with others, and strive for group maturity in all the groups where you work? How will you do this? Maybe you can change things in your workplace and maybe your boss is waiting for you to show more initiative. Have you taken any recent initiatives which stretch you and require courage to make things happen differently? Where can you get appropriate support and challenge from colleagues you respect?

These questions are posed in the context of your work but they could also be asked of your family or household situation.

The importance of the question: 'Who is in charge?' to the theme of this book is that we all need to be involved if the world in which we live is to be peaceful, economically viable, using resources wisely and respecting the biodiversity of our planet.

Who is in charge of your life? Who should be? If you need to change, how and when will you do this? Will you join those who are already making things happen? Are you already doing so?

Notes

1   This is an adaptation of a model from Gibb, Jack R. and Gibb Lorraine M., 'The Group as a Growing Organism' in Bradford, *Group Development* 1978. The Gibb model was adapted by Sheppard Moscow Ltd for their Consulting Skills Course and has been further adapted here by the author in the light of experience.

2   Bennis, Warren G. and Shepard, Herbert A., A Theory of Group Development, Human Relations, Volume 9 No 4, 1956 and reproduced in Bradford, *Group Development* 1978.

Managing Organisational Change

*I believe that educational programmes inside and outside companies will
have a major focus on education in the management of change. This will be
considered an essential part of the basic skills and abilities required for anyone in management.*

Richard Beckhard[1]

It is easier to declare intent than to carry it out.

John Harvey-Jones[2]

The management of organisational change is an issue that has been
around for a long time. Many organisations have considerable experience of major change programmes, but despite this a surprising number
find themselves taking rushed decisions and failing to use effective
processes and techniques. The number of areas in which organisational
performance is monitored have never been greater and this is stimulating the need for change. It does not really matter why an organisation
may need to change, the principles that can be applied to carry through
an effective change programme are broadly the same.

In this chapter we shall explore the options available for tackling a significant change issue, consider a model for managing change, examine
the phases of a change programme, discuss some real life examples and
draw out the learning points which can be applied in a variety of situations. These examples are not directly related to the environmental challenge because few organisations have yet undertaken large scale changes
for environmental reasons, but several are now on the threshold of
doing so.

The Options

A firm of consultants was called in by a major chemicals manufacturer to
discuss a significant change that needed to be planned and implemented
within a few months. The change involved the rationalisation of manufacturing plants, with a probable outcome that some of the existing seven
plants would no longer be required; the total work could probably be
done at three or four plants. This had not yet been investigated properly
and there was a lot of uncertainty about which locations should be kept

open. The client explained that three different approaches were being considered:

(1) Expert consultants to carry out the investigation and recommend the appropriate solution and the implementation plan.
(2) Process consultants to work alongside the company's managers and develop the appropriate solution, which they would implement together.
(3) A do it yourself strategy whereby the client would undertake the investigation and implementation without external help.

The Chief Executive wanted to investigate all three options, and recognised, through prior experience of working with both kinds of consultant, that there were at least two distinct kinds of consultancy help available. Expert consultants would bring in considerable experience of the chemicals industry, having carried out this kind of investigation before, but past experience showed that prescriptive solutions often resulted in low commitment, which created difficulties, especially during the implementation phase.

The advantage of using process consultants was that the company's staff would learn a lot. They would become familiar with the issues, the options available, how they could be assessed and how the preferred solution emerged. This would help to build understanding and commitment to the proposed changes, and this in turn would help during the implementation phase. The client knew from past experience that process consultants were particularly helpful in dealing with the myriad of issues that emerge when locations are being closed and the implications for staff are considerable. Furthermore, the learning derived from this experience might well mean that on future occasions there would be more confidence in tackling similar problems without external help.

The third option was to undertake the investigation and the implementation without external help. In many ways this was an attractive option and would certainly be cheaper than either of the other two. However, it would require a considerable investment of time and there was little confidence among board members that the staff who would be involved could do this kind of work to the required standard.

The point about this story is to illustrate that situations involving significant, complex change can be tackled in several different ways. These three options are the most common, and my preference and experience is towards process consultancy for four reasons:

(1) It ensures that the client remains in close touch with the planned change at every phase and remains in control.
(2) The client's managers and other staff learn a great deal about the organisation, the processes involved in managing successful change,

and about themselves and their ways of working with other people.

(3) The implementation phase works more smoothly because as much attention has been given to how the change will be managed as has been given to what the changes will be.

(4) Once the change has been carried out, the commitment to making the new arrangements work well is greater because of the involvement of staff in assessing the options and selecting the preferred one.

In fact the client in question opted for the process consultant and placed considerable emphasis on involvement of the company's staff at every stage of the assignment. Regular learning reviews were built in to the project and summarised at the end. The changes were successfully completed and the implementation phase worked particularly well, with strong commitment from most staff. Several commented on the fact that they had never been so well informed about organisational change. The reduction in staff numbers was mostly achieved by natural wastage, and the few people who were declared redundant received favourable severance terms and considerable help with refocusing their lives.

A Change Model

In some change situations it is helpful to ask a few searching questions in order to establish some of the main characteristics of the situation. Four questions which have proved extremely helpful in many situations are:

(1) Who is feeling the pain?
(2) Who is accepting ownership of the problem (i.e. accepting responsibility to take action – not necessarily alone)?
(3) Who has the power to act?
(4) Who has the power to block the initiative?

If the answers to the first three questions identify three different people or groups it is likely that no effective action will be taken to deal with the situation. The answer to the fourth question helps to identify key people who may need to be managed with special skill.

Let us consider an example. In a National Health Service (NHS) Region in the UK it was found that nursing staff and junior doctors were the ones who were 'feeling the pain' of a change situation, a specialist employed by the NHS in an organisation development role was 'owning the problem', while the 'power to act' lay with the senior executive officers. So long as this situation continued the problems would not be addressed and change would not occur. In another part of the NHS - a district health authority - a similar situation prevailed, but representatives of all three parties worked together to define the problems and

develop a common vision of a future desired state of affairs. This resulted in sound analysis of the situation, an agreed way forward and effective implementation.

In complex change situations the four questions provide no more than
a start, and it is desirable to have common understanding of a change
model. In this book the emphasis is placed on the significance of the
environment as a stimulus for change during the 1990s and beyond.
Financial pressures, new technology, changing customer preferences
and competitive activity will also stimulate change. However, the methods for managing individual and organisational change discussed here
are equally applicable whatever the stimulus.

Many readers will be familiar with the 'present situation - pathway -
desired situation' model, shown in chart 40. This has been adapted for
the wider issues being considered in this book. The model can be represented in a way which includes three different dimensions:

- nature of the business and its performance;
- organisation culture and staff capability; and
- environmental impacts and issues.

The current situation will be a reflection of the nature of the current business and how it performs. In addition it will be a reflection of the existing
organisation culture and the capability of staff to deliver the results being
achieved. Finally, it will also be a reflection of the ways in which the
organisation and the environment impact on one another and the issues
that arise.

There is an overall need to assess the environment and to consider its
impact on the organisation. Then the impact of the organisation on its
environment should be considered. If change is contemplated, all three
of these dimensions must be considered when thinking about the future
desired state. Each dimension influences the other two. The nature of the
business will influence the organisation culture required for the business.
and the impact on the environment. The desired impact on the environment will influence the nature of the business, and will have implications for the organisation's culture and the staff capability required to
produce desired results. The culture of the organisation and the capability of staff will influence how the nature of the business is defined and
the impact on the environment is managed.

The third element of the model is the pathway to bring about the
changes. These are the human processes, information systems and practical action plans needed to effect the changes. All three elements and
their overlapping significance are shown in chart 40.

CHART 40: AN ORGANISATIONAL CHANGE MODEL

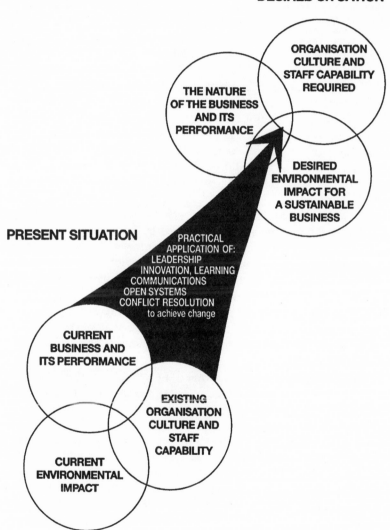

© Colin Hutchinson, *Vitality and Renewal*, Adamantine, 1994

The Phases of Change

Within an organisation it is usually one or two people who first raise the issue of a need for change. If others disagree the initiative may end there. It is often very difficult for senior executives to accept the need for change when it goes against the grain of accumulated experience. Some changes which are contrary to perceptions and practices built up over a lifetime of experience, are necessary because the future will be different and will require new products, services and working practices.

When there is support from a few other key people, the idea is kept alive and work begins in order to understand the situation and the options for dealing with it.

This phase can be described as the time when work is being done to align perceptions. Organisations vary enormously in their ability to handle this phase successfully. Those organisations which lean towards dominant top management can get through this phase quickly, with a swift decision, but the degree of understanding about the change among people lower in the organisation is often poor. Weak top managers, on the other hand, vacillate during this phase, and discussion of the issue may last a long time.

Some companies have developed effective ways to discuss major issues. These discussions are characterised by good listening as well as assertive statements, backed up with relevant facts. The robust quality of this type of discussion results in sound understanding of the issues, and an outcome whereby perceptions are genuinely aligned - not dominated by a single individual. This process is not as rapid as a unilateral decision at the top, but in an effective group the process is reasonably quick and stands the best chance of producing high quality answers. In chart 41 Company A takes six months to align perceptions, whereas Company B takes eleven months.

Once perceptions have been aligned a strategy for dealing with the issue does not take long to develop. There is less time taken to accomplish this phase in most competent organisations. In chart 41 the strategy development phase takes one month for each company.

The third phase involves implementation of the agreed strategy. The quality of implementation is often influenced by the way in which the first phase of aligning perceptions has been carried out. When the first phase has involved thorough discussion, sound investigation of options, and a mutually agreed solution, the success of the implementation phase is greater.

Chart 41 shows these three phases diagrammatically.[3] It indicates that Company A aligns perceptions more quickly than Company B. As a result A gains a significant competitive advantage by starting the implementation phase sooner.

Chart 41: The Phases of Change

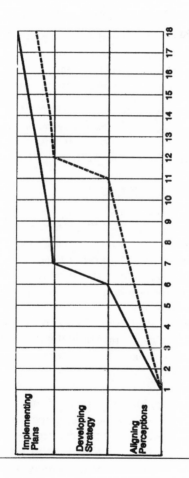

Implementing Plans

Developing Strategy

Aligning Perceptions

Months

1 2 3 4 5 6 7 8 9 10 11 12 13 14 15 16 17 18

A
B

2 companies undertake a major change simultaneously. "A" aligns perceptions within 6 months, "B" in 11 months. Both take one month to develop a strategy and implementation follows. "A" gains the competitive advantage.

In the brief descriptions of the two different health service situations described earlier it is clear that in the case of the NHS region, where the key parties did not get their act together, there was a failure to align perceptions. In the second case, the NHS district, this process was accomplished successfully.

The Process of Change[4]

The change equation has already been mentioned (chapter 5, p. 94) and this is the essence of the change process. It can now be enlarged to describe the practical work that can be undertaken in order to establish the four elements of the change equation, namely;

(1) The current situation: how dissatisfied are people?
(2) The desired situation: what is the vision?
(3) The practical steps: is there an action plan?
(4) The will to succeed: is there the will to make things happen?

There are some well tested methods for addressing each of these issues, and a checklist of questions which need answers is provided in chart 42.

Many of the approaches, frameworks, techniques and methods used to undertake this work are described in chapter 11.

Changing Organisation Culture

One of the most challenging forms of change is to modify the culture of an organisation. This is sufficiently difficult for some people to say that it should not be attempted. And yet many organisations now face the need to modify their corporate cultures in order to survive. With careful planning, effective leadership, a clear vision of the required culture and appropriate support for those who need to change their behaviour, it is possible to achieve good results.

We have already seen in chapter 7 (where organisation culture is defined) that the work of Kotter and Heskett indicates that truly effective organisations have adaptive cultures.[5] These authors also discuss whether or not it is possible to bring about culture change, and mention ICI and Nissan as companies which have done this successfully. In the case of ICI the leadership of Sir John Harvey-Jones was a crucial ingredient. However, he still needed to gain acceptance within ICI that the current situation was unsatisfactory. In effect he had to get people to be very clear about the situation they faced, and where current trends would lead the company if there was no change. He had an enormous positive impact on morale, and excited people by using the twin approaches of creating dissatisfaction with the present and involving people in a vision of the future. He devolved accountability to divisions, brought about mergers of different businesses and reduced staff at all

Chart 42: The Change Process - A Practical Guide

1 Current Situation	The Development Gap	2 Desired Situation

Assessing the present
* The organisation's mission and strategy
* Mapping the organisation's socio/economic environment
* Assessing the organisation's environmental impact

* Understanding the organisation's existing culture and staff capability

Developing a Vision:
* The world of business 5-15 years hence
* The organisation's future mission & strategy
* The organisation culture and staff capability required to achieve the mission
* Characteristics which will define how the business will become sustainable

3   Managing the Transition

* What additional information is required? From whom, where?
* How good is the organisational "FIT"? (See Chart 34)
* What is the readiness for change among managers & staff?
* What is the capability of staff to support the change and work in new ways?
* What is the level of commitment among key people?
* What are the change goals?
* Which goals are important, which urgent?
* What action is required, from whom and by when? Is there an agreed action and activity plan?
* How will people inside and outside the organisation be kept informed?
* Who will manage the transition phase? How long will it last?
* Will any procedures already established be used such as TQM, BS5750, BS7750, Life Cycle Analysis etc

4   Monitoring the Transition

* What criteria will be used to assess progress?
* Who will be responsible/accountable for monitoring the transition and making adjustments as required?
* What process & procedures will be used to review progress?

Adapted from Sheppard Moscow

levels. Above all he provided leadership which initiated hundreds of changes which, taken together, added up to a significant change in the nature of the business, in the corporate culture and in the capability of staff to perform.

Kotter and Heskett trace the history of the ICI culture from one that was strategically inappropriate to one that became adaptive. This adaptive culture had implications for corporate values, style of leadership and the behaviour of staff. The ICI story is a remarkable example of how a very large organisation can achieve a massive change. All the elements identified in chart 9, using the acronym *LILCOC*, were present in the ICI transition (*see* chapter 1).

The experience gained by large organisations such as ICI in bringing about strategic and cultural change is vitally important for the transitions that now need to be effected to achieve a sustainable society. The scale of change at society level is even more daunting, but many of the principles need to be understood and developed for the wider application now needed.

Examples of Organisational Change

Three short case histories, of very different organisations, which reflect my personal experience, illustrate how culture change was brought about. Sometimes a step change is necessary, as in the first case, at other times an evolutionary process is more appropriate. The former is more traumatic and harder to manage but may be required when the organisation and its market place are significantly mismatched. An evolutionary process is more desirable, provided that the scale and nature of change can be progressed at a sufficient pace.

Commercial Division: Shell UK Oil

Following the oil crises of 1973 and 1979, oil companies moved from an era of rapid and continuous growth to one of stagnant demand, energy conservation and considerable uncertainty. The oil producing countries of the Middle East had already nationalised or taken over the crude oil production process. There was heavy pressure to improve refining and marketing margins. Such a step change prompted the Commercial Division of Shell UK Oil to seek a reduction in staff of about one-third - from 450 to about 300 - in 1982.

Prior to the change the organisation's culture could be described as apprehensive of cutbacks, many staff had ill-defined responsibilities, information systems were poor, responsibility was focused on individual effort and morale was low. Three years later results had improved dramatically, morale was high, accountability was defined, information systems had been improved and produced timely, relevant information, teamwork had been developed, performance was being rewarded and the division was sought out by Shell UK staff because it helped them to progress their careers.

This success story can be compared with the process involved in baking a cake. Many ingredients are involved, all of which need to be present in appropriate quantities but no single ingredient is the reason why the cake tastes good. However, if any one of the ingredients is omitted the finished product will suffer.

The story began when a new head of division was appointed. He undertook his own assessment of the situation by talking to each manager in turn and seeing for himself how things functioned right through the organisation. As a result he became convinced that a major change had to be made. Two options emerged. The first would mean reducing the number of regions from eight to four with staff numbers reduced throughout. The second was to abandon the regional structure altogether and rearrange the coordinating function of the division, with strengthened departments running distinct, separate businesses from London. Staff reductions would be achieved mainly by closing the regional offices, with only a modest reduction in the staff who performed active selling roles.

The divisional head called a meeting of the seventeen executives who reported to him, including all eight regional managers, and described his analysis of the situation, the reasons why change was essential and the two options he saw. He also indicated that he preferred the second option and feared that the first option might well mean that a further change would have to be made within two years. The divisional head had worked out the impact of his proposals on those present at the meeting, and even though he had not discussed it with them he knew that there would be three retirements, three more people who were due for a move outside the division, and nine who would be required in the new structure, which left two with an uncertain future. Those attending the meeting did not know how the changes would affect their colleagues, in explicit terms, but the divisional head knew which people were likely to feel most concern. The fact that only two people faced a serious threat to their jobs probably contributed to the meeting accepting the more radical proposal to abandon the regional structure. Before the meeting closed, a series of study groups were formed, involving most of those present, to work out the details and devise an implementation plan.

The desired culture was strongly related to the business strategy, and the culture change that was required had five elements:

- strongly market related with emphasis on customer orientation;

- delegated accountability - including some pricing discretion with sales representatives;
- improved information systems to enable people to take informed decisions;
- strengthened teamwork within and between departments and improved staff development; and
- improved rewards and job security for those who performed well.

During the next few months a great deal of work had to be done; the business had to go on, and many of the senior people were involved in a series of study group meetings which worked out the details of the changes. When they were within two months of the new structure coming into being the process of making appointments began. As soon as the key appointments were known, people who were going to be working together in new teams started to contact each other. The new departmental heads were encouraged, despite their heavy work loads, to call a meeting of their key people as soon as possible, so that the new groupings could begin to work in accordance with the newly defined arrangements and the desired culture.

In order to help the managers come to terms with the new arrangements and find out for themselves what it meant to change from individually focused work to teamwork within and between departments, a workshop type programme was devised and run for the eight managers who were most keen to attend. As a result of the success of this programme. eight more workshops were run, over a two-year period, to cover most of the people who were directly affected. In each workshop programme real issues were addressed and plans made to carry changes through. There were also opportunities for the managers to understand what they personally had to do to make the changes that were required. In this sense it was a powerful learning experience for many individuals, covering management style, teamwork development and intergroup problem solving. The divisional manager was present for the final evening of each programme, and this demonstrated his commitment to the issues being addressed. It also provided a powerful example of how leadership should be exercised in the new culture.

When anyone involved faced severe difficulties, personal attention was given to help find a way through. This had not always been done in the past, and proved very significant for some key individuals. It required high degrees of leadership skill and conflict management.

One departmental manager was particularly successful and created a unique way of working in this market. On appointment, he had to face a radically different management role, without the status symbols of the time such as a big office, expensive car and a secretary. Instead the job had fewer support staff, and necessitated much travel and personal inconvenience. He also faced the need to change his own management style, with emphasis on teamwork. He demonstrated a strong desire to win, and made very effective use of his undoubted sales experience, but above all the way in which he accomplished the personal changes earned him considerable respect from his colleagues and proved personally satisfying during his last few years before retirement.

With hindsight, the particular organisational change described, became a watershed for further rationalisation within the Commercial Division of Shell UK Oil. Throughout the 1980s the oil industry had to adapt to a very different business climate. Management learnt from this radical change, with all its uncertainty, disruption and personal trauma and moved towards a process of continuous review and evolutionary development.

The principles of the 1982 organisational structure were maintained for a decade. During that time the process of change continued, albeit in a more subtle and less spectacular way, as the organisation was adjusted to meet the needs and demands of the market place.

Lloyds Bank plc

Lloyds Bank UK Retail Banking decided in 1989 that something had to be done to strengthen leadership right through the organisation and especially at branch manager level. High Street banking was changing from an emphasis on lending money towards the provision of a broad range of financial services, including the selling of various financial products. Stronger leadership was required from some 2,500 branch managers. They were unlikely to change until the way in which they themselves were managed demonstrated the new style of leadership required. This meant that all senior managers needed to appreciate that the change affected them personally. In an organisation employing 40,000 staff about 150 were senior managers. They needed to change in a reasonably consistent way, and to demonstrate through personal example what it meant to be an effective leader. In order to do this they needed a shared understanding of the business environment, a coherent vision of the future for their organisation, and 'ownership' of the need for change.

It was acknowledged that the dominance of a 'top down' style of management must change towards a style of leadership whereby there was greater willingness to influence upwards and sideways. To achieve this there needed to be wider shared ownership of the challenge, recognition of the potential to influence senior colleagues and a willingness to be influenced. The bank believed that committed people would generate better solutions from their own creativity and experience, and that service quality depended on the ability of leaders to mobilise staff behind the business strategies.

In order to ensure that the design for change would address the real issues and be appropriate for those who would attend, 25 per cent of the target managers were interviewed. This produced up-to-date information about the bank, gave those involved in running the programme additional insight into the way the bank worked, and started the process of senior bank staff and the consultant understanding each other better. The design was presented to and accepted by the top executive team of the retail banking division. Separately from this meeting, the broad principles were discussed with and approved by the Chief Executive and the Chairman of Lloyds Bank, whose support was essential.

A series of programmes was planned, and the head of retail banking agreed to attend the second programme as a participant, to give a talk at the start of each programme, and to be present on the final evening of all the other programmes.

The programme objectives were:

- to develop and own a shared vision;
- to share understanding of business strategy and the organisation culture required for the future;
- to build commitment and motivation;
- to learn about management style options;
- to strengthen support and challenge at all levels; and
- to enhance leadership skills.

These objectives include both culture change and changes in management style. The two issues are closely related because the prevailing style of management perpetuates the existing organisation culture. Culture change is brought about by managers changing their style aided by supportive processes and systems such as appropriate information, recognition and rewards. As part of the design of the programme, material developed by Human Synergistics,[6] which focuses on organisation culture and individual life styles was used. These materials are described in chart 43.

Before coming to the programme, each participant completes a questionnaire aimed at creating a profile of their management style, and gets five colleagues to each complete a complementary questionnaire, so that, on the programme, the participants can compare how they see themselves with the way in which they are seen by their colleagues. They also complete a questionnaire which describes how they see the organisation culture. Because the two questionnaires are complementary it is possible to compare personal management styles with the organisation's culture. During the programme the participants also work on the organisation culture that is required to achieve the business objectives and strategy.

Chart 43: Organisation Culture and Life Styles.

The culture of an organisation is the product of its traditions, values, working procedures and operating systems. It is manifest in the behaviour of the people who work there, and is strongly influenced by the way in which those in the most senior roles manage their colleagues and other employees. People throughout the organisation develop beliefs about what they need to do in order to 'fit in' and satisfy the expectations of the organisation. The culture that prevails has a profound effect on how people at all levels behave and the results they achieve.

Some organisations are restrictive and employees believe it is necessary to do things 'in the right way' in order to be accepted. For example, to write letters in a particular way, to control information and to accept the norms at meetings. Some organisations are very traditional, and doing things right is more important than being creative. In these organisations 'adequate' results may be the accepted level of performance. A few organisations have cultures which foster human talent, encourage teamwork, stimulate innovation and people strive for, and achieve, high standards of performance.

An increasing number of organisations are interested in their cultures and seek ways in which it can be measured, understood and changed so that it is more closely aligned with what is required to deliver high quality results in the future.

One method is called the *Organisation Culture Inventory* (OCI) which is a questionnaire designed to determine the culture of an organisation as perceived by those who work within it. The questionnaire scores are then plotted on a diagram resembling a clock face where each of the twelve segments, represented by the hours, indicates a different dimension of culture. These are well explained in the materials, including the implications of different combinations of styles. The twelve dimensions can be grouped in three broad categories (the clock face positions are shown in brackets):

Satisfying Styles:
- Achievement (11)
- Self-Actualizing (12)
- Humanistic, Helpful Style (1)
- Affiliation Style (2)

People/Security Styles:
- Approval Style (3)
- Conventional Style (4)
- Dependent Style (5)
- Avoidance Style (6)

Task/Security Styles:
- Oppositional Style (7)
- Power Style (8)
- Competitive Style (9)
- Perfectionistic Style (10)

Organisation Culture and Life Styles

Questionnaire results are plotted on a clock face diagram, and those taking part can compare the similarities and differences in the way they see their organisation's culture. This is usually an illuminating and stimulating activity. Brief notes on the main points can be summarised and shared with others.

These discussions will have clarified the meaning of the framework and enriched understanding of the dimensions of culture. Having done this, it is worth discussing and agreeing the sort of culture that will be required in future if the organisation is to perform effectively. Using a blank version of the clock face participants can shade in the extent to which each of the 12 dimensions of culture should be represented in the organisation's desired culture. This can then be compared with the various perceptions of the organisation's existing culture and notes made of the culture change required.

One of the advantages of this method of analysing culture is that *Life Styles Inventories* (LS1 & LS2) which are compatible with the OCI are available. LS1 is for completion by an individual to determine his or her own management style. LS2 is for completion by others so that they can indicate how they see their colleague's management style at work. Each individual can then compare self perceptions with the perception of others. Many people find this is a helpful and illuminating experience; a few have some shocks because their own perception differs widely from those of their colleagues.

Each individual can compare personal Life Style results with the desired organisation culture and this, together with the results from LS2s can contribute to a personal development programme. Additional materials are also available for personal learning, and some of it is organised as a self managed programme on computer.

The diagrams below indicate how the actual and desired organisation culture might compare in a particular case:

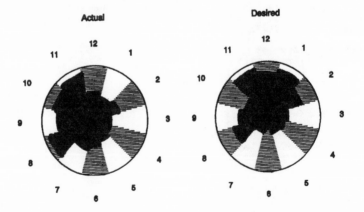

Each participant becomes aware of the organisation culture required for the future, how this compares with the existing culture, and the size of the gap that has to be bridged. They can then compare these conclusions with the information about their own management style. During the skills practice sessions, participants assess their strengths (the behaviours they use well) and their development needs (the behaviours they need to strengthen). They use all this information as the basis for creating a personal development plan.

Only a minority of participants in the Lloyds programme had a profile compatible with the desired organisation culture. Some were weighted towards the competitive, power and confrontational styles, others were weighted towards dependent, conventional, and approval styles. In every case participants were encouraged to draw their own conclusions and decide for themselves if they want to make the effort to change their management and leadership styles.

In order to help participants appreciate what is involved in making these changes an influencing skills model is used as part of the skills practice session.

The model in chart 44 broadly corresponds to the organisation culture and lifestyles profiles, in that assertive behaviours are in the top left quadrant, responsive behaviours in the top right, aggressive behaviours in the bottom left and passive behaviours in the bottom right. During the programme each of these behaviours is demonstrated and opportunities are provided to practise behaving in those ways, then get feedback. Each participant makes notes on what they have learned from these sessions.

As an aid to appreciating the distinction between leadership and management, participants are encouraged to examine a brief summary of the main differences as represented in chart 45.

At the end of the programme participants complete a questionnaire to describe their reactions to the programme, to identify the benefits, and any aspects which need to be modified. The overall reaction after the first eight Lloyds programmes was very favourable and is summarised in chart 46.

The follow-up to these programmes was undertaken in different ways, which included one day workshops to strengthen learning, team building, improved meetings, special events to carry the messages to branch managers and, in a few cases, systematic extension of the principles of leadership at every level to branch managers and assistant branch managers. On the whole the outcomes were encouraging.

Barnardos

Barnardos is a successful and expanding children's charity, which employs some 5,000 people in the UK. In 1989 they were approaching the end of their previous five year plan. The director in charge of child

Chart 44
INFLUENCING SKILLS

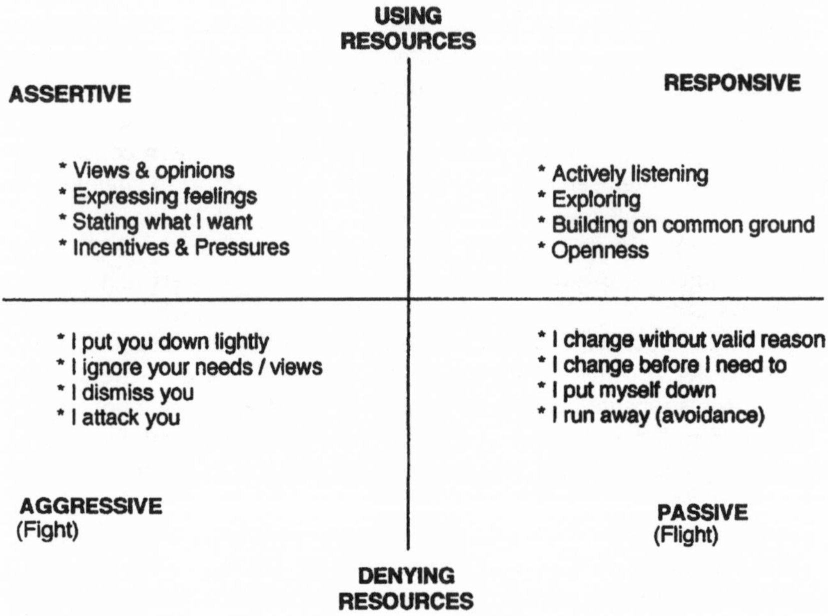

USING
RESOURCES

ASSERTIVE   RESPONSIVE

    * Views & opinions   * Actively listening
    * Expressing feelings   * Exploring
    * Stating what I want   * Building on common ground
    * Incentives & Pressures   * Openness

    * I put you down lightly   * I change without valid reason
    * I ignore your needs / views   * I change before I need to
    * I dismiss you   * I put myself down
    * I attack you   * I run away (avoidance)

AGGRESSIVE   PASSIVE
(Fight)   (Flight)

DENYING
RESOURCES

Notes:

1. The model describes how people behave when influencing others.

2. Positive behaviours which make effective use of others' resources are in the upper half of the diagram - divided into assertive (challenging) and responsive (supportive) types of behaviour.

3. The lower half of the diagram describes behaviours, often used in influencing situations, which deny others' resources (aggressive behaviour) or withdraw one's own resources (passive behaviour). These are less effective.

Chart 45
MANAGEMENT & LEADERSHIP

Both management and leadership are concerned with tasks and people. Both managers and leaders must be results-orientated and know how to delegate. However, there are significant differences, indicated in the diagram below:

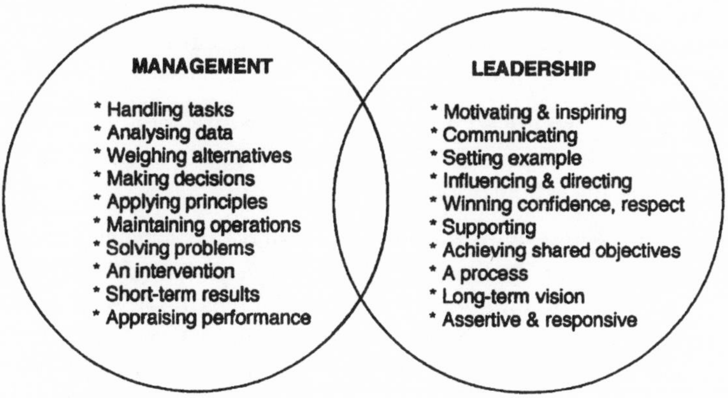

MANAGEMENT

* Handling tasks
* Analysing data
* Weighing alternatives
* Making decisions
* Applying principles
* Maintaining operations
* Solving problems
* An intervention
* Short-term results
* Appraising performance

LEADERSHIP

* Motivating & inspiring
* Communicating
* Setting example
* Influencing & directing
* Winning confidence, respect
* Supporting
* Achieving shared objectives
* A process
* Long-term vision
* Assertive & responsive

** Some bad companies have good managers
** Great companies have effective managers and outstanding leaders

© Sheppard Moscow Ltd. Reproduced by permission

Chart 46: Benefits of Leadership Programme

Three questions were asked: the degree to which the programme met the stated objectives, how the leaders performed and how they rated their time involvement as an investment, all were rated on a scale of 1 to 6. The average sores were:

Degree to which objectives were met   5.05
Rating of Programme leaders   5.00
The programme as an investment   5.38

Many participants declared their intention to do things differently and in particular mentioned their intention to do the following:

*   Improve behavioural skills - some becoming more assertive, others more responsive or better listeners
*   Strengthen the application of matrix management (this was a contentious issue at the time of the programme)
*   Better handling of poor performers
*   Organise time better, review priorities
*   Try harder to influence stubborn senior colleagues
*   Trust, respect and involve colleagues to greater extent
*   Add leadership skills to their management skills
*   Review and reorganise meetings - get more participation.

care decided to involve the staff in a major review of the charity's purpose, the values which formed the basis for its way of working, their strategies and the organisation culture that permeated the organisation. Barnardos wanted to do this review themselves but sought help in managing the processes involved. The review indicated that their work priorities required some adjustments, and that those adjustments would affect the organisation culture, so they sought help in tackling this change.

Time was precious and, as a charity, they needed to keep costs to a minimum. A plan was agreed whereby the culture change initiative would be tackled in three stages:

- introducing the ideas and approach to the directors;
- extending the approach to some thirty-five senior people; and
- involving the whole organisation.

The initial meeting with the directors lasted two days and made use of the Life Styles and Organisation Culture Inventories (chart 43) and introduced them to the influencing skills model (chart 44). As a result of this introductory event the directors decided to go ahead with the second stage. However, they wanted to keep the time commitment and costs to a minimum and therefore made use of the next regular (twice yearly) senior staff meeting.

Suitable briefings were provided and participants were required to complete the Life Styles and Organisation Culture questionnaires prior to the meeting. A similar programme was followed to that used by Lloyds Bank, but with less skills practise. At the end of the meeting people were asked to make and declare firm commitments to indicate how they intended to change their behaviour.

At the time of writing the second phase is being implemented and a further review will determine how and when to extend the initiative to the rest of the organisation. An important question that has arisen is whether the work with children requires an organisation culture similar to or different from the culture required for fund raising work. The two activities are clearly very different, but the organisation culture required is still being debated.

Key Learning Points

As a result of these experiences it is possible to summarise the following eleven key points which help to ensure that the changes are sound and carried through successfully:

(1) Effective leadership from the top.
(2) A significant degree of commitment to the required changes.

(3) An articulated, appropriate vision and clear change goals.
(4) Senior people demonstrating their commitment to and mastery of the change by modelling the required behaviour.
(5) An appropriate, tailor-made learning event (probably lasting four or five days) attended by all key people, to enable them to think through and come to terms with the change as it affects them personally.
(6) Follow-up support during implementation.
(7) Establishing appropriate systems which enable the change to work smoothly, e.g. information systems, staff appraisal criteria, and new behaviour linked into the reward structure.
(8) Creating a critical mass of people supporting the change.
(9) Regular monitoring and review of progress against predetermined landmarks or milestones; making adjustments if necessary.
(10) Regular communication with all interested parties, within and outside the organisation, throughout the process.
(11) Celebration of success, including revisiting the start point and recognising how much has been accomplished.

Every one of these learning points has been proven in complex organisational change situations. More changes will be stimulated by the environmental, social and economic challenges of the coming decade. There are powerful arguments for learning from experience and applying effective change processes to the rapidly evolving world in which we live. For example the chief executive, after consultation, can declare that the goal is to strive for a sustainable business, then authorise the necessary allocation of resources to establish detailed change goals, review of relevant systems, appropriate learning events for staff, and can then stay in touch with the progress being made.

The Potential for Change

The change drivers for organisations are:

- stricter legislation;
- changing customer requirements and buying behaviour;
- pressure from the media;
- pressure from employees;
- pressure from the financial sector, especially insurance, banks, investment assessors and trade bodies;
- the work of NGOs and pressure groups; and
- new top executives with different priorities.

There is a vast potential for change. As organisations realise that they are vulnerable if no change is attempted, they will face up to the need to consider which changes are to be given priority. Everything cannot be done at once, but some changes can be linked and undertaken at the same time because they are complementary. For example the need to redefine the purpose of the business can be linked to the need to review the organisation culture, and this can be undertaken with a review of management styles. Indeed it is helpful to make linkages such as these and to undertake the change in a combined initiative.

One way to review the possibilities and to consider which are the priorities for your organisation, is to review the potential for change described in chart 47. This is a checklist which identifies some of the areas in which organisational change needs to be made.

There is no doubt that some changes which have been accomplished by very large organisations are impressive. They have involved re-aligning business strategy, changing organisation culture, and regrouping people in new departments. Organisations employing 50,000 or even 100,000 people have been involved in such changes. A lot has been learned by many people in various sectors of the public and private sectors, working at different levels. This accumulated experience needs to be reviewed and distilled and its applicability to different situations recognised. For example there is much knowledge and behaviour which is effective at any level of application. The following points are relevant to small companies, voluntary organisations, large businesses, local authorities, multinational corporations, government departments, schools and colleges, and even Cabinet meetings and international agencies:

- the elements of effective leadership;
- getting the best out of meetings with one other person;
- creative problem solving in small groups;
- effectiveness at meetings of six to thirty people;
- understanding the concerns of people when working in groups;
- recognising how loyalties to 'own' group influence people;
- appreciating the significance of organisation culture;
- being aware of what it takes to change organisation culture; and
- knowing that organisations *can* change radically.

If we are to move towards sustainable societies as a world community, we need to make changes which influence whole countries. Compared with the scale of change required in the future, the changes that have so far been accomplished are relatively small scale. However, the experience gained by all those who have taken part in these changes should be applauded, made known more widely and used as the springboard for even more dramatic change in the future. Much that has been learned will continue to be applicable because so much *real* work is done in small

Chart 47: The Potential for Change

The scope for bringing about organisational change towards a
sustainable society is enormous. Some of the potential areas to be
considered are:

Business Performance	Staff Capability & Organisation Culture	Respect for the Environment
Economic		
Nature of business	Adaptive culture	Compatibility of economic & environmental objectives
Market standing	Achievement focused	
Sound cash flow	Staff commitment	
Profitability	Cooperative working	
Innovation		
Human Communities		
Sound development of managers	Management style appropriate to business	Effective integration with the community
Innovation and creativity encouraged	Adaptive culture	Respect for neighbours
	Good teamwork	Lobbying activity consistent with environmental policy
Physical Resources		
Efficient usage	Staff trained in conservation	Waste reduction
Sustainable supplies	High standards of public responsibility	Resource re-use
		Resource recycling
Purchasing policies consistent with environmental policy		
Biodiversity		
Application of cyclic, healthy processes for business development	Staff trained to respect Nature	Integrity of the environment respected
	High standards of openness & public responsibility.	Damaging pollution eliminated

© Colin Hutchinson, *Vitality and Renewal*, Adamantine, 1994

groups. However, there will inevitably be much more to learn as the applications move up the scale of ever larger communities from 100,000 to 1 million and on towards whole countries of 100 or even 1,000 million.

In chapter 8 we looked at change involving a small company after a management buy out. This is an example of change where the numbers involved are less than fifty. In this chapter we have looked at change involving a marketing department with rather less than 500 people, a charity employing 5,000 people, a high street bank with about 50,000 people and a multinational company with over 100,000 people. However, the challenge for the future will involve further multiples of ten. We shall need to understand how to bring about change in communities of 500,000, 5 million, 50 million and even 500 million.

The extent to which it will be possible to apply the lessons learned to much larger groups of people, who do not all work for the same enterprise, will need to be assessed, and new ideas and approaches will have to be found, but the there is a foundation from which to build. In developing the ideas for bringing about change in society it is important to recognise the obvious differences between organisations and communities such as the absence of a unifying vision and the inability to apply the same disciplinary sanctions.

Notes

1 Beckhard, 1969, p. 117.
2 Harvey-Jones, John, 1991, p. 360.
3 The formulation is one used by Brian Pitman, Chief Executive of Lloyds Bank plc, but explained here in my words.
4 Beckhard, Richard and Harris, Reuben T., 1987, is a useful source of ideas.
5 Kotter, John P. and Heskett, James L., 1992.
6 See Sources of Help.

CHAPTER 10

Personal Growth and Organisational Learning

You cannot teach a man anything. You can only help him to discover it within himself.

Galileo

Everything we have discussed so far indicates a need for personal development in one or more of the areas we have covered. This chapter provides some guidelines and 'maps' to find your way around a complex field of learning. Some of the possibilities and a broad classification are described, but personal growth and development will depend on each individual's interest, motivation and commitment to follow up.

As a framework, we return to chart 1 and use this to indicate four possible areas for learning. These relate to human communities, economics, physical resources and biodiversity, as shown on chart 48. In addition to these four elements, we now have at the centre our own inner world, our values, our spirituality and new modes of thinking.

We all learn in rather different ways, but a learning cycle has now become widely accepted as a result of the work of Kolb, Mumford[1] and the Open University. A learning model based on their work contains five elements, namely: having an experience, reflection and review of results and the reactions of others, new ideas and how to express them, identifying areas for application and then experimenting with the application of new ideas and/or behaviour. These five elements are represented in a spiral diagram, as shown in chart 49. This indicates that following any experience it is possible to reflect on the reactions of others and review the results achieved. New ideas may emerge, suggesting that different things may be done, or that what was done might be done differently to achieve a better outcome. The former is the product of a new concept, the latter a modification of behaviour. Both are valid forms of development. New ideas or new behaviours are then assessed in terms of the areas in which they can be appropriately applied. The next step is to try them out by experimenting with the new insights. If this does not go well it is worth persevering, and when it does go well, new experience results, which can be reviewed and further ideas generated. etc. This progressive, cyclical form of learning is shown in chart 49. It is a practical and effective way to learn.

CHART 48: AREAS FOR PERSONAL LEARNING

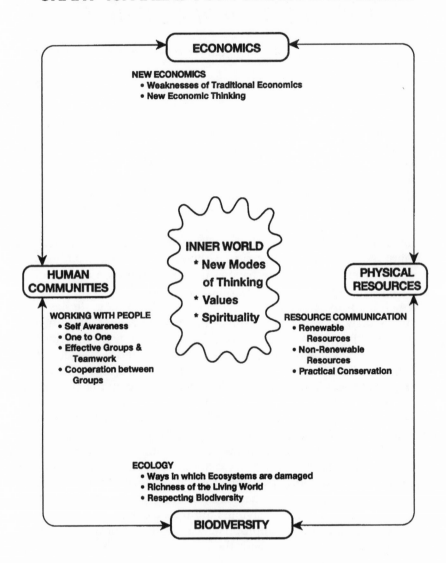

ECONOMICS

NEW ECONOMICS
- Weaknesses of Traditional Economics
- New Economic Thinking

INNER WORLD
* New Modes
  of Thinking
* Values
* Spirituality

HUMAN
COMMUNITIES

WORKING WITH PEOPLE
- Self Awareness
- One to One
- Effective Groups &
  Teamwork
- Cooperation between
  Groups

PHYSICAL
RESOURCES

RESOURCE COMMUNICATION
- Renewable
  Resources
- Non-Renewable
  Resources
- Practical Conservation

ECOLOGY
- Ways in which Ecosystems are damaged
- Richness of the Living World
- Respecting Biodiversity

BIODIVERSITY

© Colin Hutchinson, *Vitality and Renewal*, Adamantine, 1994

CHART 49: A LEARNING MODEL

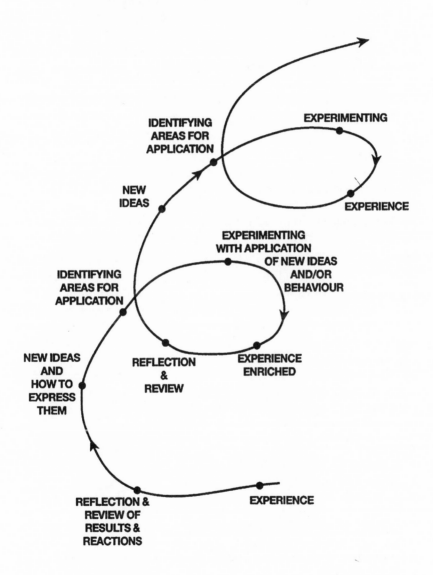

Sometimes there is a temptation to take short cuts, such as experimenting with ill-considered ideas by moving straight to experimenting and avoiding the 'review' and 'new ideas' phases. Another distortion occurs when the review and reflection phase results in confirmation of current experience, and new modes of thinking are suppressed before they have emerged. Occasionally it will be appropriate to use one of these short cuts, but if they become a habit it is likely that real learning and personal growth will be thwarted by an impoverished learning cycle. It is worth reflecting on your own preferred way of learning, and ensuring that you use all five elements most of the time.

Before we look at these areas for learning it is worth recognising some of the barriers to learning that we all encounter to varying degrees:

(1) It's too complex, I'll never understand.
(2) Contradictory information makes me wonder if anyone really knows.
(3) Habits are hard to change, I'm happy as I am.
(4) I have very negative feelings about the 'greens'.
(5) It's not *my* responsibility to do anything.
(6) Surely *they* are doing what's required.
(7) My effort/contribution will make no difference.

The answers to these thoughts are that everyone *can* understand a few simple truths and build on that understanding in their own way; it *is* possible to cut through to the best available information; determined people *can* change their habits; as more people learn about the environment the 'greens' are found in *every* sphere of life; it *is* our collective responsibility; whatever *they* may be doing, and whoever *they* may be, it will not be sufficient without *our* support; and *your and my* contribution *does* make the difference.

Now let us consider why people want to change the way they think, how they behave, and the way they lead their lives. Some of the most important reasons for learning and change are:

• to survive;
• to relieve feelings of guilt;
• to face new challenges;
• to compete effectively with colleagues;
• to support a person or an idea; and
• to develop and grow as a human being.

It is now time to explore some possibilities in each of the elements represented in chart 48.

Human Communities

The headings on the model we are using are very broad, so this section deals with all aspects of relating to and working with people. It applies to families, work groups and the communities in which we live.

We would all like to be natural human beings, able to work effectively with others in a cooperative way. We generally like to be thought of as:

- curious;
- creative;
- intelligent;
- enthusiastic;
- open; and
- honest.

We know from our experience that we and others do not always live up to these ideals. Instead we (and others) use ineffective behaviour such as:

- being critical of others;
- being impatient or irritable;
- being poor communicators: silent or long winded;
- doing silly things;
- becoming uncooperative or obtuse;
- being devious or deceitful;
- being passive or aggressive;
- behaving in a powerless way; and
- becoming angry and even occasionally violent.

Sometimes our behaviour is the consequence of what others say or do. We are stimulated because we are reminded, consciously or subconsciously, of events of the past when we felt angry, happy, sad, or frustrated. The feelings we had then are stimulated again and produce our ineffective behaviour. Once this pattern occurs in one person it is very easy for it to trigger others, and we enter a spiral of ineffectiveness. Most attempts to break out of the spiral fail. This sort of behaviour is probably a function of trying to cope with unpleasant or difficult situations. However, it seldom works and most often the situations in which these ineffective spirals occur are never satisfactorily resolved.

Occasionally we find an opportunity to get rid of some of the past distress. We might meet someone who is prepared to listen or when we get home we 'pour our heart out' to a partner about the awful meeting, or the frustrating experiences of the day. Sometimes we go to the pub and after a few drinks and a lot of laughter we feel a lot better. We can generalise about the ways in which people try to discharge their distress:

- talking, preferably to a good listener;
- yawning, shaking or sweating;

- laughing;
- getting angry;
- taking part in energetic sport;
- crying;
- gagging or vomiting; and/or
- getting away from it all; perhaps going for a long walk.

When we are with someone who is trying to discharge their distress it can easily trigger our own. Someone describes a bad situation and rather than listen we tell them about a 'worse' situation we faced. When someone starts to cry it can bring tears to our own eyes, and because it is distressing we try to get them to stop crying as quickly as possible. Many of us can recall childhood experiences when we were told to shut up, stop crying and grow up. Certain expressions are widely used such 'Big boys don't cry', 'Little girls don't get angry' and 'Don't be so childish.' The result is that hurtful experiences are not discharged. This means that distressing experiences accumulate and can be triggered next time we enter a negative spiral. When someone starts discharging their distress we try to stop them *even though it is not our intention to be unhelpful.*

The form that the discharging behaviour takes needs to be relevant to the blocked feelings. For example it is inappropriate to try and discharge anger by crying – something energetic would be better – while crying would be more relevant to discharging blocked sadness – for example, from unfinished mourning.

We can learn how to help each other avoid the ineffective spirals, and encourage others to be natural, competent human beings, by doing the following:

- listening with attention and interest;
- showing understanding by paraphrasing what others say;
- acknowledging how others feel by reflecting their feelings;
- giving support through attention;
- valuing ourselves and others;
- providing a process for tackling an issue;
- summarising what has been discussed;
- identifying progress and achievements;
- being open and sharing feelings; and
- clarifying action and tasks for the future.

The positive way to help others in distress is by showing respect and giving support. The opposite of this is ignoring them, being critical, denying their feelings and thoughts, interrupting them and putting them down. If we do the latter we perpetuate the distress. If we learn to give appreciation we help ourselves and others to become natural human beings. Chart 50 summarises how this works.[2]

Chart 50:
GIVING POSITIVE SUPPORT

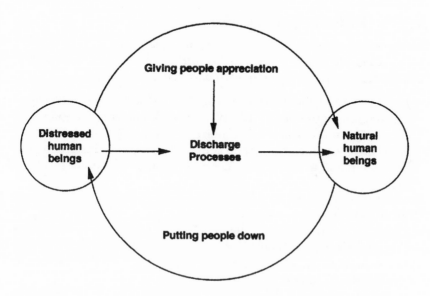

Notes:

1. People are born as natural human beings and as they grow up experience both appreciation and being 'put down'.

2. If people experience 'putting down' behaviour frequently - from parents, teachers, friends and work colleagues they become distressed.

3. Excessive distress results in ineffective behaviour and a greater tendency to put others down, thus increasing the amount of distress in a family, work group or community.

4. Distress can be relieved by giving people appreciation and support which enables them to discharge their distress and move towards becoming natural human beings.

Learning about ways of working more effectively with people is available in a great many short courses run by a variety of different organisations. The organisations tend to specialise in different sectors of the community. Some concentrate on businesses, others offer residential courses to mixed groups from the public and private sectors and some offer their services to individuals direct rather than through their employers. The appropriate source of information will differ from country to country.

Relevant Models Already Discussed

We have already discussed other ways in which we can learn to work with people in effective ways, and it is worth looking again at the following charts in the context of your own personal development:

- Chart 9: Seeking Solutions, which highlighted: leadership; innovation; learning; communication; open systems; and conflict resolution.
- Chart 15: Values, Beliefs and Culture, which dealt with: the relationship between values, beliefs and culture; the use of feedback to review behaviour; and a review of values and beliefs as a result of this feedback.
- Chart 16: Conflict Resolution, which focused on conflict: between people; within groups; and between groups.
- Chart 17: Support and Challenge Groups, which explained: What they are? Why have them? How they are organised? The benefits of this way of working; four different group climates; and behaviour which helps groups to be effective.
- Chart 29: The JIMM theory, which illustrated: the likely impact of environmentally educated people joining your organisation; and the likely impact of the JIMM theory on buying behaviour.
- Chart 37: The Trend Towards Increased Autonomy, which suggested how this might affect you and/or your employees.
- Chart 38: Effectiveness in Small Groups, which described: the concerns of people working in groups; how these concerns develop; and the characteristics of mature groups.
- Chart 39: Managing Meetings at Three levels, which covered: arrangements and procedures at meetings; task and content; and feelings and emotions.
- Chart 44: Influencing Skills Model, which identified: assertive behaviours which are positive statements; responsive behaviours which build relationships; aggressive behaviours which put people down; and passive behaviours which are signs of withdrawal.
- Chart 45: Management and Leadership, which asked: Which set of actions best describes how you work? Is there scope for personal development?

Many organisations, management colleges, business schools and other institutions provide opportunities for learning in all these areas. The skills learned are applicable at home, at work and in the community. These same skills are an essential requirement for dealing with the wide range of increasingly pressing issues that are emerging in each of the other three areas identified as the key elements in chart 48 – economics, physical resources and biodiversity. We shall now discuss these in turn, then consider our own inner world, and conclude this chapter by looking at organisational learning.

Economics

The economic systems we have created and relied on for decades make no distinction between activities which harm people and the environment, and those activities which help them. Economics takes many things for granted. For example, that the Earth's life support systems can absorb unlimited abuse. Gross National Product (GNP), as we apply it now, measures activity. This means that the activity that is required to clean up after a fatal road accident or a tanker disaster at sea is treated as if it was healthy and helpful. It is added to the GNP and contributes to our delusion that higher GNP is an adequate sign of progress, but there is no corresponding assessment for loss of life, damage to people or the environment.

If we grow our own vegetables, decorate our own houses, repair our own cars, bake our own bread, or care for an ailing relative, our only contribution to GNP is for any materials or ingredients that were purchased. However, if we buy our vegetables from a shop, employ a decorator to paint the house, take our car to the garage for service and repairs, buy bread from the supermarket or a baker and employ a nurse to care for an ailing relative we contribute much more to GNP. The economic system we have grown up to accept is selective in what it regards as productive economic activity which gets included in the GNP calculations.

Learning about the deficiencies of our current economic systems is a good starting point, for an exploration of alternatives. A good book on this subject is probably the best starting point and for most people for whom this whole subject is rather boring and difficult to understand the choice of an appropriate book is not easy. One helpful book which uses many illustrations and examples, as well as being written in accessible language, is *Wealth Beyond Measure: An Atlas of New Economics*.[3] For those who want a book that sets out a challenging programme for the adoption of 'New Economics', *Future Wealth* by James Robertson is recommended.[4]

Two highly regarded books from either side of the Atlantic are: *The Green Economy: Environment, Sustainable Development and the Politics of the*

Future, by Michael Jacobs[5] and *Steady State Economics*, by Herman Daly.[6] Another valuable book on this subject is written by Frances Cairncross, Environment Editor of *The Economist*, entitled 'Costing the Earth',[7] the subheadings of which are:

• What governments must do;
• What consumers need to know; and
• How businesses can profit.

The book contains many insights and practical suggestions.

Readers who would like to keep abreast of how this subject develops might like to join The New Economics Foundation[8] which publishes a quarterly magazine for members and a regularly updated booklist. They also organise The Other Economic Summit (TOES) which takes place every time there is a formal economic summit meeting of Heads of State from rich countries. The TOES meetings provide a challenging alternative programme which attracts large numbers of contributors and participants.

James Robertson publishes *Turning Point 2000*[9] which is mailed twice yearly to 2,000 readers who pay an informal, variable subscription (£5–£10 a year is recommended). The publication is a sixteen-page A5 format booklet and contains a wealth of information, ideas and reports of initiatives, from all around the world. It encourages networking which means that readers can make direct contact with those whose work is of interest to them. There is also a section on 'dates to note' which lists conferences, lectures, seminars and workshops. James Robertson periodically runs seminars on various aspects of 'New Economics' at his home, and will provide details on request.

Physical Resources

Learning about resources can usefully start with the distinction between renewable and non-renewable resources. A brief restatement is appropriate in the context of learning. Renewable resources are those which replenish themselves through natural processes such that the level of use does not exceed the rate at which replenishment can occur. Non renewable resources, such as minerals, metals and fossil fuels exist in limited quantities. Mankind's limited ability to extract them from the Earth means that there is a lower practical limit of availability.

Forests are a good example of a renewable resource. These can be felled if reafforestation is taking place and the cycles of use, replanting and growth are in balance. Fish catches can continue indefinitely only if the size of each annual catch does not exceed the rate at which each species can replenish itself. In fact the world catch of herring, cod, bass and mackerel all peaked around 1986,[10] then declined, as a result of over fishing. The world fish catch per capita peaked in 1988 at 19.4 kg and has since dropped to below 18 kg.[11] Governments are trying to limit catches to avoid over fishing, but this policy is unpopular with fishermen and difficult to enforce – an obvious source of conflict. Fish caught in excess of quotas are thrown back into the sea, dead, which does not assist conservation.

There are many books which provide information about different living species and the rates at which they are being used. However, for practical learning about renewable resources it is helpful to take part in some sort of field study course and to understand the issues in a practical way. This will help establish deeper understanding of the way in which the living world sustains itself and how human activity can cause damage. This theme links directly to the next heading, biodiversity, which will be picked up again below.

Facts and figures about the rate of use and known reserves of non-renewable resources only tell part of the story. This is because new reserves are usually discovered only when they are needed. Figures published in the early 1970s stated that oil reserves would last about thirty years. These calculations were based on dividing known oil reserves by consumption at the time. BP's estimates in 1993 suggested that reserves will last for over forty years. Eventually the 'years of reserves remaining' will begin to decline, and most predictions for oil suggest that this is likely to occur soon after the start of the twenty-first century. Chart 5 (chapter 1) shows the era of fossil fuel consumption, and provides a context over a much longer time perspective than we usually consider, but which puts the current era in perspective.

Having recognised that resource limitations are significant, the most important thing to do next is to learn about ways in which resources can be conserved by reducing consumption, by re-use such as returnable milk bottles, and by recycling, e.g. cans which are melted down to make new cans.

For business, the conservation of resources means exploring all possibilities for recovering resources from wastes, redesigning products so that resources are used efficiently, and replacing scarce resources with those that are more plentiful and less damaging to the environment. We have already discussed, in chapters 6 and 7 how this is being done by various companies. In addition to innovations devised, planned and implemented by staff within the company there is also plenty of scope to learn from others. To involve company staff in practical programmes, the Environment Council in the UK introduced their 'Conservers At Work' initiative in 1993 and had attracted several hundred members within weeks of the launch.[12]

Further insight into practical ways in which resource conservation can be accomplished will be derived from changing behaviour at home. Most countries in the northern hemisphere have introduced recycling schemes for glass bottles, aluminium and tin cans, paper products and textiles. By taking part in such schemes you are not only contributing to solutions but also learning about ways in which life style changes can be achieved. By taking part in the Global Action Plan for the Earth (GAP)[13] you will be participating with others in bringing about community development and moving towards a sustainable life style. The GAP programme involves changes in how to deal with household wastes, manage energy, fuel and water consumption more efficiently, how to shop in ways which conserve resources and avoid harmful products, and how to get others involved with the initiative. GAP is spreading to several countries in Europe and is already going strong in North America.

Biodiversity

The best way to learn about biodiversity is to participate in a practical way with the living world. Many of us do this to some degree by caring for a garden. However, that experience seldom brings home the diversity of plants, animals, insects and micro-organisms which abound in natural environments. The tendency is to concentrate on cultivating particular vegetables or flowers, rather than on preserving an overall healthy environment.

A field study course is a good way to achieve an appreciation of the living world in a short time. Some schools do such courses well, and as environmental education is integrated into the curriculum more and more children learn about biodiversity, life support systems, threats to species and ways in which a natural environment can be cared for and developed. Adult courses[14] are also available and have awakened latent interest in many people, while stimulating interest in local natural environment's within the overall context of the Earth's biodiversity.

In order to appreciate the extent to which current agricultural practices have steadily reduced the diversity of plant life that is used for food, it is salutary to note that:[15]

(1) Twenty plant species provide 90 per cent of our food.
(2) These come from only two plant families (legumes and grasses).
(3) There are 100 plant products on sale in USA supermarkets.
(4) And yet 70,000 plant species are known to be edible and many more may prove to be so.

The assaults on the living world threaten the number of species that exist on the planet. Some species play pivotal roles in maintaining the integrity of life.

In the 1950s malaria was rife in Borneo, so the World Health Organisation (WHO) decided to spray DDT to kill the mosquitoes which spread the malaria. This dealt successfully with the malaria but had side effects which were not anticipated. The Dayak people, who live in the area that was sprayed, found that the roofs of their houses started falling in because the DDT also killed a parasitic wasp which controlled the number of caterpillars which ate the thatched roofs. As the caterpillars increased the roofs collapsed. Furthermore, insects which died of DDT poisoning were eaten by geckos, which were eaten by cats. The cats started to die and the rat population increased. This led to outbreaks of plague and typhus. To deal with this unexpected problem, WHO parachuted live cats into Borneo![16]

Destruction of species which play important roles in the web of life can trigger massive extermination of several other species. A simple summary of how a species crash can occur is given in chart 51.

Practical learning about the living world can also take place when walking in the countryside, or on holidays. However, it is possible to walk in the country while failing to appreciate the diversity of life. A good way to avoid this is to link up with one of the many environmental and countryside organisations which provide guides and explanatory talks to draw attention to the many aspects of the environment that can be missed.

It is interesting to know what today's children are learning. For example educational attainment targets are set for children of different ages by the National Curriculum Council in the UK.[17] A few examples of what environmental geography pupil's are expected to be able to do are set out below:

(1) Level 3: describe effects on landscapes, people and wildlife of extracting natural resources.
(2) Level 5: explain why rivers, lakes, seas and oceans are vulnerable to pollution, and describe ways in which pollution problems have been addressed.
(3) Level 7: identify possible causes of global environmental change – e.g. climate change – and explain the potential effects on parts of the world.
(4) Level 10: examine critically the concepts of sustainable development, stewardship and conservation.

Inner World

At the centre of our being is our inner world. At the core of how we lead our lives are our beliefs, and values (*see* chart 15). Facing up to the complexity of the world situation we have to tackle together is very disturb-

Chart 51: Species Crash

Species are being extinguished by:

* Destruction of forest, coral reef, wetlands & habitats
* Over hunting or exploitation
* Excessive use of pesticides
* Effects of Ultraviolet (UV) radiation due to ozone depletion
* Elimination of 'keystone' species

Keystone species play a crucial role:

A BEE .... pollinates plants .... which are food for insects
.... which pollinate other plants .... and are food for birds &
mammals .... and so on. Some species are mobile links in a
pivotal relationship with many thousands of species of plants,
insects, birds & mammals. When a keystone species, such as a
particular bee, is eliminated from a region it may trigger a
cascade of extinction in that region (but the species may
survive elsewhere.)

Tropical forests are richer than most other habitats:

* Between 70 and 95 percent of all species live on just 6%
  of the Earth's surface

* They are being felled fast - all but the remotest areas
  might disappear within 25 years

* It is not just the tropical rain forests that are in
  danger. The following are also threatened:

        - temperate forests
        - arctic tundra
        - natural grasslands
        - wetlands
        - heathlands
        - hedgerows

* Habitats destroyed in Britain since 1930:

        - 95% of natural grassland
        - 80% of upland bogs
        - 50% of remaining fens
        - 30% of ancient woodland

THE WORLD IS LOSING BETWEEN 50 AND 100 SPECIES A DAY AND THE
RATE IS ACCELERATING.

Species are often being lost before their role in Nature or
their value to mankind has been assessed.

Sources:
Myers, Norman, *Gaia Atlas of Future Worlds*, R McCarta, 1991.
O'Riordan. Timothy, *Conserving Wildlife and the Countryside*,
British Gas Booklet No 7, 1990.

ing. As Mary Clark has said about 'Our Global Future', the course she inaugurated, in her book *Ariadne's Thread*:[18] '[it] forces an examination of basic beliefs and assumptions of one's inner world view, and psychologically that can be a very uncomfortable process.' She goes on to describe how the students on the course could be grouped around three very different reactions:

- faith that someone is working on the solutions;
- disowning all personal responsibility; and
- reluctant acceptance that the future is in peril.

Mary Clark says that 'at the precise moment when a person understands and accepts that it is aspects of his or her own viewpoint that have created, contributed to, and helped to sustain the world's problems, then that person suddenly becomes part of the solution.'

This perspective lies at the heart of bringing about change. Al Gore concludes his book *Earth in the Balance* with these words:

> "We can believe in [the] future and work to achieve it and preserve it, or we can whirl blindly on, behaving as if one day there will be no children to inherit our legacy. The choice is ours; the Earth is in the balance."

Exercising that choice requires us to search for new modes of thinking, and the areas in which it is important to do this have been reviewed earlier in this book and especially in this chapter. How we do this will be influenced by our own preferences, but for many it might be very appropriate to try something completely different. If you like reading and find that is an easy way to learn by all means try it, but also experiment with learning in practical ways from experience. This might involve you in group work or some outdoor event or short course. If you learn best by being challenged in face-to-face situations, then try that, but also try out some quiet reading. To be sure that real learning has taken place, summarise the main points that register with you *and* the action that needs to be taken to apply the ideas in your world. Then do it...and review the outcomes!

Edward de Bono's *Handbook for the Positive Revolution* is a useful approach to re-examining your thinking.[19] This is a book for those who like to do things logically, and who want a straightforward way to challenge their own thoughts. The book draws a distinction between positive and negative revolution and goes on to describe, with simple illustrations, how to increase your own effectiveness. It contains a section where the perspective of different groups of people is discussed, which covers women, older people, younger people, the media, business, art, political parties, trade unions, and revolutionary groups. Edward de Bono, who invented the idea of lateral thinking, is a prolific writer, who has influenced many people from all over the world by his novel approaches to creativity.

Anthony Robbins, on the other hand, is a young man who has earned a remarkable reputation in a very short time. His book *Unlimited Power* is an international best seller and has been followed by *Awaken the Giant Within*.[20] Both books are intended for those who wish to understand and develop their full potential. They contain easy to follow explanations, with copious examples, of ways by which to understand your own behaviour better, how you restrict your capabilities and how, by making some important adjustments, it is possible greatly to enhance your personal effectiveness. The second book especially, offers guidelines for taking charge of every aspect of your life – mental, emotional, physical, and your financial destiny. You will change your belief system if it is sufficiently painful to go on believing what you have always believed, and if you are prepared to move away from unquestioning acceptance that something is unchangeable. It is then important to identify new beliefs, which are tested and, through achievement, accepted for the future. This is one tiny example of many good, practical ideas for personal growth and self development which are contained in Robbins's books.

Exploration of Values

New modes of thinking may lead you into an exploration of values, but if they have not, then it may be worth finding ways in which you can do this. In an organisational context it can be done by following a series of quite practical steps:

(1) Identify current perceptions, individually.
(2) Search for agreed perceptions and note minority views.
(3) Review the processes used for agreeing perceptions.
(4) Identify underlying concerns about the organisation.
(5) Bring in external perspectives and information.
(6) Describe how these concerns influence the organisation.
(7) Receive information about policies and practices.
(8) Summarise perceptions and concerns as they are now.
(9) Review the process.

In working though this process it is salutary to gather external views to compare with your own, and see if this changes any of your perceptions or concerns. Throughout the process the aim is to identify and clarify personal values and to recognise how they evolve. If a healthy group climate exists with high challenge and high support (*see* chart 17) then it is likely that new values will emerge, and the process should move on to building wider commitment to the conclusions, so that they can be used to inform corporate action to change the way things are done. The dynamic circular process that this requires is described in chart 52.

CHART 52: AN EXPLORATION OF VALUES

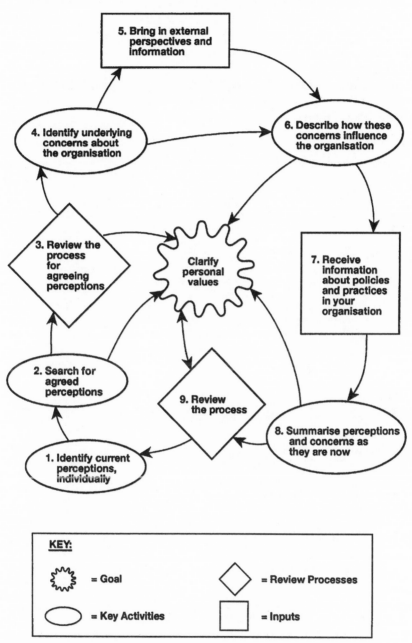

© Colin Hutchinson, *Vitality and Renewal*, Adamantine, 1994

Freeing the Spirit

There is a widespread stirring among people from many different walks of life and in all parts of the world. The stirring is about being true to oneself. People are seeking and finding ways to feel more at peace within ourselves and to believe that how we live our lives, the work we do and above all the way we work with others, is consistent with our true values.

There are many trends which contribute to an underlying awareness that a fundamental shift in perceptions is taking place. Consider the list which follows from two perspectives:

(1) How many of the following things have taken up some of your time, your thoughts and your money during the past year?
(2) How many of your relatives, friends and acquaintances are at present giving time, money or effort to these things?

The list below contains thoughts and actions which impact on each other, but each can be given attention separately:

- the desire for a healthy diet;
- the search for complementary medicine to maintain health;
- the striving for fitness;
- the wish for personal growth, development and wellbeing;
- the desire for enhanced skills in working with people;
- the search for new ways to resolve conflict;
- the need for peace and disarmament, especially nuclear;
- the move towards openness of information;
- the recognition that we are damaging the environment;
- the exploration of ethics and values in organisations;
- the trend towards ethical investments;
- the desire to help the developing world;
- the support for international cooperation;
- the need for constitutional and political change;
- the desire for greater equity and justice in society; and
- the growth in the number of self-employed people.

Trends sometimes strengthen and then weaken or even go into reverse. However, it is worth reflecting on the list above in terms of how things were twenty years ago, ten years ago, how they are now and how they might be in ten years time. Individually we seldom take stock of underlying changes in this way (although professional organisations, such as MORI, do this regularly and their findings are available). The result is that there is a tendency to believe that nothing is changing. We live in the present, and today seems much the same as any other day, so we deny the existence of underlying trends. There are ways in which we can free our own spirit, help others to do the same, and contribute to the building of a better world.

The Learning Organisation

In addition to the various ways in which individuals learn there is a need for organisations to develop the ability to learn. This is through the individual, but it is accomplished in ways which support and enhance learning as a part of organisational life. We have already seen in chapters 7 and 9 that effective organisations have adaptive organisation cultures. This adaptability is directly related to the ability of the organisation to learn and change. It means that the activities associated with learning are valued, and this is demonstrated by significant development budgets which are not automatically the first expense to be curtailed when cost cutting is undertaken.

The reference to development budgets does not imply that the only way to learn is from courses, but they often help. Learning is only partly to do with acquiring knowledge. It is also to do with the development of attitudes, beliefs and values and the acquisition of behavioural skills. There are several important ways in which people learn:

- direct, practical experience;
- taking on wider responsibilities;
- participating in projects and special assignments;
- secondments which broaden experience;
- deputising for a more senior person;
- giving and receiving feedback and valuing the learning from it;
- networking with people who have relevant experience;
- taking a sabbatical; and
- gaining unusual experiences.

The term 'learning organisation' is becoming more widely known and the theory is being developed and described in books.[21] The basic requirements for achieving organisational learning are:

- recognising learning as a cyclic rather than a linear process;
- having a clear and common understanding of important concepts such as: Mission, strategy, policy, objectives and plans;
- enabling processes which encourage people to gain satisfaction from their work;
- valuing individual competence, creativity and personal growth in ways that are relevant to the individual and the organisation;
- encouraging authentic, open and clear communication;
- seeking common ground from which shared visions are built; and
- building cooperative ways of working in teams.

When designing new organisations or redesigning well established ones it is important to remember that organisational design is much more than organisational structure. Chart 34 describes a model of an organisation and shows that structure is one element among six, all of which are important ingredients for an effective organisation. How these six elements fit together determines the degree to which the organisation will be effective. A useful, practical book on organisation design has been written by Philip Sadler.[22]

When an organisation faces up to the full complexity of the environmental challenge it recognises that new modes of thinking will be required to make realistic progress towards a sustainable future. This is never easy and may require novel forms of learning. As we noted in chapter 7, Abhay Bhushan, Manager of the Environmental Leadership Program, Xerox Corporation, saw the need to establish deeper understanding of ecology and the environment in order to make progress with the challenging environmental assignment he had taken on. He believes that we need 'to develop products and technologies in the West which are conducive to life' and as a personal statement says: 'I believe in the principle of individual empowerment.' He also believes that an institution 'can become a powerful medium for change'.[23]

Among the learning initiatives taken by Bhushan was participation in Terma's Box training,[24] which he introduced to the Xerox team working on environmental considerations in product design. The Box (literally a carefully packed wooden box) contains a variety of high quality materials which are designed to stimulate self-healing, ecological awareness, community appreciation and meditative thought. 'The journey' is experienced by going through the materials in a guided, carefully paced way, with a trained facilitator. It can be incorporated into other learning experiences or stand alone as a single unique experience. It can be linked to various forms of applications as appropriate. The materials available in 1993 are best suited for use in the USA because they have strong associations with that country, but adaptations for other cultures would be possible. Most of the materials are writings or objects, and the learning is derived from comparing the thoughts, attitudes and values that they trigger in members of the participating group. It is an intriguing and unusual experience to take part in 'the journey'.

Summary

There is plenty of scope for learning for anyone who wishes to broaden their perceptions, enhance their knowledge, review their values, enrich their awareness of the environment, discover new ways of working constructively with people and finding out how to apply their learning to the work situation to benefit themselves and their organisation. It requires a degree of discipline to decide where to start, find a relevant way to learn and persevere until real learning has taken place. Early success often leads to further exploration, and as doubts recede and self confidence is enhanced the learning process becomes a rewarding experience in its own right.

Further rewards come from taking part with others, so that organisational effectiveness is achieved on a continuing basis. As this sort of individual learning penetrates the world of work, changes the culture of organisations and leads to new, exciting futures which are in tune with vitality and renewal, people and organisations reap the benefits.

Notes

1   Mumford, *Developing Directors*, Manpower Services Commission, 1987, which refers to the work of Honey and Mumford, developing the work of Kolb.
2   These ideas and the model were developed with Robin Coates.
3   Ekins, Paul; Hillman, Mayer and Hutchison, Robert, 1992.
4   Robertson, James, 1990.
5   Jacobs, Michael, 1991.
6   Daly, Herman E, 1992.
7   Cairncross, Francis, 1991.
8   See Sources of Help.
9   Robertson, James and Pritchard, Alison, Turning Point 2000, published biannually by Turning Point 2000, The Old Bakehouse, Cholsey, OXON OX10 9NU, England.
10 Lean, Geoffrey, Hinrichsen, Don and Markham, Adam, 1990, p. 158.
11 Brown, Lester, Kane, Hal and Ayres, Ed, 1993, p. 33.
12 See Sources of Help.
13 See Sources of Help.
14 In the UK, courses of this kind are run by organisations such as the Field Studies Council, and the Environment and Training Group (see Sources of Help).
15 Myers, Norman, 1990, p. 111.
16 Rocky Mountain Institute's guiding parable (see Sources of Help).
17 See Sources of Help.
18 Clark, Mary E, 1989, p. 26.
19 de Bono, Edward, 1991.
20 Robbins, Anthony, *Unlimited Power*, Simon & Schuster, 1988, and *Awaken the Giant Within*, Simon & Schuster, 1992.
21 Senge, Peter, 1990, and Garratt, Bob, 1990.
22 Sadler, Philip, 1991.
23 Feinstein, Debra, 'Abhay Bhushan: Personal and Global Commitment', in Benchmark, October 1991, (a quarterly Xerox publication).
24 See Sources of Help.

CHAPTER 11

Managing Change: The Processes and Techniques

Leadership to move companies in more cooperative, innovative directions can come from many places, not just the Chief Executive's office.

Rosabeth Moss Kanter[1]

The purpose of this chapter is to describe some of the processes, tools and techniques which can be used to help map out the desired change and make it happen. We begin by reviewing those that have been described already. It is worth noting them again here in order to recognise the contribution they can make to effective change management. We go on to a description of several more processes and techniques which can be used in managing individual and organisational change. The chapter concludes with a summary (chart 69) which will help you to identify appropriate processes and techniques for tackling a particular situation. In describing several techniques there is no suggestion that they should all be used, any more than a surgeon, gardener or a plumber uses every available instrument for every assignment. Select those which suit your purpose.

A central theme of this book is that the many challenges we now face as a global community cannot be tackled in isolation. From the start we have recognised that human communities, economics, physical resources and biodiversity are the four elements we need to deal with together (chart 1). Now that we come to the processes and techniques which can be used to manage change, this integrative principle remains a central theme. However, the successful management of change is dependent on getting individuals, groups and organisations to work together cooperatively. The processes and techniques described all contribute to harnessing human endeavour in our common interest.

Processes and Techniques Already Described

In chapter 5 the change equation was introduced in the context of achieving a sustainable society. It is equally relevant to organisations wishing to accomplish significant change. The equation states that to achieve change, dissatisfaction with the present situation, a vision of the future, practical steps to bring about change, and the will to make it happen, are all needed. This concept is reinforced in chapter 9 with the introduction of an organisation change model (chart 40). This looks at three aspects of the present and the desired situation:

- business performance;
- organisation culture and staff capability; and
- environmental impact.

In order to get from the current to the desired situation a practical pathway has to be established. As we have already seen this requires the skills associated with leadership, innovation, learning, communications, open systems and conflict resolution. These ideas are encapsulated in the LILCOC acronym introduced in chart 9, and are particularly relevant in managing organisational change.

The management of organisational change often means that people need to be brought together in new groups to carry out the work involved. To aid understanding of this work we have discussed:

- Conflict Resolution (chart 16);
- Support and Challenge Groups (chart 17);
- Effectiveness in Small Groups (chart 38);
- Managing Meetings (chart 39);
- An Exploration of Values (chart 52).

If the change involves redesigning the organisation then the organisation model (chart 34) described in chapter 7 will be a helpful reminder of all the interacting elements which need to be considered.

One further idea, which has no model or framework to describe it, is the concept of an overarching goal. When two groups of people who are in conflict find a goal they both want to achieve, but which can only be achieved through joint effort, their disagreement can turn into cooperation quite quickly, especially if the goal is really important to both groups. This principle is a remarkably helpful force in today's world and is producing collaboration in many unexpected quarters. It is worth bearing in mind so that overarching goals can be identified in every change management situation.

Additional Processes and Techniques

The processes and techniques described in this chapter are grouped under four headings:

(1) Describing the current situation.
(2) Establishing the Desired Situation.
(3) Managing the Transition.
(4) Monitoring the Transition.

Each of these tasks can be carried out using your own concepts and methods. However, if you are looking for new, simple but powerful approaches, those described here might be helpful. Some of them may already be known to you, or something similar may be familiar. They should be regarded as a springboard for developing your own change management methods, rather than as a constraining set of rules. Each can be used on its own or in conjunction with other techniques.

A summary of the processes and techniques is given in chart 53.

Describing the Current Situation

You and your organisation will already have a lot of information about the current situation. Annual reports summarise the previous year's performance and give an outline of future intentions. The structure and reporting lines will be represented in an organisation chart. However, information of this kind seldom proves helpful in a change management project and might even act as a constraining influence by drawing attention to powerful influences which inhibit rather than encourage change. Annual reports are, after all, designed to represent the organisation in the best possible light.

SWOT Analysis

A better starting point is some form of SWOT analysis – which identifies the organisation's strengths, weaknesses, opportunities and threats. The strengths and weaknesses relate to internal factors while the opportunities and threats focus on the external environment of the business. A good way to start this process is by identifying all the pressures on the business. This can be done in a simple way, such as that suggested by chart 54. Further refinements can be added by indicating the strength and significance of each pressure with longer or thicker arrows. The approach is equally valid if a department or business unit is the focus of your interest. The important point is that you should identify your own set of pressures rather than use a generalised diagram such as the one given here.

Pressures will differ depending on the industry and the circumstances of each organisation. For example global warming, ozone depletion and acid rain will result in considerable pressures on chemical industry companies. Waste management might be the biggest headache for companies in the metals processing business.[2] Organisations in the service sector might feel little direct pressure but insurance companies will, for example, be aware of the threat of increasingly large claims arising from storms which might be localised effects of a general climate change.

Chart 53: Managing Change - Processes and Techniques

1 Current Situation	The Development Gap	2 Desired Situation

1 Current Situation

a SWOT Analysis

b Identifying the Pressures

c Spheres of Influence Analysis
d Attitude Surveys
e Current Organisation Culture

f Current Performance Criteria

g Force Field Analysis
   (for diagnosis)

2 Desired Situation

a Visualising the Future

b Revising the Mission
   Statement

c Desired Organisation
   Culture
d Inverted Pyramid Structure
e Desired Performance
   Criteria

3 Managing the Transition

a Identifying the Change Goals
b Change Management Roles
c Assessing Willingness & Ability
d Attitudes towards Change
e Enhancing the Capacity for Change
f Force Field Analysis (for action planning)
g Role Negotiation
h Negotiating Skills
j Action Planning
k Communications Strategy
l Human Reactions to Change

4 Monitoring the Transition

a Establishing criteria & landmarks
b Establishing a Procedure
c Celebrating Success

NB See also Chart 42: The Change Process - A Practical Guide and
   Chart 69: When to use a Particular Process or Technique

Chart 54
PRESSURES ON THE BUSINESS

This framework helps to identify the opportunities and threats. Allow time at the start for everyone in a group to develop their individual ideas before sharing them and working towards agreed conclusions. Develop an agreed summary of opportunities and threats facing your business.

Having worked on the external perspectives turn to the internal factors and do the same for the strengths and weaknesses of your organisation. Consider for example the financial strength and cash flow position of the business, the technology you use and your ability to adjust to a changing situation.

If the analytical work has been done by a sub-group or project team you should consider whether the analysis needs to be checked out with someone in authority. This may lead to a proposal for gathering additional data from other sources. Authority figures should be encouraged to add their ideas and to work with you until an agreed summary emerges. A quick glance at chart 41, The Phases of Change, will clarify that you are at the 'aligning perceptions' stage.

Sphere of Influence[3]

A further form of analysis which helps to establish understanding of the current situation is to look at your sphere of influence. This technique can be used for your organisation, your department or yourself. It is particularly illuminating to do this for yourself first. Get a large sheet of paper and write the word 'me' in a small circle in the centre of the page. Next draw lines radiating from this to represent all the people you have contact with and influence in the course of your work. They do, of course, also influence you, but that is healthy and influence is usually most effective when it is mutual.

Consider the people you work with most closely – your subordinates, your peers, your boss, and any secretarial or other support service people you are in contact with regularly. Are there other people you meet from different departments or in committees you attend? Add them to your chart. Next consider people outside the organisation: any professional bodies you belong to, committees you sit on, any service organisations such as accountants, bankers, insurance people, suppliers, or contractors you deal with? Add them. Are there any other work people you meet or any people you should contact to make your job more effective? Add them also.

Now look at your home and social life and add people in your immediate family, other relatives, friends, sports colleagues, acquaintances in church and social clubs, and add them. Don't forget people from whom you receive professional services at home, and your bank manager, garage mechanic, etc.

Are there any people to whom you should give time but do not do so at present, or people who will be coming into your sphere of influence in the near future? Add these to your chart.

The first time you do this you will probably be surprised at how many people are within your 'sphere of influence'. If you never seem to have enough time, this is strongly affected by the number of people you wish to see and/or people who make demands on your time, and the quality of the interaction you have with each person. When the sphere of influence map is complete, review the sort of contact you have with each person identified on it. Note beside each name the current state of your relationship:

(1) Satisfactory, continue unchanged.
(2) Discontinue, contact no longer necessary.
(3) Unsatisfactory relationship, improve.
(4) New relationship to be developed.

When this has been done, consider each category in turn. First have a quiet celebration about all those relationships which are satisfactory and need no attention. Next look at those you wish to discontinue. Plan how to close these down but make sure that the other party will not continue to make demands on your time. Think about how you can do this diplomatically. This should help to free a little time.

Next consider the unsatisfactory relationships. They probably take up more of your time than they should. Plan a strategy to raise this issue with each of these people and work with them on how your relationship might be improved. This is not your normal work agenda and will need to be introduced tactfully when you both have the time and inclination to do something about it. Obviously it will be easier to tackle this if the other party also feels that the relationship is unsatisfactory. Consider using 'role negotiation' (*see* chart 64) to change how you work together.

Finally look at the new relationships you wish to develop and plan how you will manage the first few meetings in order to establish the right relationship from the start. Invest some time in getting to know the other person so that you can agree the best way to work together. This will require careful thought to avoid the early contact being focused entirely on work issues, with both parties implicitly assuming that the relationship will take care of itself.

An example of the sphere of influence of a managing director is given in chart 55. This shows that there are 53 people within the MD's direct sphere of influence. The relationships with thirty-six are considered satisfactory and six are no longer needed or can be transferred to someone else; six relationships are unsatisfactory and need to be improved and a further five are new and need to be developed. The analysis has focused attention on a relatively small number of people where something needs to be done. The next step is to prioritise those that need attention and plan how to take appropriate action.

The whole process of analysis and follow through takes time but those who use this sort of systematic method have found that it helps enormously with time management, leads to increased effectiveness, creates space for new initiatives, cultivates friendships and makes life more enjoyable. Keep your notes and review the situation again in three months, six months and a year later. You will be surprised how much you can change your sphere of influence.

This method has been described for you as an individual, but it can also be used for your department, and it is then used by the group to work out the same answers for the departmental role, focusing on work issues only. Personal commitments should be acknowledged, but need to be developed individually. They can still be shared in the group if this is agreed.

Chart 55: Sphere of Influence

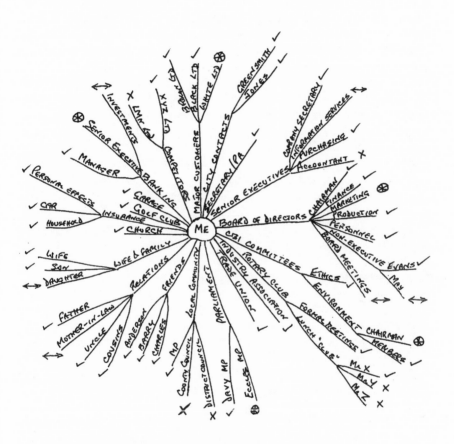

✓ Satisfactory, continue unchanged	36
✗ Discontinue, contact no longer necessary	6
↔ Unsatisfactory relationship, improve	6
⊕ New relationship to be developed	5

Attitude Surveys and Organisation Culture

Further depth can be added to your organisational analysis by carrying out an attitude survey among staff. However, bear in mind that this sort of initiative raises expectations, enhances the belief that the board or top executive group is interested in staff views, and that changes indicated by the survey findings will be addressed. Many organisations have carried out attitude surveys which have not been followed up, and the main result is that staff become cynical and disillusioned. It makes it harder to face up to change next time. It is also easy to take a top level decision to carry out an attitude survey, without middle management commitment. Staff views which are critical of 'management' usually fail to distinguish the level of management. Middle managers feel resentful that their jobs have been made more difficult by the survey which they never wanted. This does not decry the value of attitude surveys, but does suggest that they need to be carefully planned if they are to be really useful and give value for money.

Rather different information can be obtained by using a questionnaire to analyse the current organisation culture. The Organisation Culture Inventory (OCI) (*see* chart 43) has already been mentioned in chapter 9. This is one of many ways in which the culture of an organisation can be identified. The value of the OCI is that the same chart can be used later to describe the desired organisation culture, and it is compatible with other questionnaires dealing with management styles – which is very helpful when the change process begins.

Staff capability can be analysed by using various approaches to 'competency assessment', which has grown in popularity in recent years. Advice on sources of help can be obtained from various professional bodies such as the Institute of Personnel Management, or the Association for Management Education and Development.[4]

Before we leave the question of the current situation, it is important to identify the performance criteria in current use at the corporate level, as well as for main business units and departments. It is worth noting, in particular, the extent to which these criteria cover all the important areas where the business is experiencing pressure from external forces (chart 54). It may be illuminating to discover that some external pressures have increased in strength because the organisation failed to recognise them as important areas, where results matter. If they are recognised as important it is probable that explicit performance criteria will be known, specific organisational objectives will be set and performance will be reviewed regularly.

For example an organisation may not identify emissions to the environment as an area where performance needs to be measured. When objectives (and performance criteria) for emission control are clearly established, performance should be reviewed regularly with direct links to the appraisal of named people, whose rewards may be influenced by their results. Organisations which do recognise the importance of emission control (at source) are establishing appropriate standards to monitor performance regularly, and to link this to the reward system. Very few, if any, companies are yet doing this well, but several are working at it.

Establishing the Desired Situation

Creating a Mission Statement

It might be necessary to revise your organisation's Mission Statement or establish one for the first time. The purpose of the Mission Statement is to define clearly the nature of the contribution the organisation intends to make to the community. It describes why the organisation exists. It is most useful when it is expressed in a single memorable sentence. For example, the following might apply to the named organisations:

(1) A television company: We produce and broadcast audio/visual programmes.
(2) An oil company: We find oil and market products derived from oil.
(3) A home heating services business: We regulate temperature in the home to provide comfort.

Once a Mission Statement of this kind has been agreed it should not be changed very often, but an annual check and more thorough review every five years, would be appropriate. Its value to the organisation is that it provides the central focus for all other activities. Any activity which does not come within the scope of the Mission Statement should not be embarked upon. For example the television company should not get into purely audio programmes, should not build up service functions such as studio development, canteens and building maintenance services, to the point where large numbers of staff are employed in ancillary services. The oil company should not diversify into other forms of energy or other sorts of business. The home heating services company should not move into commercial and industrial properties. All such developments are entirely feasible and might be the right thing to do, but should not be undertaken without first changing the Mission Statement.

The simple, unequivocal Mission Statement also helps staff at all levels to keep in mind the central purpose which guides all other activities. If it is well conceived and can be stated from memory, it acts as a source of confidence for all staff. It also clarifies for suppliers, distributors and customers the type of business they are dealing with and the area in which they need to excel.

Some people will be critical of this approach to Mission Statements because there is no reference to profits. That does not mean that profits are unimportant, it just highlights that profits measure performance rather than describe the nature of the business. A Mission Statement focusing on profits provides little help to people in the organisation, because many different activities can be undertaken profitably.

Some people will object to simple Mission Statements because they fail to acknowledge all stakeholders and the broad area of public responsibility. Where organisations have developed comprehensive Mission Statements they do not seem very 'user friendly'. It is better to keep the Mission Statement simple, but to back this up with a clear statement of values, appropriate policies, market strategies, and objectives set, in all areas where results matter.

Once the Mission Statement, and the statement of values and policies, have been established the strategies for achieving the mission need to be determined and objectives set in all areas where results matter – including profits. The elements of organisation design are represented diagrammatically in chart 34 (chapter 7).

In summary the value of a simple Mission Statement is to:

- give the whole business a memorable guiding focus;
- help staff to feel confident about their own personal contribution;
- enable suppliers, distributors and customers to know what sort of business they are dealing with; and
- provide the basis from which strategies, policies and objectives can be developed.

If you want to develop a Mission Statement for your business, two very different approaches can be used. One is thorough, elaborate, requires external help and takes time to do well. The other is simple and quick but often produces a practical and useful result to which people feel committed.

The more thorough, elaborate method involves visualising the future of the business. It is best done in a group with the help of a facilitator who is skilled in this way of working. The facilitator's role is to get the group into a relaxed frame of mind and ready to try out an approach which will seem weird and a long way removed from the practicalities of running a business. The members of the group are then guided towards visualising the future. They are encouraged to stay with any visions they have, however strange they may seem, and to share these with others in the group. The intention is to work with the visions using them as metaphors and analogies. Each person in turn describes their vision. Once this is completed the group identifies the common ground by looking at similarities between the different visions or metaphors. Any divergent visions are also explored and insights drawn from them. Sometimes they can be linked back to a central theme. If not, they may need to be acknowledged as distinct and different possibilities. Once the common ground has been agreed a brief Mission Statement can be written.

The alternative, quick method involves the group in identifying pairs of words – a verb and a noun – which describe what the organisation does or might do. It is important to allow time for individual thought, followed by the recording of all the ideas, without editing, on flipchart paper, and displaying these in the room. It is quite likely that thirty to fifty word pairs will emerge from the group. The next step is for each individual to work alone and identify which three verb/noun combinations (not necessarily from the same original pairs) come closest to describing the core of the future business. These pairs are underlined on the flipcharts and will probably result in about a dozen words being marked. The next step is to look for any underlined words which have similar meanings and see if any can be eliminated, but making sure that all the words that are distinct and different remain.

In the next step each individual is invited to develop a single sentence, as a first attempt at a Mission Statement, from the remaining marked words. Each sentence is then read out, and one is selected for the group to edit and improve. In due course a 'good enough' agreed statement should be the result and this becomes the Mission Statement. This is a rough and ready method but it has proved effective on many occasions, with a wide range of different people working in a variety of organisations. It also generates strong commitment from those who take part.

In larger organisations the process can be carried out in several groups each of whom develop a Mission Statement. This is often regarded as wasteful of time, and many people believe it may result in widely divergent statements which cannot be reconciled. However, in practice neither fear seems to materialise. The commitment generated by involvement is worth much more than the time it takes to work through the process, and it is surprising how much common ground there is between the Mission Statements that are generated by different groups. Another meeting, with someone from each group, can then agree the preferred Mission Statement. The final step is to get the statement endorsed by the chief executive of the parent organisation. In smaller organisations the chief executive should take part in the process, but this is impractical for all sub-units in very large companies.

Desired Organisation Culture and Structure

If the Organisation Culture Inventory (OCI) has been used to describe the current organisation culture, the same framework can be used to describe the culture required to achieve the desired future organisation. Work with the OCI chart will have created good understanding of all twelve elements of the OCI framework. The task then is to shade in the clock face to indicate the degree to which each element should be present if the organisation is to become fully effective. This should be done individually then agreed as a group. Chart 43 (chapter 9) describes how this method works.

In considering the organisation's structure it is helpful to invert the pyramid.[5] Most organisation charts are drawn with one person at the top, those who report to that individual on the next level, and so on until the base of the pyramid identifies those who, for different industries, meet customers, work at the coal face, drive the buses or work in the factories. Another way to look at organisation structure is to invert the pyramid. Place at the top those who interface with the customers. This, after all, is where buying decisions are made. Without customers there is no business. Every activity in the business can then be regarded as helping those who deal with customers. Each level contributes to successful outcomes at the customer interface, until at the base of the inverted pyramid we come to the managing director, whose task is to empower and enable all others, and the board. A typical inverted pyramid is shown in chart 56.

Chart 56: Inverted Pyramid Structure

Most organisations have one crucial interface with the outside world, usually where the transactions with customers take place.

For example:

    For transport organisations with passengers
    For banks with their customers
    For supermarkets with shoppers
    For service organisations with their clients
    For hospitals with patients

If the business transacted at this interface is unsatisfactory in the eyes of the passenger/customer/shopper/client/patient then the organisation is in jeopardy of losing that business. From this it can be argued that there is no other interface that is as important and all functions of the business should be geared to ensuring that the highest standards of quality apply at the customer interface.

This has led to the development of the inverted pyramid structure for organisations which places the customer at the top of the picture and everything else in support as shown below. The diagram is inevitably a simplification and does not show all functions.

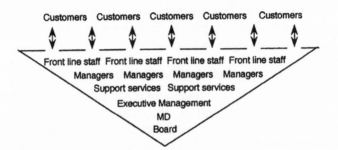

Managing the Transition

Identifying Change Goals

Make use of all the work done to identify the current situation and the work done to describe the desired future situation, to develop clarity about what needs to be changed. Clear 'change goals' are different from organisational goals. For example the organisation goal might be to have an achieving, satisfying, cooperative culture. The change goal will be different for an organisation which has a strong autocratic culture, from that of an organisation with a weak, compromising and passive culture.

Using the results of the analytical work, the organisation's change goals can be identified by summarising:

- the current situation;
- the desired situation; and
- the change goals.

This should be done to cover all three areas identified on chart 40 (chapter 9), namely:

- the nature of the business and desired performance;
- organisation culture and staff capability; and
- environmental impact.

In the phases of change model (see chart 41), this work comes under the broad heading of developing a strategy.

Change Management Roles

When a significant organisational change project is initiated it needs to be managed in the same way as any other important work. The change management roles need to be identified and some form of temporary organisation structure set up to see the change through to completion. Experience has shown that if this is not done then current work tends to take precedence and the change initiative is neglected.

The roles for effective management of change are:

- executive authority – the sponsor;
- strategic integration – the steering group;
- project responsibility – the project group; and
- resources – those who will run events and be facilitators.

Executive Authority

Executive authority rests with the most senior person associated with the change and is, in effect, the sponsor of the change initiative. It is important to identify this individual because a person with this level of authority ha˄ considerable positive influence, but is also able to stop the initiative at any time. Many change projects have ceased before completion, when they have lost their sponsor, when the authority figure finds out about a project but had not taken on the role of sponsor, or when the sponsor changes his/her mind.

Let us assume that the sponsor is the managing direction. The MD has so many other responsibilities that it is seldom possible for him or her to provide the strategic direction, unaided, for a major change project. For this purpose a steering group is required. This should be at a very senior level, probably chaired by a director. The role of the steering group is to provide the strategic direction, which includes balancing the demands of the change initiative with the need to maintain current operations and business effectiveness in the short term. If no steering group is appointed, or if it lacks authority, the urgent demands of the present business will usually take precedence over the important demands of the change initiative and the latter suffers or dies. The steering group's role, which is a part-time responsibility for senior people, is crucial for successful change management.

The steering group cannot carry out all the operational requirements for managing the change, planning specific initiatives, identifying and briefing people who will play a part, collecting information, analysing suggestions, setting up new systems, arranging the appropriate flow of information, and monitoring progress. These are the functions of the project group which, for most major change assignments, needs at least one, probably more, full time staff with appropriate skills. The project group reports to the steering group and carries out the implementation plan. This is a demanding role over a short period of a few months, or sometimes a few years depending on the complexity of the change initiative and the time it will take to establish the changes effectively.

Finally there are the specialist resources required to make the change happen. Many organisations use a mixture of internal and external people for this purpose. If all the resources are internal, it is likely that there is insufficient change management experience, and good people are diverted from other work. If all the resources are external, people within the organisation are deprived of excellent learning opportunities, and the external people have insufficiently close contact with, and knowledge of, current operations, to be able to blend the change initiative with current work. A good mix of internal and external people achieves the desired effect of bringing in relevant up-to-date experience, enabling close contact with current operations to be maintained and providing excellent development opportunities for company staff.

A summary of change management roles is provided in chart 57.[6]

Chart 57: Change Management Roles

Roles	Incumbent(s)	Key functions
Sponsor	Top executive such as the MD	Provide support, Encourage, Set example, Monitor progress (via Steering Group)
Steering Group	Senior executive level group	Set strategic direction, Balance operational and change requirements, Guide Project Group, Monitor progress (via Project Group), Set example
Project Group	Project Manager with line management experience, mix of line managers, internal and external people with change management skills	Reporting to Steering Group, Planning & implementing the change initiative, Monitoring progress
Resources	Prime requirement is for specialists - both internal and external - who understand the process of change management.	Assist the Project Group to carry through all aspects of the assignment.

Assessing and Enhancing the Willingness to Change

Let us assume that you are in a key role and responsible for a particular change involving your organisation. One thing you will do is assess which of your colleagues are likely to support you and the change initiative. This can be taken further if carried out systematically. Make a list of the people who occupy significant roles affecting the change for which you are responsible. Consider each person in terms of her or his willingness to support the change initiative and his or her ability to work in ways that are consistent with what will be required in the new situation. Record your assessment on a chart drawn up like chart 58.[7]

This is a sound basis for approaching the people from whom you can expect support, and identifies those who are likely to be less willing and able to give their support. Using the same list of people consider each person's attitude towards the change as it is now and as you would like it to be. This can be recorded on a layout such as chart 59.[8]

Chart 58: Assessing Willingness and Ability

Name	Willingness to Support Change			Ability to work consistently		
	High	Moderate	Low	High	Will learn	Poor

Chart 59: Attitudes Towards the Change

Name	Opposing	Abstaining	Allowing	Supporting	Leading

Use different symbols to indicate the present attitude P, and the attitude you believe is necessary N, to achieve the change. The gap between these two represents what needs to be done with all key people in order to bring about the desired change. In many cases it will be necessary to influence people to move towards a column further to the right, but not necessarily all the way. Not everybody should be actively leading the change initiative. In a few cases you might wish to move someone from right to left; for example if an individual is giving inappropriate support, and it would be better if that person took a more passive role and allowed the change to happen. It also enables you to check that the leadership role is located with the right person, or people, where the change involves several sub-units, each requiring a leader.

The analyses on Charts 58 and 59 provide the foundation for working out your influence strategy for each key person. When you are planning how to bring influence to bear, it is important to assess with reasonable accuracy each individual's capacity for change, which will be strongly influenced by that person's feelings of inner security. First consider their current level of security. This can be done by considering the forces which influence that person. These will emanate from pressures in society, organisational pressures and personal and family pressures. The combination of these pressures governs the feeling of inner security for each individual. If the level of security is either high or low the likelihood is that efforts to bring influence to bear will be rejected, data will be avoided and the validity of information will be denied. The high security people do this because they are over confident about the situation they are in, whereas the low security people are likely to feel threatened by changes they do not want.

The moderately secure people are most likely to react favourably to change. They will listen, search for relevant information, show tolerance towards others, seek personal development, be able to integrate new information, and show willingness to try out new ideas. A summary of the ways in which this works for most people is given in chart 60.

If you are dealing with moderately secure people it is probable that you can make good progress with your change initiative. However, in most situations there will be some people who have high or low security and fail to respond favourably to your attempts to influence them. This gives rise to the need to find ways in which to influence their levels of security rather than to influence them to accept the change.

How can high and low security people be moved towards moderate security? Two broad approaches are available. The first is to help people see the limitations in their situation, the second is to create a vision of a desirable future.

Chart 60
ASSESSING THE CAPACITY FOR CHANGE

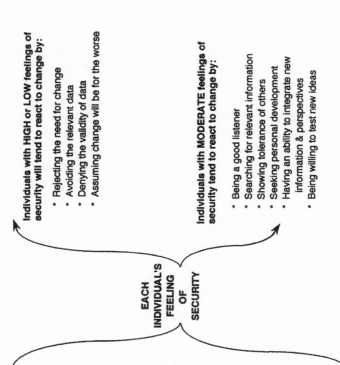

Pressures from Society

Economic tends
Unemployment
Crime rates
Changing values
Legislation
Fiscal measures
Environmental threats
Density & growth of population
Pressure groups
Prevailing political culture

Organisational Pressures

Economic performance
Market trends
Future corporate security
Personal job security
Status of department
Organisation culture
Attitudes towards risk

Personal & Family Pressures

Income / expenditure balance
Motivation for achievement
Family tensions
Knowledge & skills matched to
   nature of work & its demands
Tolerance of uncertainty
Location of home
Commitment to family

EACH
INDIVIDUAL'S
FEELING
OF
SECURITY

Individuals with HIGH or LOW feelings of
security will tend to react to change by:

* Rejecting the need for change
* Avoiding the relevant data
* Denying the validity of data
* Assuming change will be for the worse

Individuals with MODERATE feelings of
security tend to react to change by:

* Being a good listener
* Searching for relevant information
* Showing tolerance of others
* Seeking personal development
* Having an ability to integrate new
   information & perspectives
* Being willing to test new ideas

Showing the limitations in the present situation is particularly appropriate for those who tend towards over confidence – disturb their feelings of security. With people who have low security, however, this approach is likely to make them feel even more insecure. It is, therefore, important to make a correct diagnosis of the level of security of a particular person who is rejecting the change. Limitations in the present situation can be shown by providing factual information, exploring – with care and skill – possible areas of emotional disquiet, and identifying special needs. All of this is designed to get the individual to face up to and accept the situation as it really is.

The second approach, which is particularly appropriate to people with low security, is to create in the mind of the person you are trying to influence, a vision of a desirable future state. This can be done by visualising favourable features, generating options about the future, matching the relevant options to expressed needs, and creating enthusiasm. All of this is designed to stimulate a desire for the change.

The combination of showing the limitations of the present and building a vision of the future encourages dissatisfaction with the present situation. If this is successful it creates tension in the person you are trying to influence. No one likes to remain in a state of tension for long, so there is a motivation to establish a more satisfactory and comfortable state. This is achieved either by changing or by rejecting the change.[9]

Those who now accept the change are most likely to have a moderate level of inner security (you have changed their level of felt security), believe there is a reasonable chance of success and are receiving appropriate support from colleagues. Some of those who still reject the change are people whose level of security has remained low, they are doubtful that the change can be accomplished successfully, and there is little or no support available from colleagues. Those who reject the change because their level of security is high probably do so because the change is irrelevant to their own agenda. The steps involved in enhancing the capacity for change are shown in chart 61.

Although the way in which influence can be brought to bear is described in Charts 60 and 61, we have not addressed the question of who takes the initiative. If you are working alone it obviously rests with you, but in many situations a group of people will be working together and it is possible to identify who is most likely to be successful in influencing others. Sometimes the choice of person to take the initiative is the most important factor, and should be worked out with some care.

By way of summary, another method of assessing the willingness of different people to learn and change is with the help of a graph. This is shown in chart 62, and indicates that learning and change is at its greatest when the feeling of inner security is moderate. Those with high secu-

Chart 61
ENHANCING THE CAPACITY FOR CHANGE

INCREASE AWARENESS OF THE PRESENT SITUATION:

* Highlight limitations
* Provide facts and logic
* Explore emotional disquiet
* Indentify needs
* Build ownership of the true situation

NB: The above is most relevant with high security people but beware of those who mask low security with false bravado.

CREATE A VISION OF A DESIRABLE FUTURE:

* Visualise favourable features
* Generate options
* Match relevant options to expressed needs
* Create enthusiasm
* Stimulate the desire for change

Both approaches encourage dissatisfaction with the present situation which creates

TENSION

which stimulates a drive towards a more satisfactory state

Change occurs when:

* The feeling of inner security has moved to MODERATE
* There is reasonable confidence that the change will be successful
* Appropriate support from others is available

Change is rejected when:

* Inner security remains LOW or HIGH
* There is little confidence that the change can be accomplished successfully
* there is no appropriate support

rity need to be moved towards moderate security by helping them to recognise the limitations of their present state. Those with low security need to be moved towards moderate security by building confidence in a future vision.

Force Field Analysis[10]

We now turn to the analysis of particular situations, and identify the helping and hindering forces that will influence them. Force field analysis is a method that can be applied, using the back of an envelope, in a few minutes to clarify a situation you are about to face; or it can be used much more thoroughly, alone or in a group, to take stock of a complex situation. It is a technique that can be used for various purposes, including:

- analysing personal blocks in change situations;
- diagnosing any current situation; and
- analysing and prioritising action plans.

In using force field analysis to diagnose a situation, the first step is to identify the situation you want to address. Write a brief description, in a sentence or two, of the desired situation. Then identify all the helping and hindering forces that have a bearing on this situation. List all the helping forces which are driving towards the desired situation, in the left hand column, and the hindering forces which are blocking progress, in the right hand column.

Most situations are held in a state of equilibrium by a balance of hindering and helping forces. The typical way to try to bring about change is to increase the number or strength of the helping forces. This is seldom effective, because hindering forces quickly build up to resist the change. It is much more effective to look at what can be done to reduce or eliminate the hindering forces. This facilitates change because the resisting forces have been reduced and the balance altered. A diagrammatic representation of force field analysis is shown in chart 63.

Once the analysis of helping and hindering forces has been completed, it is necessary to work out which three or four hindering forces would make a significant difference if reduced or eliminated. This sharpens the focus for planning how this might be done.

Role Negotiation[11]

When two people who work together find that they are not cooperating, and the relationship is strained, it can help if they take part in a formal role negotiation with a facilitator. The focus of a meeting of this kind is to improve the way the two people work together, and to agree how this might be done. It is important to have a facilitator, because it is very easy

Chart 62
LEARNING AND CHANGE

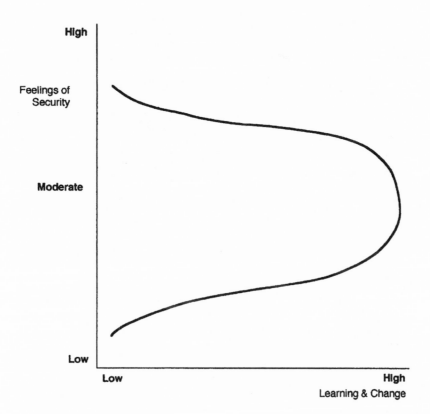

Notes:

1. People learn most and are better able to cope with change when they feel moderately secure.

2. Learning and the ability to change is less when people feel very secure (over confident) or very insecure (fearful)

Chart 63
FORCE FIELD ANALYSIS

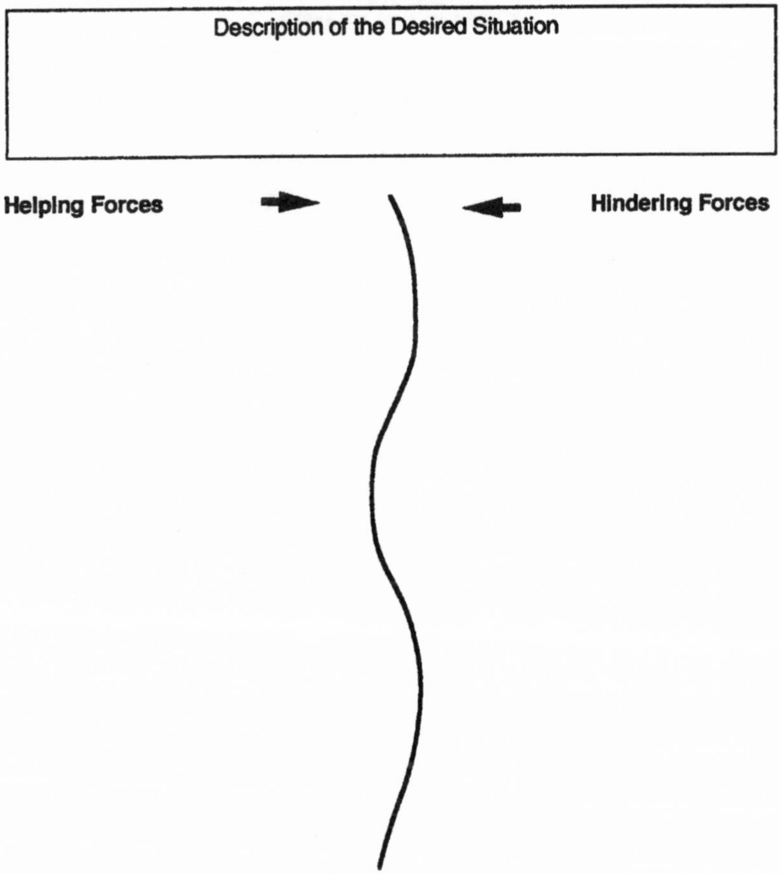

Description of the Desired Situation

Helping Forces   ➡️   ⬅️   **Hindering Forces**

Notes:

1. To develop helping and hindering forces consider many perspectives such as Human (personal, group, intergroup, organisational, and the wider community), Economics, Technological and Environmental (physical resources and biodiversity).

2. When all helping and hindering forces have been identified select the 3 or 4 hindering forces which, if reduced or eliminated, would make a real difference in achieving the desired situation.

3. Plan how to reduce or eliminate the selected hindering forces.

for the protagonists to lapse into their typical mode of communication characterised by poor listening, reluctance to share information, being obstructive, using aggressive behaviour and failing to reach agreement.

Prior to the role negotiation it is important for the facilitator to check out that both parties are agreeable to come to a meeting, away from both person's offices, are willing to prepare for the meeting, and agree to the facilitator's role. This role is concerned with setting out the process, helping to clarify and summarise as appropriate, but taking no part in the content of the meeting or the decisions. The preparation involves both parties in focusing on 'what they see the other doing' and making notes on specific examples of recent events, for their own use in answer to three questions:

(1) What I see you doing which helps me in my role, and that I would like you to continue to do, or do more.
(2) What I see you doing which gets in my way, and I would like you to stop doing, or do less.
(3) What I would like you to start doing, because if you did, it would help me in my role.

When the two people meet the facilitator sets the scene and describes the process for the meeting. This involves one person giving his or her answer(s) to the first question and the other person paraphrasing what is said. Since this is good news it is usually easy to listen to and sets a positive climate for the rest of the meeting. The roles are then reversed and the second person gives their answer(s) to the first question. Again this is paraphrased. The protagonist in the listening role should be encouraged to get the full message accurately, and should demonstrate that this has happened by accurate paraphrasing. The facilitator should not allow further comments, explanations and additions.

Once both parties have dealt with their responses to the first question the second question is addressed in the same way, and in turn. Again the listener's role is to *really* listen, and to paraphrase accurately. At this stage there should be no attempt to either agree or disagree. The task is to understand what the other person wants you to stop doing, or do less.

The third question is then addressed in the same way by each in turn. Once all three questions have been covered by both parties it is time to review the process and how both parties feel. The final step should begin with a little time for individual work, followed by each party in turn describing what they are willing to do differently, what they need more time to consider, and what they do not feel able to do.

The experience of role negotiation with managers working in different organisations and at various levels of seniority is that it usually works very well. A great deal of the dissatisfaction is because of misunderstand-

Chart 64: Role Negotiation

Objective:

To improve the role relationship of two people who need to cooperate more effectively.

Preparation

Each person prepares for the forthcoming meeting by making notes on the other person's behaviour, recalling specific events and examples wherever possible, in answer to the following questions:

1 What I see you doing which I like because it helps me, please continue to do these things.

2 What I see you doing which I dislike because it hinders me, please stop doing these things or do them less.

3 What I would like you to start doing because it would help me.

At the meeting:

A A "neutral" location should be used. Allow at least 2 hours for the meeting, preferably half a day. The improvement in relationship will enable you both to save more than this amount of time within weeks.

B It is desirable to have a facilitator to help manage the process as indicated below.

C Person "A" describes his or her answers to Q1. "B" listens and paraphrases fairly frequently before recall is lost. The goal is to achieve understanding and to demonstrate that this has been achieved. There should be no discussion or response. Roles are then reversed and "B" describes her or his answers to Q1. "A" listens and paraphrases.

D Repeat the same procedure for Q2 and then Q3. Remember that the goal is to achieve understanding of the other person's point of view and to demonstrate that this has been achieved. There should be no discussion, denial, explanations or disagreement at this stage.

E After each person has completed the response to all three Questions take a break and individually each person should prepare notes on:

   * What you are willing and able to do now
   * What you need time to think about
   * What you feel unable to do

F Meet again to describe your answers and again paraphrase what the other person is telling you. Remember that the goal is to improve your role relationship - not necessarily to meet every request from your colleague, or to have every one of your requests met.

G If the climate is favourable negotiate further progress towards meeting each other's requests, or when to meet again.

H Conclude the meeting by sharing feelings about yourself and your colleague.

ings, lack of awareness and not facing up to difficulties when they first arise. About 80 per cent of the requests for changes made by both parties can be implemented without too much difficulty. A further advantage of effective role negotiation is that the changed relationship has spin-off benefits for others, and provides both parties with a new awareness which can be used in other situations.

Role negotiation can also be used outside the work situation – for example in club committees, within families and to help partners to find out how to relate better to each other.

Negotiating Skills

Negotiating skills can be very helpful when dealing with people and situations where the parties involved are not necessarily in a close role relationship. They can be used in one-to-one situations or in a group and applied whenever an agreed solution is required.

It is important to distinguish between negotiations when one party achieves what they want while the other does not (win/lose negotiations) and a negotiated settlement when both or all parties feel they have a good outcome (win/win negotiations). The latter is emphasised here because it is consistent with the theme of this book and with the idea of empowerment. It is also important for each party to be aware of the distinction between the preferred outcome and the necessary minimum that is acceptable.

Effective negotiation depends on sound preparation and on establishing a climate which is conducive to productive outcomes in the interests of all those taking part. Once the negotiation begins four things are very important:

(1) Exploration of needs and 'coinage' or bargaining counters.
(2) Clear and effective bidding and bargaining.
(3) Effective behaviour, especially listening, and asserting.
(4) Testing for and agreeing outcomes.

Good outcomes are dependent on all four elements being used skilfully. The exploration of needs establishes the outcomes sought by those involved, while the exploration of 'coinage' discovers what each party has that can be used as bargaining counters to meet the needs of others. It is surprising how creative people can be when this step is carried out openly in an atmosphere of trust. It is also salutary to discover that people do have coinage which does not involve money directly. Being open about needs and coinage does not mean that there has to be total disclosure about bids and desired outcomes. The early exploratory stage offers many opportunities to practise listening skills and to demonstrate the ability to paraphrase accurately what others are saying.

The bidding stage is helped by clear, assertive statements of requirements at least as an opening position. Once the bids are out in the open the bargaining starts, and this is where the creative work on needs and coinage proves so helpful. During bidding and bargaining it is very important to listen accurately and to demonstrate understanding by accurate paraphrasing. Experience shows that the best negotiators are those who combine the skills of listening, summarising, and describing how each party's stated needs can be met.

Emphasis has been placed on listening, and on clear assertive statements when bidding. Those who are naturally gifted with these skills are well placed in negotiation, but others may need to develop them. Throughout the negotiation there is scope for many mini-negotiations on such things as procedures at meetings, when to take breaks, starting and finishing times and dates and venue for future meetings. These all provide less experienced negotiators with opportunities to develop their skills.

The final stage of a negotiation is often crucial and it is important to work hard for mutually agreed outcomes while avoiding the risk of giving too much away.

When an oil company wanted to drill for oil on land owned by the Coal Board there was no obvious reason why the Board should agree. However, the search for appropriate 'coinage' resulted in an offer to resurface the access road leading in to a particular coal mine, in exchange for the right to drill at the desired site. At the time, the Coal Board had very limited funds and the access road was badly in need of repair, so they agreed to the deal.

Many examples can be found in sponsorship arrangements. For example, a leading private bank arranged an exhibition of the work of wildlife artists. The bank gained favourable publicity by providing their customers with an outstanding exhibition, and associated themselves with the environmental cause, while the artists exhibited their paintings and sculptures and sold some of their work.

A framework identifying the main phases in effective negotiation towards win/win results is given in chart 65.

Action Planning

At the end of any meeting it is important to allow time to clarify what action needs to be taken, by whom and by when. This is self evident, but if left to the last minute there is insufficient time to do this important work well. Sometimes it is done in a hurry and the action required is noted, but who will do it and the time for completion or reporting back is not made clear. To overcome this problem a simple framework can be very helpful, such as that in chart 66.[12] This enables all the tasks to be list-

Chart 65:
NEGOTIATING SKILLS

The frameworks below provide guidlines for negotiating. The first explains the phases of the negotiating process, the second an outline for individual preparation prior to negotiations:

The Negotiating Process:

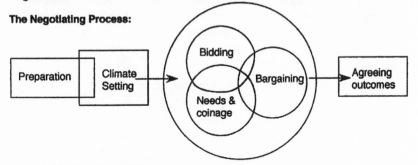

A Framework for Preparation:

My Needs	Other Person's Needs
Other Person's Coinage ↕	My Coinage ↕
My Desired Outcome	Other's Desired Outcome
My Necessary Outcome	Other's Necessary Outcome

ed in the left hand column, provides three columns to write in who will authorise the work, who is responsible for doing it, who will provide support (such as resources) and in the final column when progress should be reported and the task completed. Ideally this should be completed, and photocopies distributed to those present, before the meeting breaks up. Any other notes or minutes can follow, with another copy of the action sheet attached. Meetings which develop a discipline of this kind significantly enhance their effectiveness.

Communications Strategy

Every period of change is disturbing, and if those affected are not kept informed about what is happening and advised about progress towards desired goals, the outcomes can be seriously undermined. To avoid such problems a good communications strategy is necessary. This means thinking about who needs to know about the change – both within the organisation and outside it. Once this is clear the important questions need to be answered: what should they be told, how will it be done, who will do it, when and how frequently do people need to be given up-dated information? Chart 67 summarises a framework for a communications strategy.

Human Reactions to Change[13]

We have developed several guidelines for helping organisations to understand change and manage it effectively. As we have progressed through the various processes and techniques we have moved from the individual to groups and to the whole organisation. Let us now return to the ways in which people react to change. The change may be very close to home, such as the sudden illness or death of a loved one. It may affect home and work such as being declared redundant. It may just affect work such as an unexpected job move, a promotion, or the appointment of a new boss. It may affect the whole organisation, such as a takeover by another organisation. Some of these changes will be brought about by environmental pressures.

Everyone will have their own experience of change, and can judge the validity of the generalisations described in chart 68. There is a sequence of reactions which most people go through. When bad news breaks, the sequence usually begins with an initial state of shock, and is generally accompanied by a drop in performance. After a short while there is often a feeling that the news cannot be true; there is rejection and disbelief. During this period there may be an improvement in performance, but it tends to be short lived. This reaction is frequently followed by blaming others for the situation that exists. This phase can last for some time, but as the realisation dawns that the bad news is true, the next phase is often one of self-blame. When this starts to settle, productive work begins to be

Chart 66
ACTION PLANNING

TASKS TO BE CARRIED OUT	WHO AUTHORISES	WHO TAKES ACTION	WHO GIVES SUPPORT	DATES TO REVIEW PROGRESS / COMPLETE

Chart 67: Communications Strategy

Every significant change programme affects a lot of people. The changes always go more smoothly when people are kept informed. These guidelines provide a simple checklist of the key points to consider:

1 Who will be affected by the change?

2 Who needs to be kept informed?

- Managers
- Trade Unions
- Staff
- Senior Executives
- Members of the Board/Council
- Other Departments
- Other organisations
- Suppliers, Distributors, Contractors
- Professional bodies
- The media
- Others

3 What will each group be told? The same message for everyone is unlikely to be appropriate - each will want to know how it affects them - but consistency of the core message is important

4 How will this be done? Consider written, verbal and audio/visual - how will each message be 'packaged'?

5 An important consideration will be to decide how to handle good and bad news. Should it be mixed or separated and if so which should come first? Bear in mind what happens to the ability of people to listen after hearing news which comes as a shock.

6 Who will be responsible for which parts? The credibility of those delivering the message is important. If several people are involved how will consistency be achieved?

7 When will the message be delivered? Timing of the initial message is important as is maintaining appropriate updates

8 Most situations will require a several communications over a period of time. Plan how the overall communications will be applied and how it will fit in with other regular communications.

9 How will success of the communications strategy be reviewed and who will do this, when?

restored and there is a search for new meaning in the circumstances that now exist. This progresses to problem solving and finally to the integration of new ideas and behaviour and the restoration of good performance, often at a level higher than before the change. These phases of the human reaction to change are shown in chart 68.

Chart 68
HUMAN REACTIONS TO CHANGE

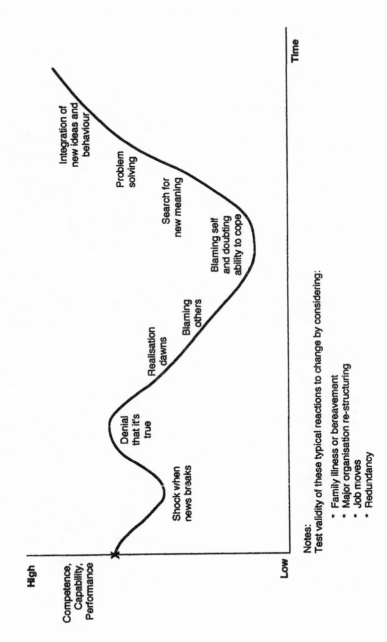

High

Competence,
Capability,
Performance

Shock when
news breaks

Denial
that it's
true

Realisation
dawns

Blaming
others

Blaming self
and doubting
ability to cope

Search for
new meaning

Problem
solving

Integration of
new ideas and
behaviour

Time

Low

Notes:
Test validity of these typical reactions to change by considering:

* Family illness or bereavement
* Major organisation re-structuring
* Job moves
* Redundancy

Chart 69: When to Use a Particular Process or Technique

Process or Technique (Chart No) What it Achieves

Understanding Self:

* The Change Equation (Chapter 5)
* Assesses personal readiness for change

* Sphere of Influence Analysis (55)
* Identifies the people within your sphere of influence and where attention is required

* Force Field Analysis (63)
* Can be used to identify personal blocks which impede your ability to tackle a change situation

* Human Reactions to Change (68)
* Describes typical human reactions to change

* Values, Beliefs & Culture (15)
* How to use feedback to modify your behaviour and review your beliefs and values

* Conflict Resolution (16)
* Analyses conflict situations you need to deal with

* Negotiating Skills (65)
* How to plan for and approach a negotiating situation

* Ideas which will make a difference (22)
* Review which of these ideas are consistent with your own thinking and actions.

* Sustainable Society - A Vision (23)
* How does this compare with your vision?

* The JIMM Theory (29)
* How does this theory affect you and your world?

Influencing Others:

* The Change Equation (Chapter 5)
* Identifies what blocks another person's ability to change

* Conflict Resolution (16)
* Suggests ways to resolve disagreements

* Assessing Willingness & Ability (58)
* Identifies key people and their willingness and ability to adjust to change

* Attitudes Towards Change (59)
* Identifies key peoples and their attitude towards a particular change

* Assessing the Capacity for Change (60)
* Assesses another person's capacity for change

* Enhancing the Capacity for Change (61)
* Shows how to enhance another person's capacity for change

* Force Field Analysis (63)
* Identifies helping and hindering forces and which hindering forces to reduce or eliminate

* Role Negotiation (64)
* To enable two people to build a more effective working relationship

* Negotiating Skills (65)
* Key principles to use in a negotiating situation

When to use a Particular Process or Technique

Working in a Group:

* The Change Equation (Chapter 5)* To identify what stops a group from changing how it works
* Support & Challenge Groups (17)* To improve individual and group effectiveness
* Effectiveness in small groups (38)   * How to help groups towards maturity & effectiveness
* Managing Meetings at three levels (39)   * Identifies the three levels at which meetings need to be managed
* Sphere of Influence Analysis (55)   * When done for a group identifies all the people with whom a group has contact and which contacts need attention
* Change Management Roles (57)   * Identifies the important roles for managing organisational change effectively
* Force Field Analysis (63)   * Identifies the helping and hindering forces and which hindering forces to reduce or eliminate
* Action Planning (66)   * A simple but powerful framework to agree action plans at the end of meetings
* Communications Strategy (67)   * A checklist for an effective communications strategy

Developing an Organisation:

* The Change Equation (Chapter 5)* Identifies what blocks an organisation from changing
* An Organisation Model (34)   * Improves understanding of organisations, how they work and might be developed
* An Organisation Change Model (40)   * Elements to consider to bring about organisational change
* The Phases of Change (41)   * How the phases need to be managed to gain competitive advantage
* Identifying the Pressures (54) * Identifies the external pressures on an organisation
* Inverted Pyramid Structure (56)* Shows another way to look at Organisation Structure
* Change Management Roles (57)   * Identifies the key roles for managing organisational change effectively
* Communications Strategy (67)   * Describes the basic requirements for communications strategy during a change initiative

© Colin Hutchinson, *Vitality and Renewal*, Adamantine, 1994

Monitoring the Transition

It is important to monitor the progress of any major project. This is especially important for projects involving organisational change, because there are so many forces striving to keep things as they are. Every effort should be made to use the strength of established procedures. If there is a planning cycle which is well established and includes preparing business plans and budgets, then these same procedures should be used to incorporate the change programme. This will help to bring the management of change alongside the management of the business. This can be done in many areas. For example if a new organisation culture requires rather different behaviour from staff, the recruitment criteria should be altered to search for the sort of staff who will be required in the future. When performance appraisals are carried out everything to do with the change programme should also be reviewed – not just the usual bottom line results. The reward system, both formal and informal, should be adjusted to ensure that those who put real effort into bringing about the change are recognised, and that this recognition is made known.

It is essential for this kind of detail to be woven into the fabric of the organisation if the change goals are to be achieved.

It is also necessary to establish clear landmarks by which it is possible to judge how well the change programme is progressing towards the desired goal. These should be as clear as the landmarks and compass bearings are for a journey. They should also have timeframes associated with them, so that delays can be recognised early and adjustments made as appropriate.

Review meetings need to be scheduled and must take place, involving all those who are able to provide the relevant data to assess progress and with sufficient influence to take action if required.

It is equally important to acknowledge and celebrate success. If a difficult assignment is completed, an important aspect of the change programme carried out despite difficult circumstances, or if a particular landmark is achieved sooner than expected, then let people know. A lot of good work goes unnoticed, but with change management it is very important to celebrate success.

How to Select Appropriate Tools

Chart 69 contains a summary of this chapter, outlining the processes, techniques and tools described, grouped under four headings, with some appearing under more than one heading:

- understanding self;
- influencing others;

- working in a group; and
- developing an organisation.

In each case there is a short description of the main result that can be achieved by using a particular method.

Notes

1 Kanter, Rosabeth Moss, 1989, p. 371.
2 Vaughan and Mickle, 1993.
3 This approach is an adaptation of a method widely used by others under the name of 'domainal mapping' or the 'clover leaf' method. Its origin is unknown.
4 See Sources of Help.
5 The origin of the inverted pyramid is not known.
6 For comparison, see Beckhard and Harris, 1987, chapter 7.
7 Based on Beckhard and Harris, 1987, p. 63.
8 Based on Beckhard and Harris, 1987, p. 95.
9 Original work in this area is attributable to David Moscow.
10 Lewin, K, Field Theory in Social Science, Harper Bros, New York, 1951.
11 This is an adaptation of a method developed by Roger Harrison, Harrison Associates Inc, Berkeley, California.
12 For comparison, see Beckhard and Harris, 1987, p. 105 - 'Responsibility Charting.
13 This an adaptation of various models describing the human reactions to change. The original work in this area is unknown but probably comes from psychological research into the stages of shock.

12

Getting the Most from the Change Process and Process Consultants

A thorough understanding of human processes and the ability to improve such processes are fundamental to any organisational improvement

Edgar Schein[1]

We have seen in earlier chapters that there are many situations involving organisational change in which the issues are complex, the degree of change that is required is considerable, original and innovative solutions are needed, and the change has to be accomplished in a relatively short period of time. Much change is now stimulated by increasing interest in the social and environmental responsibilities of organisations which must still continue to make profits. In these circumstances many organisations believe that external help is required. This chapter provides a framework for looking at the juxtaposition of social and environmental responsibility, and addresses the question of how to get value for money and derive learning from the process of change. These issues are examined from the perspectives of the organisations seeking help and of those which provide it.

Organisations are familiar with the traditional areas directly related to economic performance, in which to seek external help. However, the changing scene of social and environmental pressure is opening up new areas of concern, which often results in the need for help from outside the business. Organisations at the leading edge of environmental policy formulation have often sought help from environmental consultants. In general this has been a quest for technical advice of various kinds and there has been a rapid growth in consultancies offering this kind of help.[2] Some companies have sought a dialogue with environmental organisations or advice from people who have been environmentalists at an earlier stage of their lives.

Many organisations are wary of employing consultants and would prefer to undertake their own studies. This works well when the purpose is to find out more about the business in order to tackle the issues. It also works well when people who are well versed in change management skills are available within the organisations. It does not, however, work well when there is an absence of in-house resources and when it is necessary to provide an impartial assessment which can only to obtained from an independent, professional auditing organisation.

For those who wish to carry out an environmental review a simple guide is available from the Confederation of British Industry.[3] If a more thorough environmental investigation is desired and internal resources are to be used, a 'do-it-yourself' review is available from Business in the Environment.[4] This provides a framework for systematically reviewing all aspects of environmental impact and devising policies for dealing with the issues. Alternatively it can be used as a preliminary investigation to discover the areas in which a professional environmental audit is needed. In either case the review guide requires a significant amount of study in order to understand how to use it effectively. A third option is available whereby people can learn how to carry out an environmental audit by attending a suitable course such as Brunel's *Environmental Audit: Hands-on*.[5]

The concept of social auditing is also re-emerging. This focuses on an organisation's social and moral responsibilities which may be written into the Articles of Association but which, in practice, are given very little attention. This is because the legal requirement is to report on economic performance, while social responsibility reporting is left to the discretion of the directors. Social responsibility covers all the ways in which an organisation's activities impact on customers, staff, local communities, the wider community, and shareholders. Traidcraft Exchange and The New Economics Foundation have embarked on a joint social audit of the ways in which Traidcraft plc performs in respect of its declared social objectives. They have published details of their approach in a booklet.[6] This carefully designed approach includes many details which ensure impartiality and rigorous efforts to find out what each of the interested parties really think. Traidcraft plc published their first social audit in July 1993 and intend to publish audits each year in addition to their annual report.[7]

A Classification of Responsibility

Every business needs to achieve economic results and is required by Law to have its accounts audited and made known to shareholders and to the public. The increasing pressure for more disclosure about environmental impact, social responsibility, and environmental performance, is leading towards similar legal requirements to publish these results as well. At present this is being encouraged voluntarily and is therefore a matter of private conscience, coupled with economic prudence and a judgement about whether or not to take any action. For most organisations, developments in this area will be stimulated by enlightened self-interest. We can now examine a three dimensional model to represent the relationship between:

- environmental impact;
- social responsibility; and
- environmental responsibility.

To keep the model as simple as possible, each of these dimensions is considered in terms of two scales: high and low. The resulting cubic model provides eight perspectives as shown in chart 70.

(1) High Social Responsibility, Low Environmental Responsibility, Low Environmental Impact:
This is a traditional approach adopted by those organisations which wish to integrate with the local community and be responsible employers. The Quaker businesses, such as Rowntree and Cadbury, are examples. These are classified as 'Socially Aware'. This is a good starting point, but does not automatically cover environmental impact, which they now need to consider.

(2) High Social Responsibility, High Environmental Responsibility, Low Environmental Impact:
These are responsible companies working at the leading edge of both social and environmental responsibility, even though their impact on the environment is not great. Some of the big accountancy practices, such as Ernst and Young, and Coopers & Lybrand, are examples because of their partnership structure, and IBM because of its early move into environmental issues. They are classified as 'Service Sector Pioneers'.

(3) Low Social Responsibility, High Environmental Responsibility, Low Environmental Impact:
This is an unlikely mix because the basis for the high environmental conscience is unclear. If an example exists it is probably because of a top executive who has a high concern for environmental matters and has influenced the organisation. Such organisations need to give attention to their social responsibility in order to broaden the base of their environmental policies, ensuring that they are appropriate – and implemented. These organisations are classified as with 'Unbalanced Concern'.

(4) Low Social Responsibility, Low Environmental Responsibility, Low Environmental Impact:
This combination represents the vast majority of private sector service companies and most of the public sector organisations. Together

Chart 70: Social and Environmental Responsibility

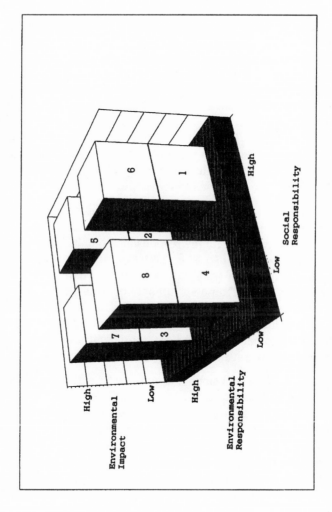

they account for two-thirds of the workforce in industrialised countries. Because their *direct* environmental impact is low they generally have a low profile and believe they do not need to be concerned about their social and/or environmental conscience. These are the most difficult organisations to influence, and yet their role in society is enormous. They are classified as the 'Silent Destroyers'[8] because the life styles of those employed in these organisations make heavy demands on other organisations which cause greater environmental damage.

Through the services they provide, these 'Silent Destroyer' organisations have an enormous impact on private and public sector organisations, who are their clients. They could make a considerable impact if they applied their minds to ways in which they could influence their clients towards increased social and environmental responsibility. This will only happen when more individuals in senior positions within the service sector organisations recognise the importance of the issues. This will probably be as a result of changing their own, personal life styles.

(5) High Social Responsibility, High Environmental Responsibility, High Environmental Impact:

These appear to be highly responsible organisations because they are aware of both their social and environmental responsibilities, but the degree to which they can be seen as virtuous will depend on whether they become sustainable organisations, and reduce their environmental impact, while relating responsibly to the communities in which they operate. An alternative perspective is that their attention to both social and environmental responsibility has become a matter of survival. They are classified as 'Searching for Virtue'.

(6) High Social Responsibility, Low Environmental Responsibility, High Environmental Impact:

This combination is likely to exist when the way in which the organisation was first formed incorporated high social concern, or when it began to be concerned with social responsibility in the last few decades. Despite causing considerable damage to the environment, little or no attention has been paid to environmental policies. These organisations are classified as 'Blind Destroyers'. Giving attention to their environmental impact should be a high priority. If this does not happen soon, they will find their business suffers because they are violating Laws, their insurance premiums have risen dramatically, banks are insisting on less favourable terms; and their high social conscience could erode because of lack of follow through to environmental matters. Many companies are in this category, without realising it.

(7) Low Social Responsibility, High Environmental Responsibility, High Environmental Impact:
This group represents those businesses which have realised their environmental responsibility and have responded by developing appropriate policies. However, effective implementation of those policies will often depend on a committed workforce, a sympathetic local community, and growing maturity as a responsible employer. Unless they give attention to their social responsibility their environmental policies may well prove unworkable. They are classified as 'Simplistic'.

(8) Low Social Responsibility, Low Environmental Responsibility, High Environmental Impact:
These are the irresponsible organisations who turn a blind eye to both social and environmental responsibility. If they do nothing their survival will be threatened because they will be in breach of new environmental legislation, vulnerable to growing pressure to be socially responsible, and increasingly regarded as high risk businesses by banks and insurance companies. They are classified as 'Dangerous and Irresponsible'.

These eight perspectives enable you to judge how any organisation is responding to the growing concerns in today's world. Which category best describes the organisation where you work? The classification can also be used to indicate the need for any organisation to:

• engage with its stakeholders;
• raise ethical standards;
• enhance environmental responsibility; and
• contribute to a better world.

Using Consultants

We can now look at the scope of the three different kinds of audit: financial, social and environmental. They overlap to some extent, as can be seen in chart 71.

The audits assess how things are now and provide a foundation for organisation development, or transformation. When this starts it will not just be a question of writing a revised Mission Statement or declaring new policies. We are dealing with issues that run deep right through the organisation. Lasting change will depend on engaging staff at every level in the new endeavour. This means learning new things, encouraging leadership at every level, social and technical innovation, personal development, culture change and creating learning organisations.

We have already seen in chapter 9 that it is possible to bring about cul-

Chart 71:
FINANCIAL, SOCIAL & ENVIRONMENTAL AUDITS

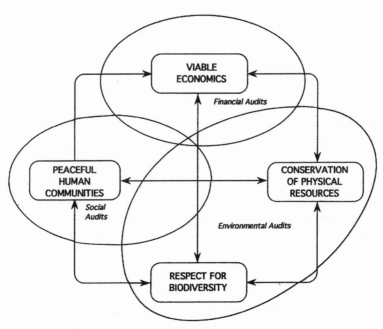

© Colin Hutchinson, *Vitality and Renewal*, Adamantine, 1994

ture change, but that it requires careful planning, appropriate leadership, supportive systems and perseverance. It also requires skilled help to devise and use processes which facilitate change. The most effective way to achieve this sort of change is by applying the principles of change management as described in chapter 9. The question we now address is how to make best use of the available resources; and we look at the issues involved, first from the perspective of the client organisation, then from that of the consultant.

The Client's Perspective

It is helpful to engage a process consultant when the work involved has the following characteristics (In this section the word 'you' refers to you the client):

(1) Changes in attitudes and behaviour are required.
(2) Staff at many different levels need to take part.
(3) Technical solutions and procedures will not be sufficient.
(4) The nature of the problem is unclear.

(5) There is uncertainty about how best to proceed.
(6) Learning through experience is desirable.
(7) You wish to create a learning organisation.
(8) Organisation development or transformation is needed.

If several of these characteristics are present in the situation, it is well worthwhile to consider bringing in external help. The sort of help that is most likely to be appropriate is process consultation. Edgar Schein, one of the great exponents of process consulting says that this type of consultant is identified by 'the attitude and philosophy that underlie the consultant's behaviour vis-a-vis the client'. He adds that evidence of their way of working is provided by the 'focus on the process by which the consultant builds readiness for change, actually conducts training, ...works with key individuals...and attempts to illustrate the importance of the attitude that the consultant takes toward the helping process.'[9] The process consultant works from the evolving needs of the client, uses live learning opportunities from the client's real world, enables practical problem solving to take place alongside personal and group development, and shows how attitudes influence outcomes. The issue for the client is how to assess the competence of process consultants, so some ways in which this kind of service can be reviewed are described below:

(1) How well does the consultant listen and demonstrate understanding of your situation at the initial meeting?
(2) Does the consultant show process awareness by using the initial meeting to demonstrate competence of this kind?
(3) Does the behaviour of the consultant demonstrate both responsiveness and assertiveness?
(4) Does the 'chemistry' of the relationship feel right?
(5) Can the consultant describe other successful work that is comparable to the assignment you have in mind?
(6) Does the consultant deal with the confidentiality issue competently, vis-a-vis previous assignments and yours?
(7) Is the consultant able to describe how a sound diagnosis of your situation will be achieved?
(8) Is the consultant confident about the next steps in the process and willing to develop a proposal with you?
(9) Is the work that the consultant will do clear and do you believe it will meet your expressed needs?

If you feel inclined to go ahead you should ask the consultant to write a firm proposal which should include the following:

(1) A clear statement of your situation and what you seek to achieve – this might be a diagnosis, in the first instance, or a description of the desired situation you wish to establish.

(2) What the consultant(s) will actually do and how many days work will be required.

(3) Name(s) of the consultant(s) who will be involved and who the lead consultant will be. You should have met this person at the initial meeting.

(4) The underlying philosophy of the consultant's approach and the ethical code which informs the consultant's work (*see* the suggested ethical framework for consultants and trainers, described in chart 72).

(5) How the learning derived from the process will be distilled.

If you go ahead and agree a contract this will also need to cover:

(6) The terms of the contract, including fee rates, expenses to be charged, VAT, method of payment, and cancellation or postponement terms.

(7) How progress will be reviewed and decisions made to adjust the work being undertaken to allow for new factors.

(8) How the consultant will deal with concluding the assignment, and withdrawing so that the benefits will continue to accrue.

You should expect the consultant to work effectively at several levels within the organisation. With some senior people there will be one-to-one sessions; where groups are involved contributions should be invited beforehand to arrange effective meetings and process facilitation when they take place. The consultant will work with the Project Group to plan the whole programme and advise on when and how to present things to the Steering Group or Sponsor (*see* chart 57). The consultant will stimulate discussion about strategic options, help the Steering Group make sound strategic decisions, develop with you the criteria for reviewing progress and help you devise review procedures.

You will be particularly keen to know if the whole assignment has delivered value for money. Ultimately this will need to be reflected in 'bottom line' results, and in improved social and environmental responsibility; but along the way, how can you judge whether appropriate progress is being made? This is never easy but there are six things you can examine:

(1) Find out how those involved *feel* about the programme and their involvement in it? A successful programme is characterised by positive feelings from the majority of those involved. It is very rare for this to be a flawed measure of progress, but it does need to be confirmed by other signals.

(2) Those involved should be able to identify ways in which their own personal development has been enhanced, and the learning they are getting from the experiences should be shared with others.

(3) Tangible evidence should begin to emerge that people are doing things differently and doing different things – consistent with the goals of the project.
(4) The overall cost of the assignment should be compared with the financial parameters of the organisation in question. For example what is the ratio of total consultancy costs to the profitability of the organisation and to the likely improvement in profits that should materialise from the assignment?
(5) What proportion of your overall development budget is taken up by this assignment? What is the ratio of development expenditure compared with the total salaries of those employed in the organisation undergoing development?
(6) Has value been added?

An assignment often produces a feeling that the achievements have actually resulted from your own efforts with little contribution from the consultant. This is a healthy outcome, because the process consultant's aim should be to empower you and your people. The more empowered you feel the better the contribution made by the consultant. You should also feel better able to tackle a similar assignment next time without external help.

The Consultant's Perspective

The client's perspective described above provides many clues to the way in which you, the consultant, should operate; but it is worth identifying some specific things the effective consultant can do. (In this section 'you' and 'your' refers to consultants, who form the group to which the section is most relevant.)

(1) Demonstrate your competence when arranging the initial meeting.
(2) At the initial meeting, demonstrate your listening skills and your ability to understand the client's situation by accurately paraphrasing what you are told, and reflecting the feelings that have been shown.
(3) Encourage the client to be open, by building an atmosphere of trust and using open questions to enable the client to describe the situation in his or her own way.
(4) Demonstrate your process skills by using them at the initial meeting and skilfully drawing attention to them.
(5) Start building an effective working relationship with each of the people present.
(6) Briefly describe relevant experiences after hearing about the prospective client's situation. Select appropriate examples and show respect for your other clients' confidentiality by describing the work without naming the client (unless you have already cleared this).

(7) Be prepared to describe briefly elements of your approach, such as how to develop a sound diagnosis, how you work with key individuals, how you develop teamwork, etc.

(8) Conclude the initial meeting on time, with a clear and confident summary of progress to date and the next step(s).

(9) Allow yourself time after the meeting to digest what has been discussed, and return with a thought through proposal which can be refined with the prospective client.

After the initial meeting, reflect on all aspects: how the client reacted to you, the impression you have created, the issues the prospective client faces, the nature of the assignment, the quality of the diagnosis that exists, your ability to make an effective contribution, how you feel about the client, who else from the client's organisation is likely to be a significant player and how you will get to meet that person. Decide what you need to do to develop the working relationships and to progress the assignment.

Remember that the initial description of the situation is likely to have focused on the symptoms presenting themselves, and may not have reached much understanding of the reasons why the situation is as it is. A more complete diagnosis may be required, and this is likely to be a sensitive issue. How you deal with this will play a significant part in achieving a successful outcome, but your next move will depend on the prospective client's readiness and willingness to do more work on the diagnosis. The areas in which you are unlikely to have heard the full story at the first meeting are the working relationships between the key people, and how these influence the way things are done. This is a always a delicate issue, but crucial to successful change management.

The second meeting will often determine the nature of the assignment, so it is important for you to find ways to raise this sort of delicate issue to demonstrate your awareness of the sensitivities involved and your skills in dealing with them. If you can do this well you are on the way towards an interesting contract. It is likely that some form of data collection phase will be your starting point and it is worth looking at some options and guidelines for this important part of in any assignment.

One of the significant contributions that you can make, especially if you are an external consultant, is in collecting information. Individual interviews, group interviews and opinion surveys all help to enrich the diagnosis. The most effective of these are individual interviews, but they are also the most time consuming (and costly to the client). If they are to be part of the assignment, those being interviewed should be properly briefed, probably in writing, by the project sponsor, and it is well worth working with your client on the wording of a briefing note. If you then create a relaxed, confidential atmosphere at each interview, it is possible to learn a great deal about how the organisation works, what its strengths and weaknesses are, and the ways in which different people would like to see it develop and enhance your credibility.

If group interviews are planned, similar principles apply and if opinion surveys are used it is still important to explain the context in which the survey is being conducted and what will be done with the results. In all cases, people want to know what was learned during the diagnostic phase, so some form of feedback or presentation of findings should be arranged. When this takes place it is a good idea to seek validation of the findings – in effect to ask if you have correctly understood what you have been told, and developed a credible and valid impression of the organisation. If necessary, be prepared to add to the diagnosis, or modify it if additional information or perspectives emerge.

Ethical Issues

There is an increasing need to establish the ethical standards by which consultants work. One initiative towards raising this issue more publicly has been taken by the Association for Management Education and Development (AMED),[10] which agreed an ethical charter at their 1993 AGM, and has suggested a set of principles for use by its members. A simplified framework for use in individual and organisational development is given in chart 72. You should consider drawing up your own ethical

Chart 72: An Ethical Framework for Individual and Organisational Development

1   To comply with the law

2   To provide services which improve economic performance, conserve physical resources, respect biodiversity and enhance community values

3   To encourage clients to develop at a pace that is reasonable and attainable

4   To help clients towards greater self-development

5   To explain the processes and techniques being used and the intended outcomes

6   To respect the confidentiality of clients' information

7   To be open about your own professional competence and personal integrity

8   To work within a commercial relationship that is agreed with the client

9   To review progress openly with the client and plan jointly how and when to conclude each assignment.

charter and using it as part of the contract for your work with clients.

From the outset you should be aware of the need to manage your own withdrawal on completion of the assignment, and should plan this with your client. Your professional reputation will be significantly influenced by your attitude towards this issue and how you handle it. Bear in mind that many clients fear that once consultants are working in their organisation it is very difficult to get rid of them. This final phase should be handled so that the relationship can be renewed, if both parties want to do this.

Getting Value for Money

In the final analysis, organisations will undertake the sort of development described in this book, using the processes and techniques which have been discussed, if they get value for money. Progress towards a sustainable society is essential but the steps along that path, many of which can and should be taken by companies, will be taken if they can be accomplished in accordance with the success criteria of today's world. The criteria are changing, but at any given stage in the process of change we must recognise that we start from where we are now. The future we strive to create is very different, and it will take courage and leadership to meet the challenge.

Ronald Higgins, in *Plotting Peace*[11], considered the question of whether the individual can do anything when the challenge seems so overwhelming. In answer to the question: 'Can the individual do anything?' he says:

> "Yes, a lot. It is a matter of applying oneself, learning the ropes, making contacts, building skills, resisting lies, spreading the facts, listening to others as well as speaking out, and trying not to be too boring."

Recognising the Challenge and Making a Difference

We began our journey by looking at the dimensions of the challenge, then at some of the myriad of things that people all over the world, and at every level, are already doing to respond to the challenge. We looked at culture, values and beliefs, how they shape our world and influence our behaviour. We examined the idea of sustainable development and appreciated some of the business opportunities that arise from it.

We explored how companies are using tactical and strategic approaches to strengthen their contribution to building a better world. We then turned our attention to the individual, and asked the question: 'Who is in charge?' You, the reader, were encouraged to ask yourself this question and to consider what else you might do to strengthen your own feelings of empowerment. We looked at how companies are managing change, and identified some of the key principles which have been shown to work. We investigated how individuals can undertake their own development and personal growth, then turned our attention to processes and techniques which can help to bring about individual and organisational change. Finally, in this chapter, we have looked at ways in which the process of change and the use of process consultants can give value for money.

The story now needs to be taken on by you. Things will change, new issues will arise, there will be successes and disappointments, but in all our interests there is a need to persevere. I hope that this book, in some small way, helps you to make a difference and encourages you to work with others, in your own way, to build a sustainable society.

Notes

1   Schein, Edgar, 1988, p.12.
2   Environmental Data Services Ltd (see Sources of Help).
3   Narrowing the Gap: Environmental Auditing Guidelines for Business, CBI (see Sources of Help).
4   See Sources of Help.
5   Brunel Environment Programme (see Sources of Help).
6   Zadek and Evans, 1993.
7   Traidcraft Social Audit 1992–93, Traidcraft plc, Kingsway, Gateshead, Tyne and Wear NE11 0NE.
8   The term 'silent destroyers' was coined by Bernard Taylor in Taylor, Hutchinson, Pollack and Tapper, 1994.
9   Schein, Edgar H, 1988.
10   See Sources of Help.
11   Higgins, Ronald, 1990, p. 211.

Appendix 1:
Environmental Checklist

A. Environmental Perspective

1 Declare attitude towards the environmental challenge and sustainable development
2 Develop scenarios for a sustainable future
3 Publish statement of corporate values
4 Establish and publish an environmental policy
5 Declare views on how communities are changing
6 Undertake research and publish findings on customer values
7 Articulate company views on the relationship between economic growth, resource conservation, protecting the Earth's biodiversity, and help for developing countries.

B. Company Policies

1 Publish a clear statement of corporate purpose, strategies and policies
2 Declare strategy and policies for purchasing, products, services, processes and sites
3 Declare intentions on new business initiatives - and the parameters for competitive confidentiality
4 Plan integration with other change initiatives, e.g. TQM, TQEM, BS5750, BS7750, etc
5 Declare Company car policy and how this relates to corporate environmental policy
6 Encourage the use of public transport and, where possible, bicycles
7 Share information openly
8 Work with other organisations on issues that cannot be tackled without them
9 Revise the focus for research and development
10 Staff training and development, especially on new challenges
11 Desired organisation culture and management style

C. Management

1 Make a Board member responsible for environmental matters
2 Check out all key appointments to ensure that the incumbents support company environmental policy
3 Provide appropriate development and training to enable staff to understand and implement new policies such as those for the environment, community, etc
4 Attract and retain high calibre staff by operating at high ethical standards and by providing job satisfaction
5 Review recruitment, appraisal and rewards - the criteria and processes in use, and required
6 Seek and respond to employee views and opinions.

D. Environmental and Social Audits

1 Assess products, processes, and services
2 Audit all sites and premises
3 Conduct social audits to assess impacts on stakeholders
4 Evaluate all suppliers, to ensure that they meet your environmental standards
5 Identify all environmental impacts and issues
6 Undertake product life cycle analysis
7 Identify where eco-labelling is appropriate and could be used

E. Resources and Emissions

1 Set standards and monitor performance
2 Purchasing policy should take account of every aspect of the declared community and environmental policy
3 Purchase recycled goods to help stimulate market demand
4 Check emission standards for existing and new products
5 Review and alter processes where necessary
6 Make managers financially accountable for waste management
7 Reduce materials used in packaging, consistent with safety standards; recycle packaging materials
8 Review all transportation contracts for goods/services - use low environmental impact criteria where possible
9 Organise practical ways in which wastes can be recovered.

F. Customer and Market

1 Ensure responsible labelling of products, with no doubtful or inaccurate claims

2   Provide for the 'green consumer' - give responsible help with buying decisions
3   Monitor market trends
4   Identify new and emerging demands for products/services
5   Recover used products, packaging and materials when relevant

G. Accounting and Finance

1   Assess the company's environmental rating and how this affects, or might affect, share value and inward investment
2   Ensure that budgets take account of environmental expenditure... and environmental savings
3   Review all insurance policies - risk assessment is changing
4   Consider novel ways in which annual reports can show environmental achievements
5   Develop new, relevant performance measures

H. Premises

1   Modernise heating (time switches, efficient combustion etc), insulation and lighting (long life, low energy light bulbs, etc)
2   Review health and safety standards - within the offices and around the site
3   Reduce, re-use, repair and recycle materials - as appropriate
4   Check sources and quality of food provided in restaurants - use socially responsible and environmentally appropriate sources
5   Check for environmental impact materials used for cleaning
6   Assess suppliers of goods and services to ensure that their environmental standards meet your own

I. Community

1   Be willing to meet others - be prepared to influence them and be influenced by them, as appropriate
2   Get involved with, and influence, industrial and professional associations
3   Support environmental groups - financially, in kind and with secondments
4   Undertake collaborative projects with community and environmental groups

Appendix 2:
Organisations with
Environmental Policies

Information on organisations with environmental policies is given in the books described below. Other organisations also have environmental policies and this listing identifies some of the organisations that are active in this area.

1   Schmidheiny, Stephan, *Changing Course*, MIT, 1992. Dr Schmidheiny was selected by Maurice Strong as his industrial adviser during the preparations for the Earth Summit (UNCED) in June 1992. He formed the Business Council for Sustainable Development by bringing together fifty chief executives from companies around the world. This is their report to UNCED and contains their perception of the issues as well as examples of how companies are responding.

2   Willums, Jan-Olaf and Golüke, Ulrich, *From Ideas to Action*, International Chamber of Commerce (ICC), 1992. ICC published the *Business Charter for Sustainable Development* (*see* Appendix 3) which has now been signed by 1,200 companies around the world. Clause 16 of the Charter requires signatories to report progress on taking action on the other 15 Clauses. This is the first report describing the action taken. The first part of the book is based on the 16 Clauses and briefly describes how some companies are tackling their declared intent, the second part describes the approach of several companies in more detail.

3   Forrester, Susan, *Business and Environmental Groups - A Natural Partnership?*, Directory of Social Change, 1990. This book is designed to stimulate wider interest in links between business and environmental groups. It includes both perspectives but the analysis here only covers those companies whose association with one or more environmental group is described.

4   Hill, Julie, *Towards Good Environmental Practice*, Institute of Business Ethics (IBE), 1992. The IBE was sponsored by the Department of the Environment to undertake this investigation and commissioned Julie Hill of the Green Alliance to do the work. The companies covered in this report are mentioned below.

5   Adams, John; Carruthers, Jane and Hamil, Sean, *Changing Corporate Values*, Kogan Page, 1991. This book explores corporate values by analysing the degree to which 130 companies meet their social responsibilities; this covers: disclosure of information, industrial democracy, equal opportunities, community involvement, environment, other countries, respect for life, politics, respect for people and military. Only those companies which are mentioned in one of the other texts referred to in this appendix are included in this survey.

6   Taylor, Bernard; Hutchinson, Colin; Pollack, Suzanne and Tapper, Richard, (eds), *Environmental Management Handbook*, Pitman, 1994. This Handbook of best practice is being completed at the time of writing. The companies contributing articles are identified here.

7   *Directory of Corporate Environmental Policy*, Industry & Environment Associates (IEA), 1st ed, 1991. The organisations mentioned in this publication are identified here, many of these are clients of IEA.

Each reference is indicated by an asterisk * in the columns below; where a tick ✓ is shown it indicates that the company is mentioned in *From Ideas to Action* in the section discussing the 16 clauses of the *Business Charter for Sustainable Development*:

	1	2	3	4	5	6	7
ABB	*	*					
ABB Zamech	*						
Akzo		✓					
Albright & Wilson							*
Alcoa	*						
Aracruz Celulose	*	*					
Arco Chemical Europe Inc							*
Argyll Group (Safeway)			*		*		*
ASDA Stores Ltd					*		*
Aspinwall & Co						*	
Atlantic Richfield		✓					
AT&T		*					
B & Q		✓					
Bass plc			*		*		
Bayer		✓					
BMW							*
Body Shop		✓	*		*	*	*
Boots		✓			*		
British Airways		✓			*		
British Gas		*	*		*	*	*
British Petroleum (BP)		*			*		
	1	2	3	4	5	6	7

	1	2	3	4	5	6	7
British Railways Board			*				*
British Telecommunications					*		*
Browning Ferris Industries		✓					
Burson Marsteller						*	
Cardiff City							*
Cheshire County Council							*
Chevron		✓					
Church & Dwight		*					
Ciba Geigy	*	*				*	
Cleanaway							*
Coca-Cola		✓					
Colgate Palmolive		✓			*		*
Con Agra	*						
Conoco		✓					
Courtaulds					*		*
Deloitte Touche Tohmatsu		*					
Deutsche Bank						*	
Digital Equipment Corporation		*					
Dow Chemical	*	*					*
Du Pont	*	*			*		
Eastman Kodak		*					
EID Parry	*						
Elkem		*					
Electrolux	*						
English China Clays			*				
ENI	*						
Eternit	*						
Fiat Auto Spa		*			*		
Forte plc						*	
Fujitsu		✓					
GE Capital	*						
General Motors		✓			*		
Glaxo		✓					*
Grand Metropolitan					*	*	
Harihar Polyfibres	*						
Henkel	*	*					
Hertfordshire County Council							*
Hewlett Packard		✓					
Hoechst		✓					
Holderbank	*						
Hovione		*					
Hydro Aluminium						*	
IBM		✓	*	*			*

| | 1 | 2 | 3 | 4 | 5 | 6 | 7 |

	1	2	3	4	5	6	7
Ibstock Johnsen plc			*				
ICI		*		*	*		*
Jaguar Cars							*
SC Johnson	*	✓	*		*		*
Jupiter Tyndall	*						
Koc Group		*					
Kodak Ltd							*
KPMG						*	
Laing	*					*	
Lasmo plc							*
Leicestershire County Council							*
Linpac Plastics							*
Lufthansa		✓					
3M	*	*				*	*
McDonald's Corporation		✓			*		
Mercedes Benz		✓					
Migros	*	✓					
Mitsubishi	*						
Mobil		✓			*		*
Monsanto		*				*	
National Westminster Bank		✓	*				
Neste Oy		✓					
New England Electric	*						
Nippon Steel	*						
Nissan		✓			*		
Nordic Environment Finance Corp	*						
Norsk Hydro	*	*					*
Norske Skog		*					
Northern Telecom	*						
Pechiney	*						
Philips Petroleum		✓					
Pick 'n' Pay	*						
Pilkington		✓					*
Powergen							*
Procter & Gamble	*				*	*	*
Rank Xerox		✓				*	
Reckitt & Colman				*	*		
Reynolds Corporation		✓					
Rhone-Poulenc							*
Rover Group plc							*
J Sainsbury plc					*		*
Salvesan Brick				*			
Schoeller International		*					
	1	2	3	4	5	6	7

	1	2	3	4	5	6	7
Shanks & MacEwan Group plc							*
Shell	*	*	*	*	*		
Smith and Hawken	*						
Statoil		*					
Surrey County Council							*
Sutton – London Borough							*
Tata Iron & Steel		✓					
Tesco				*	*		
Tetra Pak Group		*					
Texaco					*		*
Thorn EMI					*	*	
Thorntons				*			
Tioxide Group plc							*
Tomra Systems A/S		*					
Toyota		✓					
Triangle Ltd	*						
UCAR Carbon							*
Unilever					*		*
Union Carbide		✓					
Varta		✓					
Vauxhall Motors Ltd							*
Volkswagen	*	✓			*		
Volvo		✓			*	*	
Waste Management International		*				*	
Werner & Mertz		✓					
Wessex Water				*			
Wolstenholme Bronze Powders				*			
Xerox		*					
	1	2	3	4	5	6	7

Information compiled summer 1993.

APPENDIX 3

Appendix 3:
The Business Charter for
Sustainable Development

There is widespread recognition today that environmental protection must be among the highest priorities of every business.

To help business around the world improve its environmental performance, the International Chamber of Commerce established a task force of business representatives to create this *Business Charter for Sustainable Development*. It comprises sixteen principles for environmental management which, for business, is a vitally important aspect of sustainable development.

It was formally launched in April 1991 at the Second World Industry Conference on the Environment. The objective is that the widest range of enterprises commit themselves to improving their environmental performance in accordance with these Principles, to having in place management practices to effect such improvement, to measuring their progress, and to reporting this progress as appropriate internally and externally.

Principles

1 Corporate priority
To recognise environmental management as among the highest corporate priorities and as a key determinant to sustainable development; to establish policies, programmes and practices for conducting operations in an environmentally sound manner.

2 Integrated management
To integrate these policies, programmes and practices fully into each business as an essential element of management in all its functions.

3 Process of improvement
To continue to improve corporate policies, programmes and environmental performance, taking into account technical developments, scientific understanding, consumer needs and community expectations, with legal regulations as a starting point; and to apply the same environmental criteria internationally.

4 Employee education
   To educate, train and motivate employees to conduct their activities
   in an environmentally responsible manner.

5 Prior assessment
   To assess environmental impacts before starting a new activity or
   project and before decommissioning a facility or leaving a site.

6 Products and services
   To develop and provide products or services that have no undue
   environmental impact and are safe in their intended use, that are
   efficient in their consumption of energy and natural resources, and
   that can be recycled, re-used, or disposed of safely.

7 Customer advice
   To advise, and where relevant educate, customers, distributors and
   the public in the safe use, transportation, storage and disposal of
   products provided; and to apply similar considerations to the provision of services.

8 Facilities and operations
   To develop, design and operate facilities and conduct activities taking into consideration the efficient use of renewable resources, the
   minimisation of adverse environmental impact and waste generation, and the safe and responsible disposal of residual wastes.

9 Research
   To conduct or support research on the environmental impacts of raw
   materials, products, processes, emissions and wastes associated with
   the enterprise and on the means of minimising such adverse
   impacts.

10 Precautionary approach
    To modify the manufacture, marketing or use of products or services
    or the conduct of activities, consistent with scientific and technical
    understanding, to prevent serious or irreversible environmental
    degradation.

11 Contractors and suppliers
    To promote the adoption of these principles by contractors acting on
    behalf of the enterprise, encouraging and, where appropriate,
    requiring improvements in practices to make them consistent with
    those of the enterprise; and to encourage the wider adoption of
    these principles by suppliers.

12 Emergency preparedness
To develop and maintain, where significant hazards exist, emergency preparedness plans in conjunction with the local services, relevant authorities and the local community, recognising potential transboundary impacts.

13 Transfer of technology
To contribute to the transfer of environmentally sound technology and management methods throughout the industrial and public sectors.

14 Contributing to the common effort
To contribute to the development of public policy and to business, governmental and intergovernmental programmes and educational initiatives that will enhance environmental awareness and protection.

15 Openness to concerns
To foster openness and dialogue with employees and the public, anticipating and responding to their concerns about the potential hazards and impacts of operations, products, wastes or services, including those of transboundary or global significance.

16 Compliance and reporting
To measure environmental performance; to conduct regular environmental audits and assessments of compliance with company requirements, legal requirements and these principles; and periodically to provide appropriate information to the Board of Directors, shareholders, employees, the authorities and the public.

An up-to-date list of companies who have signed the Charter is available from ICC offices.

Reproduced by permission of International Chamber of Commerce.

Appendix 4:
The Earth Summit Agreements[1]

The United Nations concern for the environment, as a result of pressure from various sources, especially Sweden and THE UN Economic and Social Council (ECOSOC), resulted in the UN Conference on the Human Environment in Stockholm in 1972. This produced a declaration and an action plan focusing mainly on analysis of the problems, how to manage the issues, and education and training. It also resulted in the formation of the UN Environment Programme (UNEP), with Maurice Strong, who organised the Stockholm Conference, appointed as Secretary General.

Several other UN conferences, initiatives, conventions and protocols followed during the 1970s and 1980s. The Brandt Commission on North-South issues was set up, and later the World Commission on Environment and Development, under Norwegian Prime Minister Gro Harlem Brundtland, was established as an independent body and published its report in 1987.[2]

In December 1989 the UN General Assembly decided to convene the UN Conference on Environment and Development (UNCED), also known as the Earth Summit, in Rio de Janeiro in June 1992. National governments were invited to submit their own environment and development reports, and by the end of 1992 reports had been received from 190 countries. There was collaboration with leading non-governmental organisations (NGOs) and a series of preparatory conferences were held which developed early drafts of the conventions, agreements and action plans to be placed before the conference for signature. The conference itself was attended by over 100 heads of state and a further 78 governments were represented by delegations. While UNCED was taking place the NGOs organised their own Global Forum some 30 miles away, attended by 500 different groups.

The Framework Agreement on Climate Change

The seriousness of the issue of climate and change was set out in this agreement, with a clear recommendation that action is needed urgently without waiting for all scientific uncertainties to be resolved. Emphasis is placed on the need for the developed countries to take the lead and to compensate developing countries for any additional costs they may incur when implementing the convention. The first step towards safeguarding the Earth's climate should be to reduce greenhouse gas emissions to 1990 levels by the year 2000, but this is not a binding policy commitment. However, to add strength to the urgency of the issue the agreement urges governments to submit reports and to meet regularly to review progress and if necessary to amend the commitments.

Convention on Biological Diversity

This convention is designed to safeguard the Earth's biological diversity by protecting ecosystems and species. While acknowledging that all countries have rights over their own biological resources the convention establishes the terms under which biological resources and technology should be used and states the need to share the benefits equitably on agreed terms. Again all countries are urged to submit reports and to meet to review progress. This convention proved sensitive to some developed countries over the issue of control of funding, and to developing countries which are richly endowed with biological assets over undue external control.

Agenda 21

This is the action plan for the twenty-first century and is a formidable document of 40 chapters designed to achieve sustainable development worldwide. The document covers environment and development in an integrated way by defining ways in which social, economic and environmental development can be achieved. It sets out the roles of different groups of people and addresses the issues relating to specific natural resources. There is emphasis on the need for extensive involvement and participation of people at every level in community based projects. It includes reference to population policy – an issue not directly addressed at UNCED. Free market principles are endorsed within a regulatory framework. The document provides the basis for action at local, national and international government levels throughout the 1990s.

The United Nations Commission on Sustainable Development (UNCSD), under ECOSOC, was established in February 1993 as the principle institutional outcome from UNCED, with responsibility to follow-up *Agenda 21*. UNCSD has a membership of 53 countries (out of 180 members of the UN) and at an early meeting decided to group the chapters of *Agenda 21* as the basis of their work programme:[3]

Critical elements of sustainability – chapters 2 to 5
Financial resources and mechanisms – chapter 33
Education, Science and Technology – chapters 16, 34-36
Decision-making structures – chapters 8, 37-40
Roles of major groups – chapters 23-32

Health and human settlement issues – chapters 6, 7 & 21
Land, forests and biodiversity – chapters 10-15
Atmosphere, oceans and freshwater – chapters 9, 17 & 18
Toxic chemicals and hazardous wastes – chapters 19, 20 & 22

The Rio Declaration

This declaration contains 27 guiding principles for action on environment and development, many of which stress the need for the allevia-
tion of poverty as a right and as a pre-requisite for development. The difficulties with the final wording resulted in some ambiguity in the sections dealing with trade and the rights and roles of certain groups.

Forest Principles

This proved to be a particularly contentious issue and the final statement
of principles indicates that nations have the right to exploit their own
forests, but they are encouraged to do so within some general principles
of sound forest management.

The Earth Summit fell short of the goals desired by Maurice Strong,
the Secretary General, but enormous numbers of people throughout the
world were involved in the preparations and are taking part in the
implementation of the agreements.

Notes

1   Grubb et al, 1993; Johnson (Ed), 1993; and Quarries (Ed), 1992.
2   World Commission on Environment and Development, 1987.
3   International Chamber of Commerce document 210/432.

Annotated Bibliography

The books described briefly below are arranged in alphabetical order by authors in three sections, the third being sub-divided into two sub-sections:

(1) Nature of the Predicament
(2) Opportunities and Information for Business
(3) Individual and Organisational Learning and Change
(a) Personal Learning, Development and Empowerment
(b) Organisational Development, Change and Transformation

Nature of the Predicament

This section contains a selection of books all of which describe aspects of the environmental challenge in its broadest sense and contribute to our understanding of the predicament.

Allaby, Michael (ed.), 1989, *Thinking Greener: An Anthology of Essential Ecological Writing*, Barrie & Jenkins.
An extremely useful summary of the way in which environmental thinking has evolved. It covers brief synopses of many influential thinkers, including Rachel Carson *(Silent Spring)*, Thomas Malthus *(The Theory of Population)*, Garrett Hardin *(The Tragedy of the Commons)*, John Stuart Mill *(The Stationary State)* Edward Goldsmith, Robert Allen, Michael Allaby, John Davoll and Sam Lawrence *(The Blueprint for Survival)*, Donella Meadows, Dennis Meadows, Jorgen Randers and William Behrens *(Limits to Growth)*, Amory Lovins *(Soft Energy Paths)*, Barbara Ward and Rene Dubos *(Strategies for Survival)*, and James Lovelock *(The Gaia Hypothesis)*.
Barnaby, Dr Frank, 1988, *The Gaia Peace Atlas*, Pan Books.
This is the sequel to the *Gaia Atlas of Planet Management* (ed. Norman Myers, 1985). It broadens the scope to cover human communities, the struggle for peace, the choices for humanity and short term steps to survival. It also contains a section on a sustainable future. Contributions are from eminent people from around the world and it contains many graphic illustrations.
Brown, Lester, *et al.*, 1993, *State of the World 1993*, Earthscan.
This series of books started in 1984 and have been best selling publications all over the world ever since. Lester Brown is director of the Worldwatch Institute *(see* Sources of Help). They also produce two

other important annual publications: the *Environmental Alert* series and *Vital Signs*, as well as the *Worldwatch Papers* which are booklets on topical subjects.

Brown, Lester; Kane, Hal and Ayres, (ed.), 1993, *Vital Signs: The Trends that are Shaping our Future 1993/94*, Earthscan.
This is the second edition of a new series that will be published annually. The books provide statistical evidence of important trends. Each edition contains a summary of the topics covered to date and the edition in which the information was published. Whereas some subjects will be reported annually others will be less frequent. The grouping of topics include food, agricultural resources, energy, atmosphere, transportation, and society with special features on topics such as economics and military.

Burrows, Brian; Mayne, Alan and Newbury, Dr Paul, 1991, *Into the 21st Century: A Handbook for a Sustainable Future*, Adamantine.
An impressive analysis of the social, economic and technological developments which will influence the future. A book compiled with copious references.

Cairncross, Frances, 1991, *Costing the Earth*, The Economist Books.
A cogent analysis of the challenge to government, followed by clear indications of ways in which companies can respond to the challenge and reap benefits.

Clark, Mary E, 1989, *Ariadne's Thread: The Search for New Modes of Thinking*, MacMillan.
Mary Clark inaugurated a course on 'Our Global Future' at San Diego State University which involved fifteen academics from different disciplines providing a linked series of lectures covering biology, energy, anthropology, psychology, religion and government. The book is the result of pulling together this material and tracing the origins of our current predicament, which then leads on to ideas about new ways of thinking about solutions.

Commoner, Barry, 1990, *Making Peace with the Planet*, Gollancz.
A powerful indictment of the attempts made to safeguard the Earth over the period 1970 to 1990, followed by an optimistic view of the future if things are done very differently. The focus is primarily on the USA but many of the arguments are equally applicable to Europe.

Daly, Herman, 1992, *Steady-state Economics*, 2nd edn, Earthscan.
One of the leading exponents of new economics describes what is involved in creating a sustainable society. He sets the scene by describing the issues and explaining the concept of a steady-state economy. This is followed by a discussion of the growth debate drawing on articles written by himself and others, presenting their different perspectives.

Daly, Herman and Cobb, John, 1990, *For the Common Good: Redirecting the Economy towards Community, the Environment and a Sustainable Future*, Green Print.

Daly and Cobb state that both capitalism and socialism are growth economies but believe that these are not the only available options. This book describes their view of a realistic alternative and discusses not only economics but also looks into biology, history, philosophy, physics and theology. The practical steps which can be taken are explained and the index of sustainable economic welfare – which is another way of measuring economies – is described.

Dauncey, Guy, 1988, *After the Crash*, Green Print.

This book introduces the idea of the 'Rainbow Economy' based on seven core values – spiritual (purple), planetary (dark blue), economic (pale blue), ecological (green), personal creativity (yellow), local community (orange) and social (red). The book describes how we can act locally in accordance with these core values and is brought alive by many examples of current practices from around the world.

Department of the Environment, 1990, *This Common Inheritance: Britain's Environmental Strategy* (and subsequent annual follow-up reports) HMSO.

This is Britain's official analysis of the predicament and statement of intent. The follow-up reports provide indicators of progress. Many other countries have their own official statements and ways of reporting progress.

Department of Trade and Industry and Department of the Environment, 1993, *Advisory Committee on Business and the Environment: Third Progress Report*.

The Advisory Committee was established in May 1991 and its working groups cover global warming, recycling, environmental management, the financial sector, and commercial opportunities. This, their third report, provides a summary of their work to date before they refocus for the next phase of their work in 1994.

Ehrlich, Paul and Ehrlich, Anne, 1990, *The Population Explosion*, Hutchinson, and *Healing the Planet: Strategies for Resolving the Environmental Crisis*, Addison-Wesley, 1991.

The foremost exponents of the population crisis describe the nature of that predicament. Despite the title the book covers a much wider field than population alone and shows how pervasively the population issue affects virtually every other issue. In *Healing the Planet* the authors explain how we can save the planet by tackling issues such as biodiversity, energy policy, global warming and ozone depletion.

Ekins, Paul, 1992, *A New World Order: Grassroots Movements for Global Change*, Routledge.

Explores the 'problematique' in terms of four perspectives: militarism, poverty, environment and human rights. New approaches are then discussed using the reports from UN Commissions, Brandt and Brundtland, from which he draws out the principles of sustainable development. This sets the scene for introducing many examples of grass roots development from around the world.

Ekins, Paul; Hillman, Mayer and Hutchison, Robert, 1992, *Wealth Beyond Measure: An Atlas of New Economics*, Gaia Books.

This book follows the broad format of other Gaia books and contains many graphical presentations interspersed with a relatively brief text on a host of topical subjects including peace and security, regenerating the environment and appropriate development.

Goldsmith, Edward; Hildyard, Nicholas; Bunyard, Peter and McCully, Patrick, 1990, *5,000 Days to Save the Planet*, Hamlyn.

The authors are all associated with *The Ecologist*, a monthly magazine which has been drawing attention to the environmental challenge for over twenty years. This is a beautifully presented description of the crisis. The first part analyses the Earth's physical features, such as forests, agricultural land and rivers. This is followed by a description of the human dimension, and solutions for survival which are seen as both technological and within ourselves and our life styles.

Goldsmith, Edward, 1992, *The Way*, Rider.

This is Teddy Goldsmith's ecological world view and describes his ideas about a sustainable future. The book is divided into sixty-six chapters with four appendices and a bibliography. The first six chapters deal with aspects of ecology and this concept recurs in several other places. The Gaia hypothesis is described, as well as life processes, natural systems and how the biosphere works.

Good, Ben, 1991 (*see* page 286).

Goodland, Robert; Daly, Herman; El Serafy, Salah and von Droste, Bernd, 1991, *Environmentally Sustainable Economic Development: Building on Brundtland*, UNESCO.

The preface is jointly written by Emil Salim, Minister of State, Environment and Population, Indonesia, and Jose Lutzenberger, (then) Secretary of State for Environment, Brazil, and represents a contribution from eminent ecologists and economists to the Earth Summit. The book includes a statement describing the world's limits that have already been reached, how to adjust economic policies to take account of this, strategies for reducing inequalities and how to adjust to sustainable development on a global basis.

Gore, Al, 1992, *Earth in the Balance: Forging a New Common Purpose*, Earthscan.

Al Gore wrote this book after his own attempt to be the Democratic Presidential candidate for the 1992 elections and before he was selected by Bill Clinton as his running mate. He wrote much of the book while sitting in hospital with his son who was recovering from a serious car accident. The book is a remarkably powerful analysis of the predicament we face, drawing on many years experience of sitting on Senate Committees listening to evidence and the best factual information available. Al Gore now has a unique opportunity to bring his formidable analysis to bear on world problems.

Grubb, Michael; Koch, Matthias; Munson, Abby; Sullivan, Francis and Thompson, Koy, 1993, *The Earth Summit Agreements: A Guide and Assessment*, The Royal Institute for International Affairs, published by Earthscan.

After a brief introduction explaining the build up to the Earth Summit this book describes the outcomes and lists which countries signed which conventions. The Framework Convention on Climate Change and the Convention on Biological Diversity, both of which are binding, are summarised. The book also describes the three non-binding agreements, namely: the Rio Declaration on Environment and Development, Agenda 21, and a statement on Principles of Forest Management. Themes and lessons from the Rio experience are described and the road ahead is discussed.

Higgins, Ronald, 1978, *The Seventh Enemy*, Hodder & Stoughton.

The six threats to the Earth are described as the population explosion, the food crisis, resource scarcity, environmental degradation, nuclear arms and unleashed science and technology. The seventh enemy is identified as a combination of political inertia and individual blindness. One third of the book contains a description of possible futures, and how to mount an assault on the seventh enemy which includes self-awareness, revaluation of the feminine, the ethics of consciousness and reawakening of spirituality.

Higgins, Ronald, 1990, *Plotting Peace: The Owl's Response to Hawks and Doves*, Brassey's.

The current world security situation is diagnosed and practical steps towards peace are discussed. The central theme is to show how, as a global community, we need to move from competitiveness to a cooperative security.

Hutchinson, Colin, 1991, *Business and the Environmental Challenge: A Guide for Managers*, available from The Environment Council (*see* Sources of Help). This publication describes the dimensions of the environmental challenge, gives an outline of sustainable development, lists some of the things companies are doing, outlines how to implement an environmental programme and provides a bibliography which includes short descriptions of some of the more important books on the environment.

IUCN, UNEP and WWF, 1991, *Caring for the Earth: A Strategy for Sustainable Living.*
Three of the leading environmental organisations in the world combined to produce this book as a sequel to the *World Conservation Strategy*, published in 1980. It contains much practical and sound advice in promoting a strategy for sustainable living which includes respect for the quality of life, conservation of the earth's vitality and diversity, minimum depletion of resources, keeping within the Earth's carrying capacity and changing personal attitudes.

Jacobs, Michael, 1991, *The Green Economy: Environment, Sustainable Development and the Politics of the Future*, Pluto Press.
A widely acclaimed economic analysis of world problems. The book is presented in four parts: the analysis, objectives, programme, and measurement.

Johnson, Stanley (Introduction and commentary), 1993, *The Earth Summit*, Graham & Trotman.
This is a complete annotated report on the Earth Summit. In addition to the Rio conventions and agreements the book contains details of other agreements leading up to Rio, how UNCED's work is organised, and Maurice Strong's speech at the Summit. There is also a section on the means of implementation, which includes discussion of financial resources, technology transfer and education.

Kennedy, Paul, 1993, *Preparing for the 21st Century*, Harper Collins.
Kennedy's previous, book *The Rise and Fall of the Great Powers*, was widely acclaimed, but also criticised because it omitted subjects like population growth, the impact of technology, and environmental threats. This new book was stimulated by these criticisms and gave Kennedy an opportunity to apply his analytical powers and historical perspective to these issues. It is a formidable and impressive analysis.

King, Alexander and Schneider, Bertrand, 1991, *The First Global Revolution*, Simon & Schuster.
This a report by the Club of Rome, the organisation responsible for commissioning *The Limits to Growth*. The book provides an analysis of the predicament, which they assemble in a model called 'The Problematique', which provided the basis for the model used here in *Vitality and Renewal*. The second half of the book is devoted to 'The Resolutique', or what needs to be done to deal with the issues. This emphasises the role of government and the agents of change which include learning, science and technology and the role of the mass media.

Laszlo, Ervin, 1989 (*see* page 289).

Lean, Geoffrey; Hinrichsen, Don and Markham, Adam, *Atlas of the Environment*, Hutchinson, 1990.

A useful compilation of facts and figures with supporting charts setting out the nature and scale of the environmental challenge.

Leggett, Jeremy, (ed.), 1990, *Global Warming*, Oxford University Press. This is the Greenpeace Report, edited by their Director of Science, and contains chapters written by different authors, including Dr Stephen Schneider (a leading climatologist), Dr Amory Lovins, Dr Anne Ehrlich and Dr Susan George. The book covers the scientific aspects, the impacts on the environment and policy responses.

Lovelock, James, 1991, *The Practical Science of Planet Management*, Gaia Books. By the originator of the Gaia hypothesis, which recognises the whole Earth as a self-regulating living organism, describes how acceptance of the hypothesis can be translated into practical action. He discusses the anatomy, physiology and biochemistry of the Earth and suggests what we can do to ensure that its self-regulatory capability is not impaired.

Lovins, Hunter; Lovins, Amory and Zuckerman, Seth, 1986, *Energy Unbound*, Sierra Club Books.

The Lovins' made a name for themselves with *World Energy Strategies* (1975) and *Soft Energy Paths* (1977), both now out of print. This is the sequel and is written as a fable for America's Future. A housewife is appointed Secretary of State for Energy and most of the book is taken up by a dialogue with a wise scientist who briefs her on all facets of the energy portfolio. It advocates an approach to energy policy which starts with an understanding of what jobs require energy, the sort of energy needed and the cheapest ways in which to get it. There are also fascinating chapters on how different energy policies affect national economic and security issues. Although written for the USA and using US examples to illustrate points there are many lessons for any industrialised country.

McCormick, John, 1989, *The Global Environmental Movement*, Belhaven.

The author goes beyond national environmental organisations and describes how the global movement grew and gained strength. A well researched publication, which began as an MSc thesis.

MacNeill, Jim; Winsemius, Pieter and Yakushiji, Taizo, 1991, *Beyond Interdependence: The Meshing of the World's Economy and the Earth's Ecology*, Oxford University Press.

Jim MacNeill is a Canadian who is a former Secretary General of the World Commission on Environment and Development, Pieter Winsemius is Director of McKinsey & Company, in Amsterdam, and former Minister of Housing in the Netherlands and Taizo Yakushiji is Professor of Technology and International Relations at the Graduate School of Policy Science, Saitama University, Japan. They wrote this short book for the Trilateral Commission as a contribution to the Earth

Summit. Maurice Strong said that it 'provides the most compelling economic as well as environmental case for... reform that I have read.' It contains chapters on recasting domestic policy, global change, and the challenges and prospects for a sustainable future.

Meadows, Donella H; Meadows Dennis L. and Randers, Jorgen, 1992, *Beyond the Limits: Global Collapse or a Sustainable Future*, Earthscan.
Three of the authors of *The Limits to Growth* have now written a sequel twenty years later. Their findings are impressive and in many ways deeply worrying. However, there is a spark of hope and a declared belief that a sustainable future can be achieved if we have the will to make it happen. Their recommendations include visioning, networking, telling the truth, learning and loving, to overcome pessimism.

Moorcroft, Sheila (ed.), 1992, *Visions for the 21st Century*, Adamantine.
Twenty-one authors from around the world bring together a series of essays which describe different perspectives about the future, including a new world order, the future of democracy, the role of business, technology choice, our inner world of beliefs, education, and science. A useful book to dip into to find inspiration and ideas.

Myers, Norman, (ed.), 1985, *The Gaia Atlas of Planet Management*, Pan Books. Revised and reprinted in 1994.
A richly illustrated book, with contributions from all over the world, covering land, oceans, the elements, evolution, humankind, civilisation, and management; as well as a glossary, and six pages of sources. This was the first of the Gaia books and its success set a trend which continues.

Myers, Norman, (ed.), 1990, *The Gaia Atlas of Future Worlds: Challenge and Opportunity in A World of Change*, Robertson McCarta, 1990.
A mass of information has been assembled in an easy reference format with many illustrations. The book consists of four parts: pressures and processes, impacts and outcomes, creating the future, and conclusions about what is possible and probable.

Nicholson, Max, 1987, *The New Environmental Age*, Cambridge University Press.
One of the eminent, sometimes controversial, figures of the British environmental movement, who has been directly involved for many years, provides an interesting description of how environmental thinking has evolved. The book is a sequel to the author's earlier work *The Environmental Revolution*, first published in 1970.

OECD, *The State of the Environment*, 1991.
This publication from the Organisation for Economic Cooperation and Development contains a great deal of authoritative information about the state of the physical environment , the changing economic context and both economic and international responses to the challenge of sustainability.

Patterson, Walter C, 1990, *The Energy Alternative: Changing the Way the World Works*, Boxtree.

A review of new approaches to energy by one of the most influential energy consultants. The book includes important chapters on why we need energy, how to get more from less and options for the future.

Pearce, David; Markandya, Anil & Barbier, Edward B, 1989, *Blueprint for a Green Economy*, Earthscan.

This book is based on a report for the Department of the Environment (UK). It influenced much subsequent thinking about 'green' economics.

Porritt, Jonathon and Winner, David 1988, *The Coming of the Greens*, Fontana.

An interesting account of how the green movement evolved, as seen through the eyes of the former Director of Friends of the Earth. In particular it shows how in the 1980s, a relatively quiet period for the environment, the movement was gaining strength by attracting growing numbers of supporters who were beginning to use environmental criteria to make buying decisions and to select organisations they supported.

Porritt, Jonathon, *Save the Earth*, 1991, Dorling Kindersley.

This book was prepared for the United nations Conference on Environment and Development (UNCED), in June 1992, and has been printed in over twenty languages. It contains contributions and powerful pleas from many eminent people from around the world.

Quarrie, Joyce (ed.), 1992, *Earth Summit 1992*, The Regency Press.

A report on the United Nations Conference on Environment and Development which took place in Rio in June 1992. The book contains details of the Rio Declaration and an abridged version of Agenda 21, which is the programme of action to implement the Rio conventions. The book is divided into four sections: Social and Economic, Conservation and Management of Resources for Development, Strengthening the Role of Major Groups and Means of Implementation.

Renner, Michael, 1991, *Jobs in a Sustainable Economy*, Worldwatch Paper No 104. This booklet answers the fear that pursuit of environmental goals will increase unemployment. The argument is supported by examples to demonstrate that there are many ways in which environmental policies contribute to the creation of jobs.

Robertson, James, 1989, *Future Wealth: A New Economics for the 21st Century*, Cassell.

A useful analysis of the way in which new economics could evolve. It also contains information on landmark events during the 1990s which provide opportunities to influence global thinking.

Roszak, Theodore, 1993, *The Voice of the Earth: An Exploration of Ecopsychology*, Bantam Press.
A deep thinking exploration of underlying issues relevant to the environmental challenge. The author explores psychology, cosmology and ecology and indicates the magnitude of the challenge we face if we are to scale down, slow down, democratise and decentralise as he proposes.

Russell, Peter, 1992, *The White Hole in Time*, Millennia.
This interesting book shows how many different aspects of the 'predicament' are moving towards a crescendo. These include the environmental crisis, the speed and scale of communications. the growth of tension and fear and the role of spirituality. He describes how, despite our best intentions, we have created our problems, and discusses the need to face up to this reality and seek the wisdom to find solutions.

Schumacher, E. F., 1973, *Small is Beautiful: A Study of Economics as if People mattered*, Blond and Briggs.
An extremely influential book which resulted in the formation of at least three organisations: the Intermediate Technology Development Group, the Schumacher Society, and the New Economics Foundation, all of which are described in the Sources of Help section. Schumacher was also President of the Soil Association.

Government Statistical Service, *Social Trends*, 1993, HMSO.
This is an annual publication providing an analysis of social trends in Britain.

Starke, Linda, 1990, *Signs of Hope*, Oxford University Press.
This is the sequel to the World Commission Report, *Our Common Future* (*see* below) and was prepared for the follow-up conference which took place in Bergen, Norway, in May 1990 to review progress. It brings together an array of positive action which reveals good grounds for optimism, but also describes the unfinished agenda.

Suzuki, David, 1992, *Inventing the Future: Reflections on Science, Technology and Nature*, Adamantine.
As a Canadian of Japanese origin, a geneticist of some renown and with considerable experience as a journalist, David Suzuki brings a refreshing mix of perspectives to his work. His book is a delight to read and contains numerous examples of the damage that certain sorts of science and technology are doing to the environment and highlights choices we need to influence if a sustainable future is to be achieved.

Toffler, Alvin, 1980, *The Third Wave*, Collins.
The author who became famous with his earlier book, *Future Shock*, succeeds again with an impressive dissection of topical issues. The third wave is comparable in its significance to the agricultural and

industrial revolutions. We are living in the transition and struggling to find ways in which to describe and understand it. Toffler's insights are impressive and helpful. The sequel, *Power Shift*, was disappointing and had little new to add.

The World Bank, 1989 to 1992, *World Development Report*, Oxford University Press.

These annual reports began in 1977 to provide information on indicators of development, country by country. 1990 witnessed the introduction of a slight variation on this approach. That year the theme was 'poverty', in 1991 it was 'development strategies' and in 1992 'the links between economic development and environment'. The documentation and presentation is impressive and shows signs of a change of heart towards developing countries, with greater understanding of the need for development from within and for more appropriate development.

Union of International Associations, 1991, *Encyclopedia of World Problems and Human Potential*, 3rd edn, K.G. Saur, Germany.

Published in two volumes and extending to 2,000 pages (and costing DM 898) this impressive analysis brings together not only a comprehensive summary of problems but also information on human potential which can be harnessed in our mutual interest.

United Nations Development Programme (UNDP), 1992, *Human Development Report 1992*, Oxford University Press.

`Never before has there been broader consensus on what is needed for development. Economic development can be sustained only by unleashing the creative energies of all people through competitive and efficient markets.' This is taken from the foreword. The report describes how to measure development, provides statistics country by country, discusses political freedom, explores opportunities and offers a vision for global human development.

World Commission on Environment and Development, 1987, *Our Common Future*, Oxford University Press.

This is the report that launched the idea of sustainable development. It contains a great deal of information drawn together from many parts of the world and includes several quotes from prominent people. It is also known as The Brundtland Report after Gro Harlem Brundtland who chaired the Commission.

World Wide Fund for Nature, 1986, *The Assissi Declarations*.

This booklet arose from a WWF initiative to bring together, at Assissi, the leading religions of the world – Buddhism, Christianity, Hinduism, Islam and Judaism – to make declarations about the environment. Their statements are contained in this useful booklet and reveal encouraging elements from all five religions.

Opportunities and Information for Business

These books all relate to the broad theme of opportunities for business arising out of the social and environmental challenge.

Adams, Richard; Carruthers, Jane and Hamil, Sean, 1991, *Changing Corporate Values*, Kogan Page.
This book contains the research findings of *New Consumer* (*see* Sources of Help) and describes how 130 companies shape up in terms of their social and environmental responsibilities (*see* also Appendix 2).

Baden-Fuller, Charles & Stopford, John, 1992, *Rejuvenating the Mature Business*, Routledge.
There is nothing in this book that directly identifies the environment as an issue. However, it contains many useful and practical ideas for rejuvenating the mature business, which may well be required as a result of the pace of change often stimulated by environmental trends.

Business in the Environment, 1993, *Buying into the Environment: Guidelines for Integrating the Environment into Purchasing and Supply*.
This is a loose leaf publication, thus enabling it to be up-dated. It is the result of a consultation process involving over 100 firms and it sets out seven principles to guide purchasing departments in their procurement policies. The principles are: understand the business reasons, know your environment, understand your supply chain, adopt a partnership style, collect only information needed, validate suppliers environmental performance, and set a timetable for performance improvement. Many examples from different sectors illustrate the principles in action. The one regret is that there was not more emphasis on identifying real market needs and the best ways to meet them.

Charter, Martin (ed.), 1992, *Greener Marketing: A Responsible Approach to Business*, Greenleaf Publishing.
The book is divided into three parts: strategic implications, practical implications and case studies, which include examples from ICI, B & Q, British Gas, McDonald's, Traidcraft, Gateway, Sutton Borough Council, British Telecom and Pilkington Glass.

Davis, John, 1991, *Greening Business: Managing for Sustainable Development*, Blackwell.
Written from the perspective of a chief executive who wishes to move his company towards a sustainable business. It provides practical guidelines from a former chief executive, starting with vision and values and continuing through a series of steps which explain how issues can be identified and worked through.

Drucker, Peter, *The Practice of Management*, (1955), *Managing for the Future*, *The Age of Discontinuity* and *The New Realities*, (1989).
These are four of Peter Drucker's many books. He is one of the most

influential writers on business matters since the mid 1950s. *New Realities* in particular contains many insights which are very significant to the challenges we face.

Good, Ben, (1991) *Industry and the Environment: A Strategic Overview*, Centre for Exploitation of Science and Technology.

The twelve most prominent environmental problems are identified, together with the industries which cause most damage and the technologies which might provide solutions. Estimates are also provided for the likely expenditure that will be incurred during the current decade in tackling these issues.

Handler, Thomas (ed.), 1992, *Regulating the European Environment*, Baker & McKenzie.

This is a succinct summary of European regulation of the environment and provides a useful foundation from which to plan new business initiatives in order to keep ahead of legislation.

Handy, Charles, 1989 and 1991, *The Age of Unreason*, Business Books.

This book challenges us to think about how we manage when so much is unpredictable and how important it is to shape our future rather than be shaped by it. It provides the basis from which to consider new opportunities for business and new ways of doing business.

Harper, Malcolm, 1984, *Small Business in the Third World*.

A practical guide to doing business in developing countries in ways which contribute to their development.

Schmidheiny, Stephan, 1992, *Changing Course*, MIT.

This is the contribution from industry to the UN Conference on Environment and Development (the Earth Summit, June 1992). It contains an analysis of the issues and many examples of ways in which business is contributing to the solutions. (*See* Appendix 2 for identification of some of the companies whose environmental initiatives are mentioned in this book.)

Sklar, Scott & Sheinkopf, Kenneth, 1991, *Consumer Guide to Solar Energy: Easy and Inexpensive Applications for Solar Energy*, Bonus Books, Chicago.

An optimistic book which describes how solar energy can be used now for heating water and swimming pools, providing electricity, making water safe to drink, cooking and space heating. It also goes into financial matters and gives tips for taking action. There is also a helpful glossary.

Taylor, Bernard; Hutchinson, Colin; Pollack Suzanne and Tapper, Richard (Eds), 1994, *The Environmental Management Handbook*, Pitman.

The first section sets the scene by providing information about the environmental challenge. Thereafter the authors all describe leading-edge activities with which they and their organisations are associated in tackling the problems. (*See* also Appendix 2.)

Tromans Stephen and Grant, Malcolm (ed.), 1993, *Encyclopedia of Environmental Law*, Sweet & Maxwell.
This is a loose-leaf service in two volumes. Part 1 is an introduction, Part 2 covers treaties and conventions, Part 3, EC legislation, Part 4, statutes, Part 5, subordinate legislation, and Part 6, government circulars, codes of practice and miscellaneous materials. This book includes commentary by experts, and a reliable updating service is promised.

Vaughan, Dion and Mickle, Craig, 1993, *Environmental Profiles of European Business*, The Royal Institute of International Affairs, published by Earthscan.
The Centre for Exploitation of Science and Technology and the Association for Conservation of Energy undertook this survey to find out how companies in Europe viewed the environmental challenge. Six sectors were involved: automotive, chemical and petrochemical, steel, metal processing and electricity. The findings revealed useful insights into the significance of different environmental threats to each industry, where the pressures were coming from and which level of government – local, national, European or global was most significant to each sector.

Wells, Phil and Jetter, Mandy, 1991, *The Global Consumer: BestBuys to Help the Third World*, Gollancz.
A classification of products which are deemed to be less damaging to the environment. These include currency, furniture, food products, oils, soaps and detergents, tobacco, clothing and textiles, footwear, electronics, and holidays.

Williams, Jonathan, 1992, *Environmental Opportunities: Building Advantage out of Uncertainty*, Centre for Exploitation of Science and Technology.
This is the sequel to Ben Good's report on industry and the environment and describes ways in which cooperative action can alleviate environmental problems and provide good opportunities for business.

Willums, Jan-Olaf and Golüke, Ulrich, 1992, *From Ideas to Action*, International Chamber of Commerce.
The International Chamber of Commerce (*see* Sources of Help) published the *Business Charter for Sustainable Development* and over 1,200 companies had signed by mid-1994. This book is the first summary of information received by the ICC, describing the action taken to implement the 16 Clauses of the Charter. (*See* Appendix 2, which identifies some of the companies mentioned in this report.)

Individual and Organisational Learning and Change

This section contains books which describe practical and effective approaches to learning and change. It is divided into two sections:

A. Personal Learning, Development and Empowerment

Acland, Andrew Floyer, 1990, *A Sudden Outbreak of Common Sense*, Hutchinson.

Bennis, Warren and Nanus, Burt, 1985, *Leaders – The Strategies for Taking Charge*, Harper & Row, New York.

Extensive research was carried out by spending up to three days with the top executive in different US organisations to find out what they did as leaders. An enormous amount of data was gathered and almost overwhelmed the authors. After much analysis of the findings they published this book which identifies the common themes which could be associated with effective leaders. These include vision, communication, trust, and self-regard – not in themselves surprising, but the ways in which different chief executives put this into effect provides stimulating reading.

Block, Peter, 1990, *The Empowered Manager: Positive Political Skills at Work*, Jossey-Bass.

A description of the constraints of the bureaucratic mentality is followed by an appreciation of the politics that retain it. This leads on to much good advice about ways in which managers can learn positive skills, gain support from colleagues and make things happen.

de Bono, Edward, 1991, *Handbook for the Positive Revolution*, Penguin.

A new contribution from the prolific author who invented 'lateral thinking'. This is a practical tool with many good ideas for applying logic in order to become more effective.

Button, John and Bloom, William, 1992, *The Seekers Guide*, Thorsons.

This is a resource book and is ideal for anyone wishing to understand better the wide variety of options available for embarking on systematic personal development.

Elkington, John and Burke, Tom, 1987, *The Green Capitalists: Industry's Search for Environmental Excellence*, Gollancz.

Written before most companies had recognised the environment as an important issue, this book identifies some of the leading-edge work carried out by those who were the first to recognise entrepreneurial opportunities.

Elkington, John and Hailes, Julia, *The Green Consumer Guide*, (1988), and *The Green Consumer's Supermarket Shopping Guide*, (1989), Gollancz.

The first of these became a best seller and remained in the top ten UK paperbacks for several months. It has provided the basis for similar books in other countries and provides guidelines for aiding customers to make informed choices. The sequel provided the same help for shopping in supermarkets.

Fisher, Roger and Ury, William, 1981, *Getting to Yes: Negotiating Agreement without Giving In*, Hutchinson Business.

A best selling book on practical ways in which to conduct win/win negotiations.

Fisher, Roger and Brown, Scott, 1989, *Getting it Together: Building a Relationship that Gets to Yes*, Business Books.

The authors work with the Harvard Negotiation Project and this provides guidelines for conducting any level of negotiation. Considerable emphasis is placed on building the right climate and relationships to make negotiation possible. There is a useful analytical table of contents which can also be used as a checklist for managing a negotiation.

Garratt, Bob, 1990, *Learning to Lead: Organising Yourself and Others*, Fontana.

From experience of running courses for directors the author distils the blocks to learning and discusses how these can be overcome. He goes on to describe the requirements for successful development and concludes with ideas for creating learning organisations.

Gershon, David, 1990, *The Household Ecoteam Workbook*, Global Action Plan (UK). This book originated in the USA and has now also been published in special editions in Canada, Germany, Holland, Sweden, Finland and the UK. It provides practical guidelines for households to enable people to change their life styles and move towards sustainability. The book is made available to those joining the programme and not sold separately. (See Sources of Help – Global Action Plan).

Gregg, Sue; Pike, Graham and Selby, David, 1987, *Earthrights*, WWF and Kogan Page.

This is a compilation of many useful insights and ideas which can be applied to the process of education – 'as if the planet really mattered'.

Laszlo, Ervin, 1989, *The Inner Limits of Mankind*, One World.

Both Alexander King and Aurelio Peccei, Chairman and Founder of The Club of Rome make a contribution to introduce this book. The proposition that is explored is that the real limits are those we impose on ourselves, rather than the physical limits of the planet. Every reader is challenged to consider a set of beliefs which appear to be widely accepted in today's world, based on the evidence of how people behave, which contribute to the crisis we now face.

National Curriculum Council, 1990, *No 7: Environmental Education*.

This booklet spells out the proposals for teaching about the environment as a cross curricular theme in UK schools. It describes what should be taught and indicates how this can be done when teaching subjects such as English, Science, Mathematics, Technology, Geography and Art. Several practical projects are described.

Robbins, Anthony, 1988, *Unlimited Power*, Simon & Schuster.

Anthony Robbins is a remarkable man who became a millionaire by the age of twenty-four and has established several companies in the

USA, mostly focused on promulgating his ideas about personal growth and development. This book is a worldwide best seller and is written for anyone who wishes to tap his or her full potential.

Robbins, Anthony, 1992, *Awaken the Giant Within: How to Take Immediate Control of Your Mental, Emotional and Financial Destiny*, Simon & Schuster.

This is the sequel to *Unlimited Power* and is destined to become another best seller. The essential ingredients of learning and change are identified and explained in a powerful and compelling way with many examples.

Schumacher, E F, 1977, *A Guide for the Perplexed*, Jonathan Cape. Having written *Small is Beautiful*, Schumacher turned his attention to more philosophical matters. This book, which some people claim is more significant than the book that made him famous, provides guidelines for resolving inner confusion. Several writers in the 1990s (e.g. Clark, Gore, King, Laszlo, Meadows, Russell, Vittachi) have claimed that lasting solutions to world problems will only be achieved as a result of coming to terms with our own inner world. Schumacher addresses this issue in this book.

Schwarz, Walter and Dorothy, 1987, *Breaking Through*, Green Books. Walter Schwarz is the *Guardian*'s religious affairs correspondent and his wife, Dorothy, writes children's books and teaches. They had not previously attempted to write a book together but did so on this occasion because they originally maintained that there was no common theme to issues such as complementary medicine, deep ecology, organic farming and new economics. This book was their 'repentance' and describes the breakthrough they personally experienced.

Shields, Katrina, 1991, *In the Tiger's Mouth: An Empowerment Guide for Social Action*, Millenium Books.

Practical experience, mostly in Australia, provides the basis for this helpful guide to ways in which learning about empowerment takes place in counselling and group work. The book owes its title to a Buddhist monk from Thailand who visited a rural community in Australia where the author was living. The monk stayed only one day then departed quietly, early one morning, leaving a drawing of a rampant tiger with the caption: The best place to meditate is in the tiger's mouth.

Seymour, John, 1991, *Changing Lifestyles*, Victor Gollancz.

The author is well known for his personal efforts to achieve a sustainable life style through self-sufficiency. In this short book he describes some of the compelling reasons why we need to change our life styles and brings home the force of his arguments with wonderful, powerful examples.

Skinner, Robin and Cleese, John, 1993, *Life and How to Survive it*, Methuen.
This is the sequel to *Families and How to Survive Them* and is presented in similar format, with many cartoons which vividly illustrate the points made in the text. The juxtaposition of Skinner's knowledge and insights and Cleese's down to earth summaries of key points works well.

Susskind, Lawrence and Cruickshank, Jeffrey, 1987, *Breaking the Impasse: Consensual Approaches to Resolving Public Disputes*, Basic Books.
A practical book about current work being done in the USA to achieve breakthroughs in resolving conflicts, some of which have been around for a long time. It also describes the process of facilitation and the skills required to be effective.

The Commission on Social Justice, 1993, *Social Justice in a Changing World* and *The Justice Gap*, Institute for Public Policy Research, 30-32 Southampton Street, London WC2R 7RA.

Vittachi, Anuradha, 1989, *Earth Conference One: Sharing a Vision for our Planet*, New Science Library.
In a foreword to this book James Lovelock describes this conference, which took place in Oxford in April 1988, as 'the most significant gathering I have attended in a lifetime. It changed my life irreversibly.' The gathering brought together 100 spiritual and parliamentary leaders from around the world and became a mutually rewarding experience which is described in this book.

B. Organisation Development, Change and Transformation

Beckhard, Richard, 1969, *Organization Development: Strategies and Models*, Addison-Wesley.
One of the earliest expositions on the subject of organisation development from the man who became a pre-eminent practitioner.

Beckhard, Richard and Harris, Reuben T, 1987, *Organizational Transitions: Managing Complex Change*, 2nd edn, Addison-Wesley.
The issues addressed cover the management of change and go on to deal with the question of stability following a period of change. A case study brings together all the elements in a coherent whole.

Beckhard, Richard and Pritchard, Wendy, 1992, *Changing the Essence: The Art of Creating and Leading Fundamental Change in Organisations*, Jossey-Bass.
Wendy Pritchard joins Richard Beckhard in writing this book and contributes from her experience, gained mainly with Shell.
Learning while doing is a central theme as is the need for clear vision to stimulate the change initiative and build commitment to the future. A particularly interesting chapter deals with the leader's personal dilemmas during change. Examples and cameos bring the book to life.

Benedick, Richard Elliot, 1991, *Ozone Diplomacy: New Directions in Safeguarding the Planet*, Harvard University Press.

This book acknowledges the changing world of international diplomacy which now goes beyond peace and war to environmental issues such as global warming and ozone depletion. The book describes the process whereby the Montreal Protocol on Substances that Deplete the Ozone Layer was agreed in 1987 and revised in London in 1990. The process involved scientists, industrialists and government officials and this account is provided by a person with many years experience as a diplomat and negotiator.

Bradford, Leland (ed.), 1978, *Group Development*, University Associates.

This book covers both research findings and practical applications of group development, with contributions from many of the leading American practitioners, including Warren Bennis, Herbert Shepard, Ronald Lippitt, Gordon Lippitt, and Jack Gibb. A useful source of ideas.

Elkington, John and Knight, Peter, 1991, *The Green Business Guide: How to take up and profit from the environmental challenge*, Gollancz.

This book begins with a table which shows the growth in the number of industries that are in the firing line – five in the 1960s, fifty-four in the 1990s. How to spot environmental opportunities is discussed, and supported by examples. The scope of environmental management covers all main departments and a chapter is devoted to each, with copious examples.

Global Environmental Management Initiative (GEMI), 1991, *Corporate Quality/Environmental Management: The First Conference*, GEMI, Washington.

These are the proceedings of the conference held in January 1991 and attended by some 250 people, including representatives from companies such as Procter and Gamble, IBM, Coopers & Lybrand, Dow Chemical, AT&T, and Union Carbide. The proposition that TQM and environment can be combined into TQEM was first explored at this conference and shown to be feasible.

Harvey-Jones, John, 1991, *Getting it Together: Memoirs of a Troubleshooter*, Heinemann.

His first book *Making it Happen*, described his philosophy as both an agent for change and a chief executive. This sequel provides more information about how he faced up to issues with his family and friends while tackling ever more difficult work assignments.

Kanter, Rosabeth Moss, 1989, *When Giants Learn to Dance*, Routledge.

A leading American consultant provides many insights into ways in which large organisations can discover how to develop and change. The book covers strategic issues, the management of change, and how to deal with career issues.

Kotter, John P Heskett, James L, 1992, *Corporate Culture and Performance*, The Free Press.

This book describes research findings, firstly to explore the validity of the saying that successful companies have strong cultures, secondly that they have strategically appropriate cultures. Both sayings are found to be untrue. The most effective companies are those which have adaptive cultures. Many examples and facts are quoted to support the findings. The question of how to change organisation culture is then explored, with examples of companies that have done this successfully, such as ICI and Nissan.

Morgan, Gareth, *Images of Organization*, Sage, 1986 and *Riding the Waves of Change: Developing Managerial Competencies for a Turbulent World*, Jossey-Bass, 1988.

One of Canada's leading authorities on organisation learning, change and development provides many useful insights in these two important books. One of the strongest elements in the books is the way in which many perspectives are brought to bear on the challenges of our times. The emerging managerial competences which are riding the waves of change include: reading the environment, proactive management, leadership and vision, human resource management, creativity, learning and innovation, and information technology.

Sadler, Philip, 1991, *Designing Organisations*, Mercury.

A useful guide to organisation design, although it does not specifically identify environmental pressures as a reason why such redesign may be necessary, it does contain helpful frameworks and practical advice.

Schein, Edgar H, 1985, *Organizational Culture and Leadership: A Dynamic View*, Jossey-Bass.

A thorough exploration of what culture is, how it influences organisations, how it develops and how cultural change can be managed.

Schein, Edgar H, 1988, *Process Consultation: Its Role in Organization Development*, 2nd edn, Addison-Wesley.

One of the great exponents of process consultation lucidly describes what it is and how it works. An outstanding book for practitioners and one that will help any manger to understand better what process consultation can contribute to the management of change.

Senge, Peter, 1990, *The Fifth Discipline: The Art and Practice of the Learning Organization*, Century Business.

This book put the idea of the learning organisation on the map. It is, in effect, the process whereby people are learning while doing their job and thereby enabling the organisation to benefit. The disciplines of the learning organisation are: systems thinking, personal mastery, mental models, building shared vision, and team learning.

Stead, W. Edward and Stead, Jean Garner, 1992, *Management for a Small Planet: Strategic Decision Making and the Environment*, Sage Publications. A sound practical guide for managers and students. The book covers a brief summary of the environmental issues, a conceptual model for understanding how new economics apply to business, and management of sustainability through total quality.

Zadek, Simon and Evans, Richard, 1993, *Auditing the Market: A Practical Approach to Social Auditing*, published jointly by Traidcraft Exchange (Kingsway, Gateshead, Tyne & Wear NE11 0NE), and New Economics Foundation (*see* Sources of Help).

Describes the issues and the approach used to strive for an objective assessment of how social responsibility targets are being met.

Sources of Help

Organisations

Advisory Committee for Business and the Environment (ACBE), Department of the Environment, 2 Marsham Street, London SW1P 3EB (071 276 3732). Jointly established, in May 1991, with the Department of Trade and Industry to achieve closer dialogue with business on environmental policy. Working Groups have been revised in 1994 to focus on the financial sector, transport, achieving environmental goals, waste management and agriculture and industry. The groups publish periodic reports.

Applied Futures, 2101 Crystal Plaza Arcade, 233 Arlington, Virginia 22202, USA. Tel: (202) 895 5226. Fax: (202) 895 2915. Recently moved from the UK to the USA and concentrate their work on business consulting. Christine McNulty is MD.

Association for Management Education and Development (AMED), 14/15 Belgrave Square, London SW1X 8PS. Tel: 071 235 3505. Members come from industry, the public sector, academic institutions and consultancies. They have an active Sustainable Development Network.

British Library Environmental Information Service, 25 Southampton Buildings, London WC2A 1AW. Tel: 071 323 7955.

British Standards Institution (BSI), Linford Wood, Milton Keynes, MK14 6LE. Tel: 0908 221166. Responsible for the Quality Standard, BS5750 and the Environmental Management Standard, BS7750.

Brunel Environment Programme, Brunel University, Uxbridge, Middlesex UB8 3PH. Tel: 0895 256461. This is part of the Brunel Management Programme, which includes Organisation Development, Change Management and New Business Imperatives. The Environment Programme covers topics such as: Life Cycle Assessment, Environmental Marketing, Purchasing Policies, Market Research, Environmental Auditing, Design and Packaging, Business Strategy for the Environment, Priorities for R&D, Environmental Training and Environmental Management is Change Management.

Business Council for Sustainable Development (BCSD), World Trade Centre Building, 3rd Floor, 10 Route de l'Aeroport, CH-1215 Geneva 15, Switzerland. Tel: +41 22 788 32 02. Fax: +41 22 788 32 11. Founded by Dr Stephan Schmidheiny, BCSD produced the book *Changing Course* for the Earth Summit in Rio in June 1992 and are now focusing on phase 2, which will concentrate on implementing their proposals, under the chairmanship of Anand Panyarachun.

Business in the Community (BiC), 8 Stratton Street, London W1X 5FD. Tel: 071 629 1600. Fax: 071 629 1834. Business in the Environment (BiE) is a Business in the Community initiative. It devises and promotes practical steps that support the UK's progress towards understanding and applying the principles of sustainable development; publishes *Your Business and the Environment, A D-I-Y Review for Companies* (prepared by Coopers & Lybrand) and *Buying into the Environment.*

Centre for Alternative Technology plc, Machynlleth, Powys SY20 9AZ. Tel: 0654 702400. Became a plc in 1990 in response to growing demand for their ideas and services. They had 72,000 visitors in 1990 – an increase of 17 per cent on the previous year.

Centre for Dispute Resolution (CEDR), 100 Fetter Lane, London EC4A 1DD. Tel: 071 430 1852. CEDR is a non-profit-making organisation supported by industry and professional advisers. It aims to encourage the use of Alternative Dispute Resolution (ADR) to achieve better solutions to domestic, business and international disputes.

Centre for Exploitation of Science and Technology (CEST), 5 Berners Road, London N1 0PW. Tel: 071 354 9942. Fax: 071 354 4301. CEST manages the process which aims to identify and establish exploitable areas of science. Their environmental work has included the publication of *Industry and the Environment: A Strategic Overview* and *Environmental Opportunities: Building Advantage out of Uncertainty.*

Centre for Sustainable Industry (CSI), The Rookery, Adderbury, OXON OX17 3NA. Tel: 0295 810993. Fax: 0993 813244. CSI promotes sustainable industry by assisting companies to adopt sustainable systems, to generate such systems in partnership with poor communities, and to foster understanding of sustainable industrial activity.

Charter 88, Exmouth House, 3-11 Pine Street, London EC1R 0JH. Tel: 071 833 1988. Promotes the idea of constitutional change in Britain which includes freedom of information, a fair electoral system, reformed Houses of Parliament and the judiciary, independence for local government and a written constitution.

Confederation of British Industry (CBI), Environment Management Unit, Centre Point, 103 New Oxford Street, London WC1A 1DU. Tel: 071 379 7400. The Environment Unit publishes booklets on topics such as environmental auditing, pollution control and eco-labelling. It has also established the Environment Business Forum and publishes an Environment Newsletter.

Conflict Management Plus, 47 Cranleigh Road, London N15 3AB. Tel: 081 802 3535. Offers training courses, mediation, dispute resolution, consultancy and research.

Conservation Foundation, 1 Kensington Gore, London SW7 2AR. Tel: 071 823 8842. Fax: 071 823 8791. Creates and manages sponsorship schemes involving all environmental interests. The Foundation has an Environmental Managers Group.

Earthscan Publications Limited, 120 Pentonville Road, London N1 9JN. An editorially independent subsidiary of Kogan Page and publish a wide range of books on environmental matters.

Environmental Business Association, 1150 Connecticut Avenue NW, 9th Floor, Connecticut Building, Washington DC 20036. Tel: (202) 862 4363.

Environmental Data Services Limited (ENDS), Finsbury Business Centre, 40 Bowling Green Lane, London EC1R 0NE. Publishes the *ENDS Report* and the *ENDS Market Analysis of Environmental Consultancy*.

Environmental Law Foundation (ELF), 42 Kingsway, London WC2B 6EX. Formed by a group of environmentalists, scientists and lawyers to promote the solution of environmental problems through the legal processes.

Environment Training Group (ETG), is an informal group of people from the Field Studies Council, Capel Manor, Peak National Parks, and Kindrogan Field Centre. Their mission is to empower the integration of environmental responsibility with management development for successful and sustainable business. They will arrange special events to suit the needs of clients. Further information can be obtained from the member organisations.

Field Studies Council, Preston Montford Field Centre, Montford Bridge, Shrewsbury, Shropshire, SY4 1DX. Tel: 0743 850380. Runs courses on environmental awareness for senior managers, and environmental policy and audit for local authorities and business.

Friends of the Earth (FOE), 26–28 Underwood Street, London N1 7JQ. Tel: 071 490 1555. Fax: 071 490 0881. Encourages and empowers the public through their network of 300 branches in the UK. FOE is an international initiative which is active in many countries.

Gaia Foundation, 18 Well Walk, London NW3 1LD. Tel: 071 435 5000. Fax: 071 431 0551. Highlights the importance of cultural and ecological diversity and works in accordance with the priorities of the South.

Global Action Plan (GAP), 84 Yerry Hill Road, Woodstock, New York 12498, USA. Tel: (914) 679 4830. Also 42 Kingsway, London, WC2B 6EX. Tel: 071 404 0837. GAP has offices in Canada, Denmark, Finland, Germany, Norway, Poland, Sweden and The Netherlands. It is an initiative arising out of Earth Day 1991 to help households change their lifestyles by using the *EcoTeam Workbook*, available in the appropriate languages, focussing on household wastes, energy, water usage, transportation, shopping, and empowering others.

Global Environmental Management Initiative (GEMI), 1828 L Street NW, Suite 711, Washington DC 20036. Tel: (202) 296 7449. Organised the first conference on Corporate Quality and Environmental Management, in 1991, and published the proceedings.

Green Alliance, 49 Wellington Street, London WC2E 7BN. Tel: 071 836 0341. A non-profit organisation which works on implementation of environmental strategies, developing the environmental agenda into new areas, enhancing the capacity of other environmental organisations and developing the integration of environment with other policy areas.

GreenNet, 23 Bevenden Street, London N1 6BH, England. Tel: 071 713 1941. GreenNet is a global computer network for the environment, peace, human rights and sustainable development.

Greenpeace, Canonbury Villas, London N1 2PN. Tel: 071 354 5100 or 071 359 7396. Fax: 071 359 4372 or 071 359 4062. An international environmental pressure group. They now publish their own journal for business.

Group for Environmental Manufacturing (GEM), Jasmine House, The Walled Garden, South Wanborough, Hampshire RG25 1TN. Tel: 0256 862721. Created by Dr Jonathan Williams, previously of CEST, this group facilitates the resolution of problems facing manufacturers in three ways: through problem-driven projects, identification of critical areas of science and technology, and highlighting opportunities for new management and design procedures.

Holden Meehan, 40 Park Street, Bristol, BS1 5JG, England. Tel: 0272 252874. Fax: 0272 291535. Financial advisers specialising in ethical and environmental investments, and publish *An Independent Guide to Ethical and Green Investments*. They have an office in London. Tel: 071 404 6442.

Human Synergistics-Verax, 60 High Street, Odiham, Hants RG25 1LN, England. Tel: 025671 3355. Market a range of materials for use in training and development of staff at all levels. They are also UK agents for the Life Styles Inventory (LS1 and LS2), the Organisation Culture Inventory (OCI) and compatible computerised learning material developed by J. Clayton Lafferty, Human Synergistics Inc, 39819, Plymouth Road, Plymouth, Michigan 48170. Tel: (313) 459 1030.

Industry Associations. These are often the first source of information for any business, but are too numerous to list here.

Industry Council for Packaging and the Environment (INCPEN), Premier House, 10 Greycoat Place, London SW1P 1SB. Tel: 071 222 8866. Fax: 071 976 7178.

Information Technology Centre for Educational Research, Development and Training in the Environmental Sciences (IT CERES), School of Education, Southampton University, Highfield, Southampton, Hants SO9 5NH. Tel: 0703 592 385.

Institute for Business Ethics (IBE), 12 Palace Street, London SW1E 5JA. Tel: 071 931 0495. Seeks to clarify ethical issues in business and propose positive solutions to establish common ground with people of goodwill of all faiths.

Institute of Environmental Assessment, Holbeck Manor, Horncastle, Lincolnshire LN9 6PU. Tel: 0507 533444. Fax: 0507 533522. Focuses on improving standards of environmental assessment, working through its membership drawn from industry, environmental consultancies, local authorities and educational establishments.

Institute of Personnel Management (IPM), IPM House, Camp Road, London SW19 4UX, Tel: 081 946 9100. Members cover all aspects of human resource management and development.

Institute of Waste Management (IWM), 9 Saxon Court, St Peter's Gardens, Northampton NN1 1SX. Tel: 0604 20426. Fax: 0604 21339. An association of professional and technical people qualified in all aspects of waste management. The Waste Management Forum and the Waste Management Industry Training and Advisory Board (WAMITB) work from the same address.

Intermediate Technology Development Group (ITDG), Myson House, Railways Terrace, Rugby CV21 3HT. Tel: 0788 560631. Fax: 0788 540270. An international development agency working with communities in the Third World to enable poor people to gain greater control over their lives and contribute to long-term sustainable development.

International Chamber of Commerce (ICC), The World Business Organisation, 38 Cours Albert 1er, 75008 Paris, France. Tel: (33)(1) 49-53-28-28. Fax: (33)(1) 42-25-86-63. ICC UK, 14-15 Belgrave Square, London SW1X 8PS. Tel: 071 823 2811. Fax: 071 235 5447. Publishes the *Business Charter for Sustainable Development* (*See* Appendix 3) and has a Committee on Environment which meets regularly, and an initiative on sustainable development. ICC have recently established the World Industry Council for the Environment (WICE).

IDR Europe Ltd , Three Quays, Tower Hill, London EC3R 6DS. Tel: 0272 252090. IDR (International Dispute Resolution) provide services which analyse disputes, help to prevent disagreement escalating, and mediate in conflict situations. They also train people to acquire negotiation and mediation skills.

International Institute for Environment and Development (IIED), 3 Endsleigh Street, London WC1H 0DD. Tel: 071 388 2117. Fax: 071 388 2826. IIED emphasises the intrinsic interdependence between the environment and economic development.

IUCN – see World Conservation Union and World Conservation Monitoring Centre.

Local Exchange Trading Schemes (LETS), LETS LINK UK, 61 Woodcock Road, Warminster, Wiltshire BA12 9DH. Tel: 0985 217871. A LETS system is a locally initiated and controlled non-profit scheme which provides a community information exchange service and records transactions of members exchanging goods and services within the system. It enables people to exchange goods and services at 'prices' they determine themselves using the 'currency' created for each local scheme. LETS schemes are active in Canada, USA, Australia and New Zealand, and in the UK where over 200 such schemes exist.

MORI, 32 Old Queen Street, London SW1H 9HP. Tel: 071 222 0232. Carries out market and opinion research surveys, many of which track societal trends; also conducts surveys on behalf of businesses.

National Curriculum Council, Albion Wharf, 25 Skeldergate, York YO1 2XL. Tel: 0904 622533. Fax: 0904 622921.

New Consumer, 52 Elswick Road, Newcastle upon Tyne, NE4 5BR. Tel: 091 272 1148. Fax: 091 272 1615. Promotes the idea of environmental awareness when shopping; publishes *Changing Corporate Values, Career Values* and *Shopping for a Better World*.

New Economics Foundation (NEF), 88/94 Wentworth Street, London E1 7SA. Tel: 071 377 5696. Fax: 071 377 5720

Open University Environmental Education, The Open University, Business Development and Marketing Office, Walton Hall, Milton Keynes, MK7 6AA. Tel: 0908 652029. Published The Report of the Environmental Education and Training Task Force, in 1992.

Organisation for Economic Cooperation and Development, (OECD), 2, Rue Andre-Pascal, 75775 Paris CEDEX 16, France.

Osho Multimedia Ltd., 3-5 Neal Street, Covent Garden, London WC2H 9PU. Provides Environmental Information Systems and Eco-consultancy using multimedia methods.

Robbins Research Institute, 1223 Camino Del Mar, Del Mar, California 92014, USA and 5 Cornwall Crescent, London W11 1PH. Tel: 071 221 9096. RRI conduct personal and professional seminars in the USA, Canada, the UK and other countries on topics such as business effectiveness, sales training, influencing skills and the treatment of phobias and personal relationships.

Rocky Mountain Institute (RMI), 1739 Snowmass Creek Road, Old Snowmass, Colorado 81654-9199. Tel: (303) 927 3851. Fax: (303) 927 4178. RMI is a non-profit research and educational foundation, established by Amory and Hunter Lovins, with a vision across boundaries to foster efficient and sustainable use of resources as a path to global security. They are actively involved with projects on energy, water, economic renewal, agriculture, global security, transportation and the provision of green development services. The Lovins's books on energy, *Soft Energy Paths* and *Energy Unbound*, have been widely acclaimed.

Saferworld, 82 Colston Street, Bristol BS1 5BB. Tel: 0272 276435. Fax: 0272 253305. They have undertaken the 50 per cent initiative as a strategy for survival, which is aimed at cutting world military expenditure by half, in real terms. They also run Rapid Response, a letter writing scheme to enable concerned individuals to be actively involved. Members of Rapid Response receive postcards, each month, providing background information on a topical subject and some suggested questions to put to a named person in an individually composed letter. Twice yearly, members receive a newsletter reporting the results achieved.

Schumacher College, The Old Postern, Dartington, Totnes, Devon TQ9 6 EA, England. Tel: 0803 865934. Fax: 0803 866899. Provides a programme of courses for people from all over the world to stimulate learning designed to build understanding of a balanced and harmonious worldview.

Schumacher Society, Ford House, Hartland, Bideford, Devon EX39 6EE. Tel: 0237 441621. Fax: 0237 441203. Builds on the legacy of E.F. Schumacher, author of *Small is Beautiful* and *A Guide for the Perplexed*. The Society publishes *Resurgence* magazine (*see* under journals), manages the Green Books publishing house, the Schumacher College (*see* previous entry), The Small School at Hartland, and organises the Schumacher Lectures, a popular annual event in Bristol.

SETAC-Europe, Av. E. Mounier 83, box 1, 1200 Brussels, Belgium. Tel: +32 2 772 7281. Publishes *LCA News*, a newsletter on life cycle analysis, distributed to members and available for non-members on request.

Sheppard Moscow Limited, Beaumont House, Willow Grove, Chislehurst, Kent BR7 5DA. Tel: 081 468 7975. Consultants in organisation development and manager training, organising a wide range of open and in-house training programmes on subjects such as influencing, consulting and negotiating skills, managing organisational change, developing change resources and facilitation workshops. Their in-house consulting services include work on changing organisation culture.

Soil Association, 86-88 Colston Street, Bristol BS1 5BB. Tel: 0272 290661. Campaigns to maintain and improve the quality of food, health and the environment by promoting organic agriculture and running the Soil Association Symbol Scheme.

Synergy Brand Values, 5th Floor Bilton House, 54-58 Uxbridge Road, London W5 2TL. Conducts values related research.

TERMA Box Training, is provided by various individuals in a network (Circles of Trust), including John Wallace, Seventh Generation Consulting, PO Box 2352, Sante Fe, New Mexico 87504, USA. The training is based on a collection of materials designed to challenge and inform those taking part so that values are examined and current thinking about the world is reviewed and developed.

The Centre for International Peace Building, 9 West Street, Chipping Norton, Oxon OX7 5LH. Tel: 0608 642335. Strives to influence the armed forces to accept a wider role which includes peace keeping, peace building and environmental matters. Run by Brigadier Harbottle who is the author of *Proper Soldiering*.

The Environment Council, 21 Elizabeth Street, London SW1W 9RP. Tel: 071 824 8411. Fax: 071 730 9941. An active Business and Environment programme, an Information programme, and Environmental Resolve – an initiative designed to help prevent and resolve environmental disputes. The Council publishes *habitat* (*see* under journals, below). The Business and Environment programme has a membership of over 700 Environmental Managers and has initiated *Conservers at Work* to enable more people to get involved with their company's programmes.

The Hunger Project, One Madison Avenue, New York, NY 100100. Tel: (212) 532 4255. Fax: (212) 532 9785. And in the UK at, 2nd Floor Mezzanine, 92 New Cavendish Street, London W1M 7FA. Tel: 071 255 2404. Fax: 071 637 0951. This is a worldwide campaign with offices in many countries to give priority to ending hunger globally .

The Natural Step, Box 70335, S – 107 23 Stockholm, Sweden. Also Natural Step UK, 3rd Floor, Theba House, 49 – 50 Hatton Garden, London EC1N 8YS. Promotes the idea that we need to change the industrial infrastructure from one that is linear, wasteful of resources and producing toxic wastes to one that is cyclic, resource-conserving and healthy. They work with scientists, farmers, the media and industry and encourage people to find their own solutions to environmental problems, within guidelines.

The Royal Society for the Encouragement of Arts, Manufactures and Science (RSA), 8 John Adam Street, London WC2N 6EZ. Tel: 071 930 5115. The RSA, founded in 1847, has a varied programme of work which includes granting awards, providing lectures, publishing a journal and undertaking projects. A current major project is *Tomorrow's Company: The Role of Business in a Changing World.*

The Technology Exchange Ltd., Wrest Park, Silsoe, Bedford MK45 4HS, England. Tel: 0525 860333. Fax: 0525 860664. Established in 1985, as a non-profit company, the Exchange helps firms to form partnerships with firms in other countries with the objective of improving their products and processes in terms of quality, environment, reduction of waste and increased efficiency. They have established links in seventy countries and work in cooperation with the United Nations Industrial Development Organisation (UNIDO), for whom they have prepared catalogues, which are used at 'Techmart Fairs' in countries such as China, India, Vietnam, Costa Rica and Zambia.

Turning Point 2000, The Old Bakehouse, Cholsey, OXON OX10 9NU, England. Tel: 0491 652346. Created and run by James Robertson and Alison Pritchard, who publish *Turning Point 2000*, twice a year, distributed to 2,000 people in North America, Europe and Australia, giving information on a host of alternative subjects. James Robertson is the author of *Future Wealth: A New Economics for the 21st Century* and other earlier books.

UK Ecolabelling Board, 7th Floor, Eastbury House, 30-34 Albert Embankment, London SE1 7TL. Tel: 071 820 1199.

UK Centre for Economic and Environmental Development (UK CEED), Suite E, 3 Kings Parade, Cambridge CB2 1SJ. Tel: 0223 67799. Fax: 0223 67794. Formed as a result of the Conservation and Development Programme for the UK. Promotes a productive partnership between environmental protection and development.

United Nations Environment & Development: UK Committee (UNED), C/o United Nations Association, 3 Whitehall Court, London SW1A 2EL. Tel: 071 930 2931. Fax: 071 930 5893. The committee is chaired by Jonathon Porritt, former director of Friends of the Earth (UK). Its primary objective is to promote global environmental protection and sustainable development through support for the UN Environment Programme, UN Development Programme and the UN Commission for Sustainable Development.

UNEP – United Nations Environment Programme, Nairobi, Kenya. Its programme is promoted in the UK by UNED and IIED.

Waste Management Forum (*see* Institute of Waste Management).

Waste Management Industry Training and Advisory Board (*see* Institute of Waste Management).

World Conservation Monitoring Centre, 219c Huntingdon Road, Cambridge CB3 0DL. Tel: 0223 277314. Created as a joint venture by the three organisations who launched the World Conservation Strategy: IUCN, UNEP and WWF.

World Conservation Union (IUCN), Rue Mauverney 28, CH-1196 Gland, Switzerland. Tel: (41 22) 999 0002. Fax: 419 624 iucn ch. Promotes a common approach for the world conservation movement to ensure that human use of natural resources is appropriate, sustainable and equitable. Publishes *Caring for the Earth* and produces a quarterly bulletin for members.

World Development Movement (WDM), 25 Beehive Place, London SW9 7QR. Tel: 071 737 6215. Fax: 071 274 3232. WDM strives to influence Britain and the European Community to play a leading role in creating a just world in which people everywhere can enjoy adequate food, education, health care, housing and jobs.

World Industry Council for the Environment (WICE)- see under International Chamber of Commerce.

World Resources Institute (WRI), 1735 New York Avenue NW, Washington DC 20036, USA.

Worldwatch Institute, 1776 Massachusetts Avenue, NW, Washington DC 20036- 1904. Publishes the *Worldwatch Paper* series, initiated in 1976. The Institute has published over 110 papers as booklets, most of which have been highly acclaimed. They also publish three books as a series: the annual *State of the World* reports, *Vital Signs*, which defines the trends that are shaping our future, and the *Worldwatch Environment Alert Series*.

World Wide Fund for Nature (WWF), Panda House, Weyside Park, Godalming, Surrey GU7 1XR. Tel: 0483 426444. Fax: 0483 426409. The largest international voluntary organisation devoted to the care and protection of the natural living world, with twenty-three national offices.

Journals, Bulletins, Reports and Directories

Business and the Environment: Critical Issues of the '90s. Cutter Information Corporation, 37 Broadway, Arlington, MA 02174-5539, USA. Launched in 1990, provides benchmark information and practical experience of leading organisations. Guarantees that subscribers will be able to save or earn ten times the annual subscription ($497 outside USA, $397 within USA) in the first year.

Business Strategy and the Environment. Published quarterly by European Research Press, Tel: 0274 729 315.

Conservers at Work. Available from The Environment Council (*see* above). Provides practical information on conservation topics relevant to employees at any level.

Directory of Environmental Consultants. Published by Environmental Data Services Limited (see above).

Earth Matters. Published quarterly by Friends of the Earth for members (*see* above). Contains FOE campaign news, topical environmental information, new publications and book reviews.

Earthwatch. Published by the International Planned Parenthood Federation, Tel: 071 486 0741.

ECO Directory of Environmental Databases in the UK. Published by ECO Environmental Education Trust, Avon Environmental Centre, 10–12

Picton Street, Montpelier, Bristol BS6 5 QA. Tel: 0272 420162. Describes what is available in some 250 UK environmental data bases.

Eco-Management Auditing. Published three times a year by European Research Press, Tel: 0274 729315.

ENDS Report. Published monthly by Environmental Data Services Ltd (see above). Provides useful summaries of environmental trends, topical issues and legislation.

Environment and Industry Digest. Published monthly, ISSN 0958 2126.

Environment Business. Published fortnightly by Information for Industry, 521 Old York Road, London SW18 1TG, England, Tel: 081 877 9130. Fax: 081 877 9938. Provides topical information on environmental issues relevant for business. Information for Industry also publish special reports on environmental auditing, air pollution regulations, environmental policy guidelines and industrial waste management.

Environment Risk. Published ten times a year, ISSN 0965 3813. Information available from Quadrant Services, Tel: 0444 440421.

European Environment. Published six times a year, ISSN 09S61 0405. European Research Press, Tel: 0274 729315.

habitat. Published ten times a year by The Environment Council for Associates and members (*see* above). Contains brief news items on a wide range of topical subjects (mostly UK focused) and short book reviews.

IUCN Bulletin. Published quarterly by IUCN (*see* above). Provides useful information on worldwide environmental news and longer special reports on countries and issues.

LCA News. A newsletter on life cycle analysis published bi-monthly by SETAC (*see* above). This short newsletter is written by business people for business people and gives up-to-date information on the state of the art in life cycle analysis.

New Consumer. Quarterly publication for members of the organisation of the same name (*see* above).

Resurgence. Published six times a year by the Schumacher Society (*see* above). A thoughtful and stimulating publication on a wide range of social, philosophical, spiritual and environmental issues. Contains an extensive book review section.

RSA Journal. Available to Fellows (*see* above). Covers news of forthcoming events, extensive reports on recent lectures and meetings and a book review section.

Sustainable Development. Published three times a year by European Research Press, Tel: 0274 729315.

The Ecologist. Published six times a year. Agriculture House, Bath Road, Sturminster Newton, Dorset DT10 1DU. Tel: 0258 73476. Fax: 0258 7378. A challenging publication on environmental topics.

The Third World Directory. Published by The Directory of Social Change, Radius Works, Back Lane, London NW3 1HL. Gives details of 200 organisations based in the UK and working for Third World Development.

Tomorrow: Global Environmental Business. Published six times a year. Kungstgaten 27, S-111 56 Stockholm, Sweden. Tel: +46 8 24 3480. Fax: +46 8 24 0809. Provides very helpful topical, worldwide information in a very readable style. Contains a supplement from the Business Council for Sustainable Development.

WARMER Bulletin. World Action for Recycling Materials and Energy from Rubbish, Bridge House, High Street, Tonbridge, Kent TN9 1DP. Tel: 0892 524626. The *WARMER Bulletin* is published quarterly and is free of charge. They have offices in Germany (Tel: +49 511 39 38 36) and Spain (Tel: +34 6 380 6912). Provides authoritative information on all aspects of waste management in a global context.

Who's Who in the Environment. Published by The Environment Council (*see* above). Separate editions are available for England, Scotland, Wales and Northern Ireland. *Who's Who* – England is available on disk and covers some 700 environmental organisations which are active in England.

Index

About the Author

COLIN HUTCHINSON, formerly chairman of the management consultants Sheppard Moscow, is an independent environmental management consultant specializing in strategic approaches to individual and organizational change. While with Sheppard Moscow he led major assignments with companies such as Shell UK, Lloyds Bank, British Petroleum, Rank Xerox, ICI, and Hewlett Packard. His lifelong interest in the environmental threat to the Earth's life support system led him in 1971 to become chairman of the Conservation Society, and in 1978 chairman of their educational charity. He was a director for the Environment Council from 1992 to 1994 and chairman of their Environmental Resolve Committee. He is currently a director of the Global Action Plan UK Limited and also a council member of AMED, the Association for Management Education and Development.

ISBN 0-275-95233-9

90000>

HARDCOVER BAR CODE